W9-BVC-436
3 3420 00655 357 3

Waterloo
Public
Library

AUG - 2004

Reference Collection
Adult Department

How It Works®

Science and Technology

Third Edition

Marshall Cavendish
99 White Plains Road
Tarrytown, NY 10591

Website: www.marshallcavendish.com

© 2003 Marshall Cavendish Corporation
HOW IT WORKS is a registered trademark of Marshall Cavendish Corporation

Third edition updated by Brown Reference Group plc.

All rights reserved. No part of this book may be reproduced or utilized in
any form or by any means electronic or mechanical, including photocopying,
recording, or by any information storage and retrieval system, without
prior written permission from the publisher and copyright holder.

Library of Congress Cataloging-in-Publication Data
How it works: science and technology.—3rd ed.
p. cm.
Includes index.
ISBN 0-7614-7314-9 (set)   ISBN 0-7614-7323-8 (Vol. 9)
1. Technology—Encyclopedias. 2. Science—Encyclopedias.
[1. Technology—Encyclopedias. 2. Science—Encyclopedias.]
T9 .H738 2003
603—dc21   2001028771

Consultant: Donald R. Franceschetti, Ph.D., University of Memphis

Brown Reference Group
Editor: Wendy Horobin
Associate Editors: Paul Thompson, Martin Clowes, Lis Stedman
Managing Editor: Tim Cooke
Design: Alison Gardner
Picture Research: Becky Cox
Illustrations: Mark Walker, Darren Awuah

Marshall Cavendish
Project Editor: Peter Mavrikis
Production Manager: Alan Tsai
Editorial Director: Paul Bernabeo

Printed in Malaysia
Bound in the United States of America
08 07 06 05 04   6 5 4 3 2

Title picture: Cooling of machine cutting tools, see *Lubrication*

How It Works®

Science and Technology

Volume 9

Instant-Picture Camera

Lumber

WATERLOO PUBLIC LIBRARY

Marshall Cavendish

New York • London • Toronto • Sydney

Contents

Volume 9

Instant-Picture Camera

Since the first instant-picture camera was introduced in 1948, over 100 million have been produced, mainly by Polaroid, who were the originators of the concept. Color prints can now be produced instantly; the image appears on a blank sheet in seconds, without the need for the darkrooms, negatives, printing papers, and sequences of chemical baths that are so much a part of the normal photographic process.

The first instant camera, developed in the 1940s by Edwin Land, the American scientist and chairman of the Polaroid corporation, was similar in appearance to the folding cameras popular at the time and was a roll-film model. The prints were sepia in color rather than the more generally preferred black and white, and the film was insensitive to red light. However, the entire developing and printing process lasted only 60 seconds. For the

first time, a photographer could point the camera, adjust the simple exposure controls, take the picture, and then see the result almost immediately.

Land's attempts to duplicate the normal photographic procedure inside the camera itself obviously required a great deal of ingenuity. The film included the negative and the printing paper sandwiched together with all the chemicals required to process them.

Wet processing

With the original instant-development system, an imprinted negative is formed in the same way as a conventional negative, then the transparent negative and the print paper are drawn, either manually or automatically, between rollers that squeeze them together. As the two materials pass through the rollers, a pod of chemicals attached to the

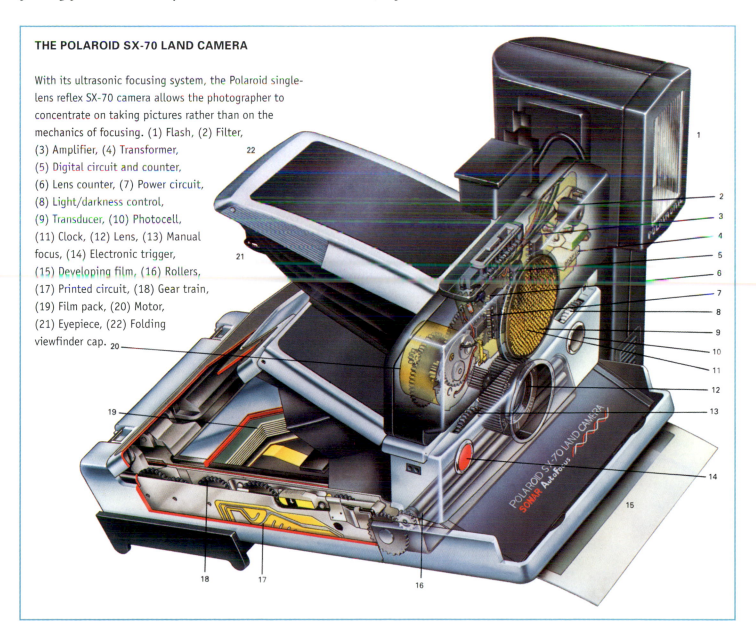

THE POLAROID SX-70 LAND CAMERA

With its ultrasonic focusing system, the Polaroid single-lens reflex SX-70 camera allows the photographer to concentrate on taking pictures rather than on the mechanics of focusing. (1) Flash, (2) Filter, (3) Amplifier, (4) Transformer, (5) Digital circuit and counter, (6) Lens counter, (7) Power circuit, (8) Light/darkness control, (9) Transducer, (10) Photocell, (11) Clock, (12) Lens, (13) Manual focus, (14) Electronic trigger, (15) Developing film, (16) Rollers, (17) Printed circuit, (18) Gear train, (19) Film pack, (20) Motor, (21) Eyepiece, (22) Folding viewfinder cap.

negative is burst and is spread evenly between negative and positive. Initially, the pod acts as a developer on the negative, but instead of washing away the unexposed parts of the image and leaving them clear, as in a conventional negative, it transfers the chemicals as a dark dye across to the print paper that is now held in contact with the film negative.

The result is a positive image on the paper, exactly the same size as the negative. After either 10 or 20 seconds, depending on the type of film, the negative is peeled away and discarded, leaving a print on the paper, which develops a little further over the next five minutes as the paper dries. A development of this process gives a permanent negative as well as the print.

Instant-picture film

Instant-picture film uses a system of metallized dyes, and the process is effectively dry because the processing chemicals are sealed within the film covering. When the shutter is fired, exposing the film, the print is automatically wound out of the camera by an electric motor. It consists of a rectangle of white plastic on which the color image gradually begins to appear, taking up to four minutes for complete development.

Any normal film would be immediately ruined if exposed in daylight in this way before the processing procedures are complete. Therefore, this film consists of a complex sandwich of a number of physical layers, most of which are coated on the two plastic sheets of which the film is made up. At

▼ The complex layered structure of Polaroid color film. The color components are metallized dye developers over which lie sensitized emulsions to control the developers during the processing of the picture. As the film is fed out of the camera between the processing rollers, developing chemicals are forced between the layers and also prevent light from reaching the sensitive lower layers.

the bottom of the sandwich is a dark plastic base on which are coated the many layers that will make up the negative and supply the dyes for the print. At the top of the sandwich is a clear, transparent plastic layer that forms the protective surface of the print. On its underside is coated the image-receiving layer in which the final picture will be formed when the film is developed.

Between the multicoated base and the image-receiving layer, there is a weak bond. When the film is exposed and is forced out of the camera, it passes through two rollers. As with the earlier instant film, a pod of chemicals in the film is burst by the rollers and chemicals are forced evenly between the layers. In this case, it is a thick, milky substance that, as it is spread through the interior of the film sandwich, prevents light from reaching the light-sensitive layers lower in the sandwich. At the same time, it acts as a developer and sets in motion the processing of the film.

Apart from space layers, the negative portion consists of six active layers. Three of these are coated with silver halide layers that are sensitive to different colors of light, and three contain cyan (blue), magenta (red), and yellow dye developers. Moving down through the film from the image-receiving layer, the layers are blue-sensitive halide, yellow dye developer, a spacer layer, green-sensitive halide layer, magenta dye developer, a spacer layer, red-sensitive halide layer, and cyan dye developer. The arrangement of the layers is such that they act as filters for the layers below them so that, as the light passes down through them, colors are progressively filtered out, and each of the light-sensitive layers responds to only one particular color.

During exposure, three negative imprints are thus formed in the layers, one each for blue, green, and red light (in order moving down toward the bottom of the film). When the developer is added, it develops the three negatives and releases the dyes from the other three layers. These dyes move freely up through the film. When they meet an exposed section of the negative of the appropriate color, however, they are immediately trapped and neutralized. The dye that is not trapped in this way continues up through the film to the image-receiving layer under the print surface and is trapped there along with the white developer layer.

Two things happen next. First, the colored pigments mixed with the white pigment begin to form a positive

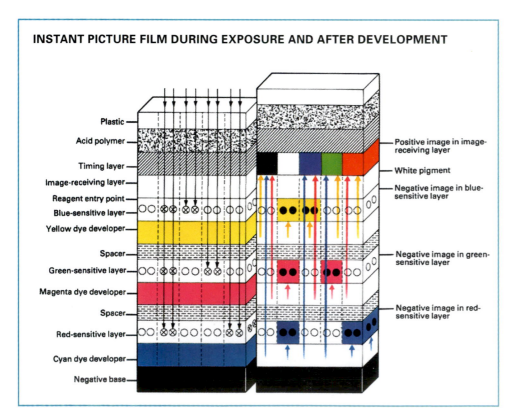

INSTANT PICTURE FILM DURING EXPOSURE AND AFTER DEVELOPMENT

Plastic
Acid polymer
Timing layer
Image-receiving layer
Reagent entry point
Blue-sensitive layer
Yellow dye developer

Spacer
Green-sensitive layer

Magenta dye developer
Spacer
Red-sensitive layer

Cyan dye developer

Negative base

Positive image in image-receiving layer
White pigment
Negative image in blue-sensitive layer

Negative image in green-sensitive layer

Negative image in red-sensitive layer

systems, automatic exposure control, built-in flash, and even automatic focusing. The last works by measuring the echoes of an ultrasonic sound wave. A microprocessor calculates the distance, and the lens is adjusted with a miniature electric motor in the instant before the shutter is opened and the film exposed.

Instant photography users

While the greatest market for instant photography has proved to be in the snapshot market, the development of the technology has been extended into diverse fields. There is a surprisingly high use of instant equipment by professional photographers, in both the creative and the industrial fields. Special Polaroid film backs can be fitted to a number of professional cameras, and they are used extensively for planning the composition and complex lighting of a shot. The photographer simply fits the Polaroid back to his or her camera and checks the result on instant film, before switching to conventional film when satisfied. There are also industrial photographic uses; professional instant cameras available are capable of producing high-quality records of engineering works in progress, for example. Similarly, systems are available for making instant records of computer displays.

Electronic cameras

Although Polaroid introduced an instant home movie system in the 1970s, it was not a commercial success because it came into direct competition with video systems that were cheaper and more versatile. Similarly, electronic systems are gradually being adopted for still photography. A number of electronic and photographic companies have developed digital cameras in which the pictures are captured with an image sensor and stored on miniature floppy disks. These systems have many advantages over instant-picture cameras. Digital images can be downloaded directly onto a computer and fed to a printer to form a hard copy. Alternatively, the images can be transmitted on the Internet. One advantage digital cameras lack, however, is the ability to print out instant images from the camera itself. Manufacturers, such as Polaroid, have responded to this shortcoming by producing cameras such as the I-Zone Digital and Instant Combo Camera that combine the functions of instant-picture cameras with those of digital cameras.

image, and second, the opaque coloring elements in the reagent mixture are gradually cleared by the materials released in the development process. After about a minute, the opaque white barrier becomes clear in accordance with the level of chemical activity beneath it, revealing the picture, which rapidly becomes fast on the image-receiving layer. Another, slower-working layer now fixes the activity, and the image becomes as permanent as any other print.

Cameras

A major drawback with instant-processing systems is that because of the direct image-forming process, the cameras have to be fairly large to give an acceptable size of print. Considerable effort has been applied to minimize the effects of this limitation; folded light paths are being used in the cameras to give the lens-to-film distance needed to make a large image. While the basic system is the same in most models, the more expensive cameras offer considerable sophistication with features such as single-lens reflex (SLR) viewing

▲ Professional photographers make extensive use of Polaroid stock before committing their work to film. This step allows them to check that their equipment is working properly, that the composition of the photograph is acceptable, that the lighting is correct, and that the overall shot is exactly what is wanted. What such tests cannot do is give an accurate indication of color rendition on film.

SEE ALSO: Camera • Camera, digital • Lens • Light and optics • Movie camera • Photographic film and processing • Shutter

Insulation, Thermal

Wherever there is a difference between two temperatures, heat will flow from a warmer to a colder environment. Heating living spaces accounts for nearly 70 percent of the energy used in the average home, but a significant portion of this energy can be wasted unless steps are taken to prevent the heat from escaping through walls, floors, roofs, and windows. Most modern houses make use of energy-saving insulating materials to prevent heat loss, many of which can also be fitted to older buildings to make them more energy efficient. Thermal insulation not only can prevent heat from flowing out from a house, it can also keep a house cool in the summer. It even has the added benefit of reducing noise levels.

The insulating properties of a material are rated according to its thermal resistance, or R value, which indicates its resistance to heat flow. This value varies with the type of material, its density, and the thickness that is used. When a number of layers of different materials are used, the R values are added together to give a combined rating. Compressing the insulator will decrease its rating, as will structural joists and studs, which act as thermal short-circuits through the insulating material.

Heat can be lost from a building in four ways: by conduction through structural materials, through convection by currents of air within the rooms or cavity walls of a building, by air leaking through cracks and gaps in the structure, and by radiation. Materials used in thermal insulation depend on the space being insulated. Cavities can be filled with blown-in loose fibers or pellets or with a polyurethane foam. Blankets of mineral fibers can be produced in a variety of widths to suit the spaces between wall studs and floor joists, and they can be bent around curved surfaces. Fibrous materials and foams can also be compressed or extruded into more rigid structures and faced with a reflective foil surface to radiate heat in the preferred direction.

Glass and mineral fibers

Fiberglass is the most common form of thermal insulation used in buildings. Made from molten sand or recycled glass, it is produced in two forms: wool-like fibers and textile fibers. It is the wool-like fiber that is commonly used for insulation materials. Molten glass is poured onto a rapidly spinning disk that has thousands of holes around its rim. The glass is forced through the

▲ New houses are built to much higher energy-saving standards than older properties. As a result, new houses frequently include filled-cavity outer walls, board or fiberglass-lined inner walls and floors, lagged pipework, and double-glazed windows.

holes by centrifugal force to create a fiber that is immediately coated with a chemical binder to stick the fibers together. The glass fiber is then cured in an oven before being cut into lengths of insulating batting or blanket or chopped into loose-fill material that can be blown into cavities. Fiberglass batts and blankets are available with R values that vary according to thickness and fiber density, typically between R-11 and R-15 for a 3½ in. (9 cm) thick blanket. Loose-fill fiberglass blown into a cavity will have three times the density of batting and an R-value of 14.3 for a 3½ in. cavity. However, fiberglass has come under scrutiny by environmental groups and government health agencies over fears that it may prove to be carcinogenic in the same way as asbestos fiber, once used extensively as a fire retardant and insulating agent.

Two other synthetic vitreous fibers are used for thermal insulation. Rock wool is made from a mineral such as diabase or basalt. Slag wool uses the waste from iron ore smelting. Both are produced much as fiberglass is and have the same resistance to the growth of molds and mildew. Because mineral wools can resist temperatures in excess of 2000°F (1100°C), they are also used for fire protection in pipe and process insulation, in ships, and in domestic cooking appliances.

Polyurethane foam

Filling wall cavities with foam has proved one of the most effective ways to prevent heat loss, as it seals the cavity almost completely and has the highest R value of any form of insulation at R-7 per inch. It is, however, expensive and there was initially concern about the chlorofluorocarbon propellants used to make the chemical foam, though they have since been replaced by pentane. A modified form of urethane foam, called Icynene, has now been developed that uses water as the propellant. The resulting foam is much lighter and retains its pillowy structure when set, making it able to expand or contract with the building, but it has a much lower R value of 3.6 per inch.

Rigid insulation boards

Another thermal insulation product used in building construction is the rigid board, which can be made of fibrous material or extruded polymer pressed into a board or into molded fittings for pipes. Polystyrene can be used in its extruded or expanded form as a lightweight beadboard. Polyisocyanurate is spongy and less brittle and, like polystyrene, is often backed with paper, plastic, or foil to increase its strength. Boards typically have R values between 4 and 7 per inch.

Radiant-barrier systems

Radiant barriers and reflective insulation systems consist of a thin sheet of aluminum or a similar reflective material applied to one or both sides of a substrate, usually kraft paper, plastic films, cardboard, or plywood. Radiant barriers work by reducing the amount of heat radiated across an air space adjacent to the barrier, for example, that between the attic floor and the roof. For barriers to work effectively they must have high reflectivity (a measure of how much radiant energy is reflected by a material) and low emissivity (that is, they must not emit too much radiation). Most barrier materials have reflectivities of 0.9 or more and emissivities of 0.1 or less.

Composite wall systems

Rather than fit insulating materials to the inner or outer surface of brickwork, researchers have investigated the use of bricks that have insulating material as part of their internal structure. These concrete masonry units (CMUs) work on the principle of thermal mass in that the blocks help to regulate the structure by dissipating the heat they have absorbed during the day back into the building during the night. In summer the process works in a similar manner, the temperature of the blocks falling to that of the ambient air and staying cool for up to eight hours.

The interior of the concrete brick can be filled with either natural or synthetic insulating materials, such as polystyrene, polyurethane, or perlite. The thermal insulation values for CMUs are very good, ranging between R-15 and R-28, depending on the filler material.

▼ A false-color scanning electron micrograph of vermiculite, or micafill, used as a loose-fill insulator. Vermiculite is made from expanded mica, a silicate mineral composed of very thin sheets of atoms. The expansion process introduces air between the layers, increasing its insulating properties.

SEE ALSO: Fiber, mineral • Glass fiber • Heating and ventilation systems • Thermogram

Insulator, Electric

Insulators constitute a class of substances, sometimes called dielectrics, that resist the flow of electrical current. As such, they are useful in isolating electrical conductors one from another. Insulators help prevent the loss of current from electrical circuits by electrically isolating circuits from grounded conductors. Insulators also help prevent electrocution—in which case one of the potential conductors is a living being—and they are an essential component of capacitors, which are electrical charge-storage devices.

Examples of insulators

Ceramics, such as glass and porcelain, are examples of rigid insulators; porcelain pots are used to suspend conductors from electricity-transmission towers, for example. Flexible insulators include polymers such as plasticized polyvinyl chloride (PVC), polytetrafluoroethene (PTFE), and polypropene (PP); these materials are used as flexible coatings for electrical cables.

Some polymers—the phenol-formaldehyde thermoset bakelite, for example—are tough materials that are useful for making rigid casings for electrical equipment. Hydrocarbons and certain inorganic compounds—notably sulfur hexafluoride (SF_6)—are liquid insulators. They are useful for cooling and immersing electrical equipment in an insulating medium. Sulfur hexafluoride is

▲ Electricity substations interconvert high-tension power for long-distance transmission and lower-tension power for local and regional distribution. Here, V-shaped insulating struts support high-tension conductors to prevent discharges to ground.

used to quench electrical arcs between the contacts of one type of heavy-duty circuit breaker, for example. Other insulators include air, paper, mica (a mineral), and most metal oxides.

Resistivity and resistance

Resistivity is a measure of the intrinsic ability of a material to impede the flow of electrical current. As such, an ideal insulator—if one existed—would have an infinitely large resistivity.

Resistance, measured in ohms (Ω), is defined as the theoretical voltage required for a current of one amp to flow through a sample. In the case of insulators, however, the current is often much less than one amp, and the resistance is calculated by dividing voltage by current.

The resistivity, ρ (the Greek letter rho), of a material is derived from resistance measurements by compensating for the dimensions of samples of that material. If the distance between two electrodes separated by a resistive material doubles, for example, the resistance to the flow of current between those electrodes will also double. Resistivity is therefore measured as the resistance per unit length of sample. If the cross section of the sample doubles, the amount of current that flows at a given voltage doubles, and the resistance falls to half its original value. Resistivity is therefore calculated by multiplying resistance by the cross-sectional area of the sample.

Combining the two factors that account for sample dimensions, the resistivity of a material is calculated according to the following expression:

$$\rho = RA/l$$

In this expression, ρ is resistivity (in Ωm), R is resistance (Ω), A is the cross section (m^2) of the sample between two measuring electrodes, and l is the length (m) of sample between electrodes.

Resistivity values

A typical resistivity value for glass is 10^{12} Ωm, which corresponds to a one-inch (2.54 cm) cube of glass having a resistance of around 4×10^{13} Ω between two opposite faces. In contrast, copper—an excellent conductor of electricity—has a resistivity of 1.7×10^{-8} Ωm, corresponding to a resistance of around 6×10^{-7} Ω for a one-inch (2.54 cm) cube. Rubber has a resistivity of around 10^{14} Ωm, PTFE has a value greater than 10^{19} Ωm, and fused quartz has a value of almost 10^{17} Ωm. The difference between the resistivities of a typical good conductor and a typical good insulator is therefore a factor of around 10^{25}.

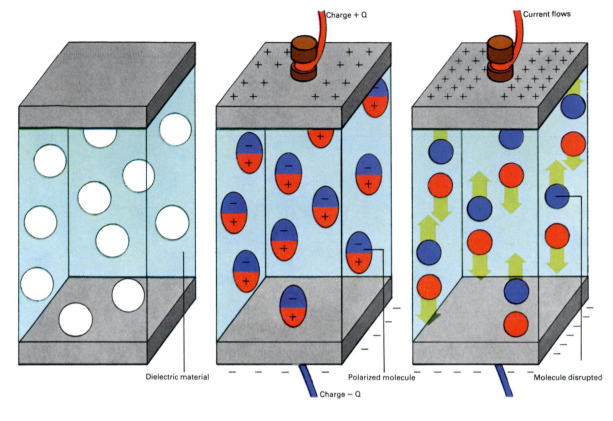

▶ When an insulator, or dielectric material (left), experiences an electrical field, its molecules become polarized (center). Above a certain field strength, the dielectric molecules are ripped apart by the field, forming positive ions and free electrons (right). A current can then flow.

Charge + Q   Current flows

Dielectric material   Polarized molecule   Molecule disrupted

Charge − Q

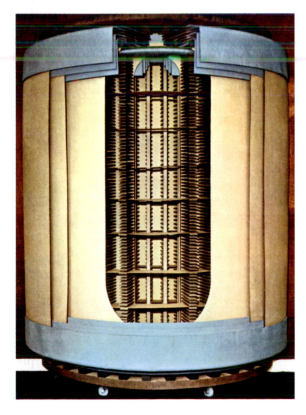

▼ This cutaway of a transformer casing shows the insulating supports that carry conductive copper windings (absent in this picture) and prevent potentially dangerous short circuits when the transformer is in action.

Structures of insulators

The two broad classes of insulators are ionic solids and molecular solids, liquids, and gases. In either case, the insulating property stems from the absence of charged species that are free to move and therefore carry a current.

In the case of ionic solids, their component negative and positive ions are held firmly in lattice structures by extremely strong electrostatic attractions between neighboring ions that have opposite charges. The force caused by an electric field between two electrodes is weak in comparison. When an ionic substance melts or dissolves, it becomes a good conductor as its ions become free to move.

Molecular solids, liquids, and gases are insulators because their component molecules have no overall charge. Hence, they have no means of carrying an electrical current.

Polarization

Some molecules have electrical dipoles. An example is molecular hydrogen chloride (HCl), which has a slight negative charge on its chlorine atom owing to the great affinity of chlorine atoms for electrons; in compensation, the hydrogen atom carries a slight positive charge. In electrical fields, polar molecules tend to become aligned such that their negative portions point toward the positive pole of the field, and vice versa.

Nonpolar molecules, such as methane (CH_4), acquire dipoles in electrical fields. These temporary dipoles, called induced dipoles, arise because an electrical field draws electrons in bonds toward the positive pole of the field. Induced dipoles also enhance charge separation in polar substances.

Breakdown

Extremely strong electrical fields are capable of ripping electrons from the bonds in molecular insulators. At that point—a condition called breakdown—an insulator starts to conduct as electrons are liberated from their bonds.

The field strength at which breakdown occurs depends on the insulator. Rubber, for example, requires a field strength (voltage gradient) greater than 2.5 megavolts per in. (1 MV/cm) for breakdown to occur. Breakdown can cause irreversible changes in the bond structure of an insulator.

SEE ALSO: CAPACITOR • CONDUCTION, ELECTRICAL • ELECTRICITY • FUSE AND CIRCUIT BREAKER • ION AND IONIZATION • RESISTOR

Integrated Circuit

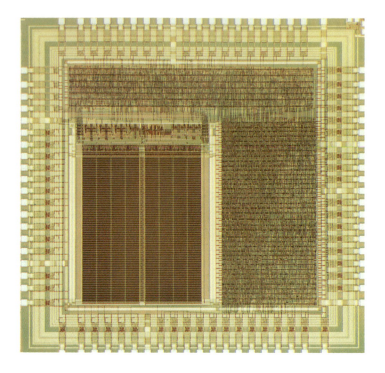

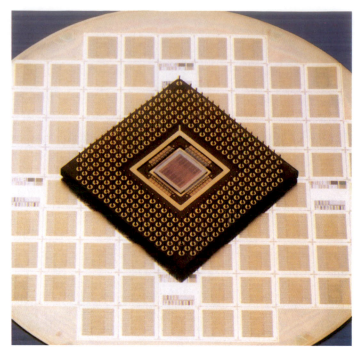

An integrated circuit is a monolithic (one-piece) device, built by forming conducting and semiconducting paths on the surface of a single chip of semiconductor, that has all the electronic components necessary to perform a specific function. Integrated circuits include the central-processing and memory units of computers and the microprocessors that control the functions of appliances such as automatic washing machines.

Before integration

The applied science of electronics by no means started with the invention of the integrated circuit in the 1960s. From the start of the 20th century, vacuum tubes had been used in combination with resistors, capacitors, and other electrical devices to control the flow of electrons so as to produce signals, tune radios, and perform calculations. The component parts of an integrated circuit merely perform the same functions as such pieces of equipment, but in much more compact devices and in a much more reliable manner.

A great step toward the integration of circuits on semiconducting material occurred in 1947, when the first semiconducting (solid-state) transistor was invented. The term *transistor* is a contraction of *trans*fer–res*istor*, which refers to the component's ability to allow or impede the flow of electrons according to conditions.

The core of one type of transistor is a three-layer sandwich of alternating variants of the same semiconducting material—usually silicon. The semiconductor variants are of two types—*n* and *p*

▲ Left: a silicon chip, typically about ¼ in. sq. (5 mm²) viewed through a microscope so that its intricate patterns can be seen clearly. Right: a complex state-of-the-art microchip such as might be used for advanced microprocessors. The chip is photographed on top of a wafer containing a number of microchip dies.

(negative and positive)—which are produced by doping (allowing impurities to diffuse into a crystal of pure semiconductor). In the case of silicon, an *n*-type semiconductor is produced by diffusing phosphorus into pure silicon, producing an excess of negative-charge carriers (electrons); a *p*-type semiconductor is produced by diffusing boron into silicon, producing positive-charge carriers (electron vacancies, or holes).

In such a device, called a bipolar transistor, an *n-p-n* or a *p-n-p* sandwich prevents the flow of electrons between electrodes attached to the two outer layers, because a junction between an *n*-type and a *p*-type semiconductor resists the flow of electrons from the *p*-type and *n*-type in either case. A current can flow, however, if an appropriate voltage is applied to a "gate" electrode attached to the central layer of such a sandwich. A negative voltage applied to the middle layer of an *n-p-n* sandwich will neutralize the center layer or convert it into an effective *n*-type semiconductor, thereby reducing the *p-n* barrier and allowing current to flow. A similar effect occurs if a positive voltage is applied to the center of a *p-n-p* sandwich.

Since the amount by which the barrier-to-electron flow reduces depends heavily on the voltage applied to the center layer of a transistor, small changes in that voltage result in large variations in the current that flows between the electrodes attached to the two outer layers. A transistor the size of an electrical fuse can therefore act as an amplifier—a task previously performed by a triode valve the size of an electric lamp.

Early integrated circuits

The first electronic component incorporated in the surface of a semiconductor crystal was developed in 1958. The potential of semiconducting devices to replace larger conventional components was then extended to whole electrical circuits in 1961, when the U.S. electronics engineers Jack Kilby and Robert Noyce independently produced the first integrated circuits. Their devices consisted of transistors, and other electronic components, produced by selectively doping regions of crystals of pure silicon and linked by conducting paths to form complete electronic circuits. A typical early integrated circuit consisted of around 10 components linked together on a slice of silicon around 0.1 in. (2.5 mm) square.

Developments

Since the early 1960s, the pace of development of integrated circuits has been unrelenting. By 1974, the sophistication of integrated circuits had become sufficient to provide the calculating power for the first home computers: the Intel 8080 had a circuit that contained 6,000 transistors joined by conducting paths no more than 6 μm wide. The 8080 could perform around 2 million basic calculations per second—a clock speed of 2 MHz. Within five years, the Intel 8088 had almost five times the number of transistors, joined by conducting paths half as wide as in the 8080, and achieved a clock speed of 5 MHz. By the end of the 20th century, the Intel Pentium 4 had 42 million transistors, 0.18 μm conducting paths, and clock speeds around 1.5 GHz.

Developments in integrated circuits for computer applications have had spin-off benefits for the manufacturers and users of electrical appliances. Ever-cheaper and more sophisticated integrated circuits have revolutionized the capabilities of microprocessor-controlled devices as

diverse as mobile telephones, sound systems, and so-called white goods, such as washing machines and microwave ovens. The automobile industry has also reaped the benefits of advances in integrated circuits, by using microprocessors as the "brains" of advanced braking, suspension, and engine-management systems.

MOSFETs

A major contributing factor to the increased compactness and computing power of integrated circuits was the replacement of bipolar transistors of the type already described by MOSFETs—metal-oxide semiconductor field-effect transistors. A MOSFET dispenses with the gate electrode that feeds electrons to (or drains them from) the middle layer of a bipolar transistor and has two layers of different types of semiconductor rather than three. The two layers lie side by side in the surface of the semiconductor, and one of them is separated from a metal electrode on the surface by a layer of insulating silicon dioxide. A voltage applied to this electrode produces an electrical field that causes electrons to shift within the layer below so as to neutralize or reverse its character and create a channel through which electrons can flow.

Since no current passes between the metal electrode and the semiconductor, MOSFETs use less power than do bipolar transistors. Their simpler structure allows them to be packed more tightly and reduces the rejection rate in production.

▲ The surface of an integrated circuit viewed through an electron microscope. The conducting paths are clearly visible.

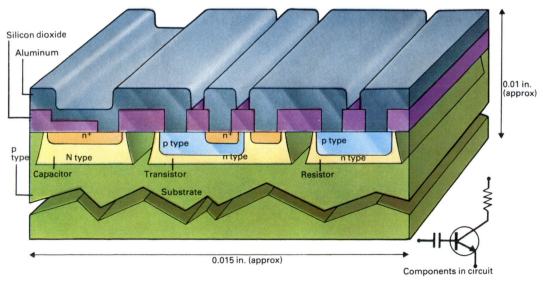

◄ The components of an integrated circuit are built up from regions of doped semiconductor, insulating silicon dioxide layers and conducting aluminum.

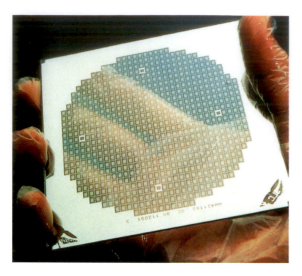

◄ Integrated circuits are etched onto silicon chips using glass masks such as this. Each mask contains hundreds or even thousands of exact replicas of one circuit layer.

Wafer preparation

The manufacture of integrated circuits always starts with the purification of the basic semiconducting element or compound, because impurities modify the electrical properties of semiconductors—an effect that is used in a controlled manner to create circuit components.

The purification of silicon for semiconductor devices starts with 98-percent-pure silicon, which is produced by the reduction of sand (almost-pure silicon dioxide, SiO_2) using coke (a form of carbon) in a furnace. Impure silicon is treated with hydrochloric acid (HCl) to give a mixture of silicon tetrachloride ($SiCl_4$) and trichlorosilane ($SiHCl_3$), which are purified by fractional distillation to remove boron and phosphorus impurities.

The purified silicon compounds are reduced using pure hydrogen, and solid silicon then forms polycrystalline deposits on fine rods of pure silicon heated to around 1800°F (1000°C). These rods may be up to 3 ft. (0.91 m) long with a final diameter of around 6 in. (15 cm). Typically, the silicon that results has no more than one part by weight impurities in 10^9 parts silicon.

The silicon is then further purified and formed into a single crystal. In one of the methods used, a single seed crystal is dipped into the surface of a bath of molten silicon at just over 2550°F (1400°C). Before it melts, the seed crystal is slowly withdrawn at such a speed that pure silicon solidifies at the base of the crystal and forms a columnar single crystal. Any impurities remain in the melt, and the crystal structure continues that of the original seed crystal. The operation is performed in an inert gas atmosphere to prevent the hot silicon from reacting.

The single crystals produced by the above method have an irregular shape. The next stage is to grind them to a uniform diameter, usually around 4 in. (10 cm). The resulting cylinder is sliced using a thin, high-speed diamond saw to form wafers around 0.02 in. (0.5 mm) thick. These wafers are then ground smooth on both sides and highly polished on one side. These operations are done in stringently clean conditions to avoid contamination of the wafers.

Doping and circuit preparation

Silicon is doped by heating it in the presence of volatile compounds of the doping elements phosphorus (for *n*-type silicon) and boron (for *p*-type silicon). To create the components of an integrated circuit requires the formation of distinct regions of *n*-type and *p*-type silicon. The photoengraving process that achieves this separation takes advantage of the fact that silicon dioxide is impermeable to the doping reagents.

Wafers are first heated in an oxidizing atmosphere so that a continuous layer of silicon dioxide forms on their surfaces. The oxidized wafer is then coated with a light-sensitive emulsion and exposed to light through a mask that casts shadows on the areas to be doped. The emulsion in the remaining areas hardens to form a polymer film at this stage, and unhardened emulsion is then washed away from the areas to be doped. The hardened emulsion resists the acid etch that follows, while the unprotected areas lose their silicon dioxide coating as it dissolves in the acid. Finally, the hardened emulsion is removed and the slice is ready for selective diffusion.

When the various components have been formed by a series of diffusion steps, they are interconnected by a metal film, usually of aluminum, deposited on the surface and insulated from it in most parts by a layer of silicon dioxide. Where the aluminum is intended to come into contact with the semiconductor, the silicon dioxide must first be removed by a photoengraving process similar to that used for doping.

Assembly and testing

Up to this point, the circuits have been processed in a batch of many slices, each one containing hundreds, thousands, or even millions of individual circuits. This mass production is a feature of the process and is a dominant factor in the economics of integrated circuit manufacture. For the user, however, each circuit must be individually assembled in a suitable package to provide protection and convenience in handling and further assembly into equipment. These later stages contribute a major part of the manufacturing cost of the finished circuit. Therefore, before packaging, each circuit must be thoroughly tested.

Wafers are tested using a multiprobe technique, in which tens of needle probes are brought into contact with the aluminum pads of the chips

MEMORY DEVICES

The processing function of any integrated circuit requires memory devices from which instructions and other data can be retrieved and to which processed data can be stored. Some of this memory capacity may be present as part of the processor chip itself, while the majority is usually devolved to separate memory devices, which take a variety of forms.

One type of memory is ROM—read only memory. Such memory is stored in a form that cannot be overwritten, as is the case of the data of a CD-ROM or DVD-ROM. In the case of the standard ROM of a chip, information is permanently stored in the circuitry of the chip. Such information includes the BIOS (basic input-output system) of a personal computer (PC). Some types of ROM chips are bought blank and programmed only once. Such chips are called PROMs (programmable read only memories); others can be erased by ultraviolet light and then reprogrammed (EPROMs—erasable-programmable read only memories); while yet others can be reprogrammed at will using task-specific software (EEPROMs—electrically erasable–programmable read only memories).

A hard drive provides the long-term memory that a computer uses for storing information that is subject to change but that may remain unchanged for long periods. A hard drive has several magnetizable rotating disks and a read-write head that stores information as magnetic pulses on those disks. Drives for floppy and other removable disks function in the same way.

The memory that works most intimately with the processor of an integrated circuit is the RAM—random access memory. RAM is classed as volatile memory, since its content disappears once its power supply is disconnected, unlike the content of a ROM or hard drive.

The function of RAM is to store all the information, including software, that a processor requires for a computer's tasks at any given time. Such information might include word-processing programs, images that are being edited, and open documents. Provided the RAM capacity satisfies

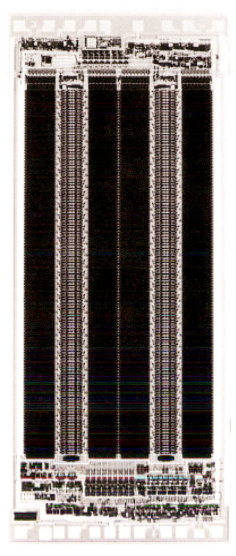

▲ A close-up view of Japanese manufacturer Fujitsu's 64-kilobyte SD-RAM. Random access memory acts as a temporary store for data that are frequently used by a computer's CPU.

the total memory requirement for all the programs in use, the effect of RAM is to make the processor more agile by keeping the information it requires "close at hand" (access to and retrieval from RAM is more rapid than with other forms of memory).

The process of keeping a temporary supply of data in readiness for use by the central processor unit (CPU) is called caching. A small amount of cache memory, the level-one (L1) cache, forms part of the integrated circuit of the CPU. While its capacity is relatively small—typically 2 to 64 kilobytes—the close physical link between the CPU circuit and the L1 cache

makes it the fastest to access. A memory-controlling circuit directs the most often used data to the L1 cache.

The next-fastest cache after the level-one cache is the level-two (L2) cache, which may be around 2 megabytes in capacity. While some computers have the L2 cache directly connected to the CPU but mounted on a separate card—making L2 significantly slower than L1 cache—some high-performance computers have both the CPU and the L2 caches on the same card, so the speed difference is less. The term *onboard* is used to describe L2 caches that share a card with the CPU.

The largest part of the RAM of a computer is located in memory modules. Memory modules are multichip cards that may each accommodate around eight 4-megabyte chips, typically providing 32 megabytes of RAM in total. The advantage of modules is that a number of such cards may be plugged or soldered into the motherboard—the card that supports the CPU and onboard L2 cache memory. This allows one type of computer to be configured with different amounts of RAM so as to offer options of cost and performance. Furthermore, additional memory modules can usually be installed to meet growing demands on RAM from new software.

The two basic physical formats of RAM are static and dynamic. Both consist of one-bit memory cells in grids, whose nine-bit rows each store a byte of information and an error-correction bit. Data is written to and read from the cells by signals that pass along the wires of the grid to intersect at the appropriate cells. In the case of static RAM (SRAM), the memory cells are multitransistor latch circuits, which do not need to be rewritten provided their power supply is maintained. In the case of dynamic RAM (DRAM), each memory cell consists of a transistor switch and a capacitor that represents "1" when charged beyond a certain value. The charge must be topped up millions of times per second, thus slowing the operation of DRAM relative to SRAM. On the other hand, the simpler cells of DRAM make it cheaper and more compact than SRAM.

and an appropriate electrical test is performed. Full functional testing can be extremely complex, but acceptable production rates are achieved by using computer-controlled test sequences.

Such systems may perform thousands of test steps per second, at the same time recording the results for statistical analysis, listing failures, and sorting the devices for further processing. The probe machine then marks imperfect chips with ink so that they can be isolated and destroyed.

After the probe test, the slices are separated into individual chips, sometimes by scribing between rows of chips with a diamond point, then breaking the wafers mechanically along the scribe lines. This method is slow, so large-scale production lines tend to use fine automatic saws or lasers to cut wafers into individual chips.

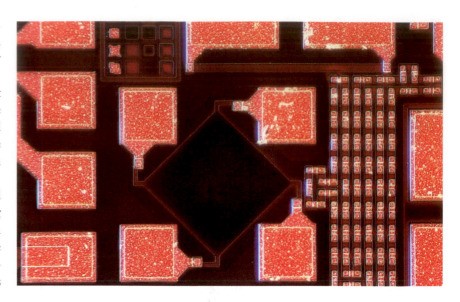

FACT FILE

- In the early 1980s, integrated circuit engineers recognized a phenomenon, called circuit aging, that has the potential to degrade the performance of integrated circuits. The effect is caused by fast-moving electrons escaping from the conducting channels of integrated circuits and striking silicon atoms in their paths. Some of these collisions release free electrons, which cause physical damage and compositional changes in integrated circuits. Significant circuit-aging problems became apparent only in the late 1990s, when channel lengths decreased to around 0.18 μm (7.1 x 10^{-8} in.).

- In 2000, a team of U.S. researchers announced they had built a biointegrated circuit, or BBIC (bioluminescent bioreporter integrated circuit). The biological component of the chip is a strain of Pseudomonas—a microorganism that digests naphthalene ($C_{10}H_8$), a bicyclic aromatic hydrocarbon present in petroleum-based pollution. The researchers genetically modified the bacteria to glow in the presence of naphthalene. In the BBIC, this glow is detected by light sensors, and the circuit then generates a signal that reports the concentration of naphthalene in the vicinity of the BBIC. Such devices have great potential for pollution monitoring in the soil around petroleum processing and storage installations and for monitoring the spread of pollution after oil spills at sea.

Chips that have not been rejected during the test stage are next fixed onto mountings, called headers, that form the basis of the final package. The chip may be welded onto the header by an alloying process between the silicon and a gold coating on the header, or it may be simply stuck down using a conducting epoxy resin.

Once mounted, the chip must be electrically connected to the pins of the header. It is most often done by wiring, using aluminum or gold wire 0.001 in. (0.025 mm) in diameter bonded to the pads and the pins by ultrasonic welding. The final stage is then encapsulation. This may be an injection-molding process using epoxy resins or, in more critical cases, a hermetic cap welded over the circuit with an inert gas environment to ensure exclusion of reactive gases and water vapor, which could damage the product.

Future trends

As the scale of integrated circuits continues to diminish, the useful lifetime of the photoengraving technique is reaching its end, because the finest detail that can be described by ultraviolet light is 0.1 μm—slightly more than half the size of the finest detail of a Pentium 4 chip. X-ray etching might provide a means of achieving finer detail, as might the direct removal of the oxide layer using beams of ions or electrons.

Researchers are currently investigating ways to increase the speed and reduce the power demand of integrated circuits beyond the capabilities of silicon technology. These goals might one day be achieved by using single electrons or photons to carry information, rather than the electronic currents in present use.

▲ This photomicrograph shows an example of a process-control module. Such devices are used to test the performance of integrated circuits at several stages during their manufacture. Significant proportions of any given batch of integrated circuits must be rejected at some stage of manufacture, adding considerably to the cost of the chips that are acceptable for sale.

SEE ALSO: CAPACITOR • COMPUTER • DIODE • ELECTRONICS • MICROPROCESSOR • RESISTOR • SILICON

Internal Combustion Engine

Development of the internal combustion engine was largely made possible by the earlier development of the steam engine, which established many of the engineering principles and techniques that were needed. Although both types of engines burn fuel to release energy that is then used to perform useful work, they are otherwise totally different.

The steam engine is an external combustion engine in which the fuel is burned in a separate section of the engine to heat a working fluid—steam—which then drives the work-producing part of the engine, the piston in its cylinder. In the internal combustion engine, the fuel is burned in a combustion chamber formed inside the working cylinder. The combustion process is very rapid, amounting to a sudden explosion that forces the piston down the cylinder to produce work. There are two main classes of reciprocating internal combustion engine, the distinction being made according to the working cycle used, the alternatives being the Diesel cycle and the Otto cycle used for spark-ignition gasoline engines. Continuous-flow engines, such as the gas turbine, are also of the internal combustion type.

Development

Early internal combustion engines were mainly gas engines and worked on the atmospheric principle; the combustion products were cooled in the cylinder to give a vacuum so that atmospheric pressure drove the piston into the cylinder to give a power stroke. A number of such engines were built by Samuel Brown in London, and in 1826, he used one of his engines in a road vehicle. The engine had two working cylinders, each of a 12 in. (30 cm) bore and 24 in. (60 cm) stroke. Also in 1826, the first American internal combustion engine, built by Samuel Morely in New Hampshire, was one of the first designs to use liquid fuel and a form of carburetor.

In 1860, J. J. E. Lenoir, a French engineer, started production of a successful engine design that used expansion of the combustion products to drive the piston. This design was similar to a double-acting horizontal steam engine and used town gas as the fuel. In 1867, the German firm of Otto and Langen began producing an engine that transmitted the power of a freely moving piston to a shaft and a heavy flywheel by means of a rack-and-gear device, using a freewheeling clutch in the gear so that it turned freely in one direction and transmitted power in the other.

Meanwhile, in 1862, Alphonse Beau de Rochas had published in Paris his theory of a four-stroke engine of the type used in the modern automobile. While de Rochas never built any engines, his theory included compression of the fuel mixture in order to raise its temperature, and he also realized that a four-stroke design would be more efficient at scavenging (intake of fuel mixture and exhaust of burned gases) than the two-stroke.

▲ The invention of the internal combustion engine revolutionized the transportation of people and goods over large distances. Constant refinements in engine size and performance are enabling designers to build vehicles that are more aerodynamic and fuel efficient, while minimizing the pollutant effects of burning fossil fuels.

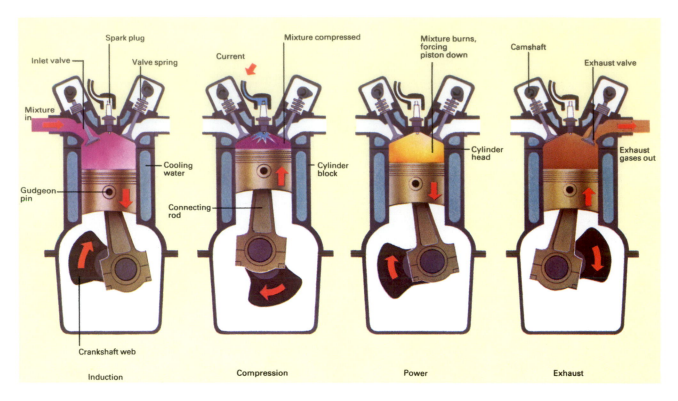

Induction — **Compression** — **Power** — **Exhaust**

Labels in figure: Spark plug, Inlet valve, Valve spring, Mixture in, Cooling water, Gudgeon pin, Connecting rod, Crankshaft web, Current, Mixture compressed, Cylinder block, Mixture burns, forcing piston down, Camshaft, Cylinder head, Exhaust valve, Exhaust gases out

A two-stroke engine provides for intake of fuel, combustion, and exhaust of burned gases with each back-and-forth motion of the piston (that is, with each revolution of the crankshaft). A four-stroke engine requires four strokes, that is, two complete back-and-forth movements of the piston (two revolutions of the crankshaft). The two-stroke engine delivers twice as many power impulses as the four-stroke engine to the crankshaft, but the four-stroke is much more efficient at scavenging, if all other things are equal. The two-stroke design is also wasteful, because unburned fuel is exhausted along with the burned gases.

In 1876, Otto and Langen began building the Otto silent engine (it was a good deal quieter than their earlier model). It was the first modern internal combustion engine, a four-stroke design that compressed the fuel mixture before combustion. After 1878, it was also manufactured in the United States, where it was an inspiration to Henry Ford in his early research.

Although the four-stroke, or Otto, engine was a notable success there was also considerable interest in the possibility of increasing the output by having a power stroke for every engine revolution. In 1879, the Scottish engineer Sir Dugald Clerk developed an effective two-stroke engine.

These early engines used a gas as the fuel—in Morely's engine the heated carburetor was used to vaporize turpentine into a gas for use in the engine—but gas was an expensive fuel and of limited availability. The solution lay in the use of petroleum-based fuels, with engines being devel-

oped to use both the volatile fractions (gasoline engines) and the less volatile oils. In early oil engines, the fuel oil was injected into the engine cylinder during the engine compression stroke. The heat in the cylinder vaporized the oil to give a fuel–air mixture that was then ignited by hot-tube or spark-ignition systems, as in gas engines. In a development of this arrangement, the fuel was injected into a separate vaporizing chamber, and the resulting gas charge was drawn into the working cylinder. In 1892, Dr. Rudolf Diesel obtained a German patent for an oil engine in which compression of the air to a high pressure resulted in a high enough temperature to ignite fuel sprayed into the cylinder. The first successful working version of the diesel engine was produced in 1897.

The other main stream of engine development was directed to the production of lighter, higher-speed engines more suited to vehicle applications, such as automobiles and aircraft, with the German engineers Gottlieb Daimler, Wilhelm Maybach, and Karl Benz laying the foundations for the continued development that has resulted in modern automobile engines.

The arrangement of a reciprocating piston working in a cylinder still forms the basis of most modern automobile engines, but an alternative approach is offered by the Wankel engine. In this design, the piston and cylinder are replaced by a triangular rotor working in an oval chamber. The rotor turns eccentrically within the chamber giving three separate chambers that move around the chamber with the rotor, altering in size to give induction, compression, ignition, and exhaust

▲ A cutaway showing the four cycles of the four-stroke spark-ignition engine. When the piston begins its downward movement, the intake valve opens and the engine takes in a cylinder full of air and gasoline. The piston then moves up to compress the mixture, and thus make the explosion more powerful. As the piston reaches the top of its stroke, the spark plug ignites the mixture and pushes the piston back down. When the piston reaches the bottom of the cylinder, the exhaust valve opens and the gases escape. The cycle then starts again.

strokes at successive positions around the chamber. A gear system inside the rotor transfers the motion to an output shaft.

Four-stroke design

The four-stroke cycle operates as follows: On the first downstroke of the piston, the intake valve opens, and the fuel mixture is pulled into the combustion chamber. On the following upstroke, all valves are closed, and the fuel mixture is compressed. At the beginning of the second downstroke, combustion takes place; the fuel mixture is ignited by a spark from the spark plug, and the expanding gases drive the piston downward. On the second upstroke, the exhaust valve opens, and the burned gases are expelled. Thus, the four parts of the cycle are intake, compression, combustion, and exhaust.

The fuel mixture is a mixture of fuel and air in the form of a vapor, which is prepared by the carburetor. The fuel is usually gasoline, but internal combustion engines of various types can be designed to run on anything from kerosene to high-test aviation fuel and gas. Fuel-injection systems use a high-pressure pump and injection nozzles to supply measured amounts of fuel to the engine. The carburetor must be adjusted properly: if the mixture is too lean (does not contain enough fuel), the engine will not run properly; if it is too rich, the result will be carbon deposits fouling the spark plugs, the valves, and the inside of the combustion chamber, wasting fuel and affecting the performance of the engine.

Two-stroke design

The two-stroke engine must accomplish intake, combustion, and exhaust in one back-and-forth movement of the pistons. Since scavenging (the removal of the exhaust gases) is incomplete and inefficient, the proper mixture is difficult to obtain. Small two-stroke engines such as are still used in some motorcycles, lawn mowers, and small cars must have oil added to the gasoline and constitute an air pollution problem; the blue smoke from the exhaust pipe of these engines is one of their familiar characteristics.

One way of improving the scavenging of the two-stroke engine is to build opposing pistons, which reciprocate in opposite directions and share a common combustion chamber. This design was chosen by Henry Ford for his first car, which was built in 1896. A big disadvantage is that each piston must drive a separate crankshaft, and the motion of the two must be combined through a system of gearing.

The modern diesel engine pulls in air only on the intake and compresses it to between $\frac{1}{12}$ and $\frac{1}{25}$ of its original volume, compared with $\frac{1}{6}$ to $\frac{1}{10}$ for compression in a gasoline engine. Compression raises the temperature of the air to over 1000°F (538°C). At this point, the fuel is injected and ignites spontaneously, without the need for a spark plug. Diesel engines may be two- or four-stroke (both types can be turbocharged), though most road-going diesels are four-stroke.

Fuel injection

As the volume of air drawn into the cylinder is always the same in a diesel engine, its speed is controlled by the amount of fuel that is injected. The fuel is delivered to each injector by a fuel pump, and there is either one pump for each injector or else one main pump supplying all the injectors in turn by means of a distributor valve. Where there is a pump for each injector, the pumps may be grouped together in a single unit, supplying the injectors through feed pipes, or else the pumps and injectors may be combined into individual units with a separate unit mounted on each cylinder. The pumps are of the reciprocating type, with spring-loaded plungers actuated by a camshaft driven by the engine. The accelerator control is connected to the pump mechanism and

▶ Electronic control units are playing an increasing role in the smooth operation of internal combustion engines. Sensors monitor the position of the twin camshafts in this engine, which also benefits from twin-output, plug-top coils that provide a higher spark voltage than remote coils, which gives the spark plugs a longer life.

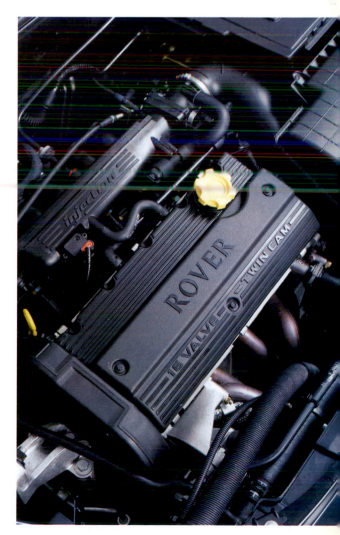

▲ A Mazda RX7 rotary engine. This type of engine has fewer moving parts and is smaller, lighter, and quieter than a conventional piston engine.

alters the running speed of the engine by varying the amount of fuel that is delivered to the injectors. The injectors have spring-loaded needle valves that are opened by the pressure of the shots of fuel delivered by the pumps at the correct instant in the firing cycle. The fuel is sprayed out through holes in the end of the injector, which break it up into a fine mist and distribute it correctly and evenly around the combustion chamber.

Supercharging

The power output of internal combustion engines can be increased significantly by supercharging, and the diesel engine is well suited to this, as only air has to be blown in as opposed to a gasoline–air mixture needed by a gasoline engine. The supercharger drives more air into the cylinders than can be drawn in by the downward motion of the pistons alone, so more fuel–air mixture can be burned in a given cylinder volume than on an unsupercharged engine, and thus, more power is obtained without increasing the size of the engine. The supercharger is a form of compressor, driven by the engine, and several types are

used, including reciprocating, screw, and centrifugal versions, on both two-and four-stroke diesels. Turbochargers are superchargers driven by a small turbine.

Engine design

The block, the head, and the crankshaft are all castings that require extensive machining before the engine can be assembled (some larger crankshafts are forgings, for extra strength). The cylinders must be bored and finished precisely in the block. The top of the block and underside of the head are machined to fit smoothly together, and the tops of the compression chambers are also machined on the underside of the head—except in bowl-in-piston designs, where the head is flat and the tops of the pistons are recessed. Both the block and the head must have numerous surfaces machined and holes drilled and tapped where various components will be mounted. Where the head is bolted to the block, a head gasket is fitted to the joint in order to prevent escape of compression.

Internal combustion engines have been built with as many as 16 cylinders or more in several configurations: opposed, radial, V-formation, and in-line (all in a row). The most common type of engine today is the in-line four- or six-cylinder engine used in cars; V-8 engines are also common.

The underside of the block is open; at the bottom of each cylinder wall, bearing surfaces are machined to accept the main bearings of the crankshaft. Bearing caps are screwed down to hold the crankshaft in place. The pistons slide up and down in the cylinders and are connected to the crankshaft by means of connecting rods that pivot in the pistons and turn on the throws of the crankshaft. An oil pan made of sheet metal or cast light alloy is screwed to the bottom of the block, covering the crankshaft; a gasket is included to prevent leakage of oil, and there is also an oil seal at the end of the crankshaft where it protrudes from the block.

The crankshaft itself is a mechanical adaptation of the hand crank, used for centuries to operate simple machines such as early lathes. For each cylinder in the engine, there is a separate throw (offset section forming a crank) that revolves around the axis of the crankshaft, pushed by the operation of the piston when the engine is running. Opposite each throw on the crankshaft is a web (a mass of metal) to balance it. The throws in a multicylinder engine are arranged equidistantly around the circle described by their revolution, and the firing sequence of the combustion chambers, which depends on the crank position, is timed in such a way as to balance the engine and provide for smooth running.

On the front of the crankshaft, where it protrudes from the engine, is mounted a pulley wheel from which are operated, by means of a belt, the generator and the water pump, if the engine is water cooled. The crankshaft also drives the oil pump by means of a skew gear.

Also mounted on the crankshaft is the timing gear. The timing gear is a pair of gearwheels, or a sprocket linked by a chain to a smaller sprocket, which turns the camshaft, which is generally located in the block, at half crankshaft speed. The camshaft in turn operates the valves and also drives the distributor to spark the mixture at the correct moment.

If the valves are located in the block, the engine is a side-valve, valve-in-hand, flat-head or L-head design. In this case, the valve stems are operated directly by the cams. If the engine is an overhead valve design, the valves are operated from the camshaft by means of an assembly of push rods and rocker arms, and access to the valves for repairs is more easily obtained by removing a sheet metal cover on top of the head, instead of having to remove the head itself. In the overhead cam, the camshaft is also on top and drives the valves directly.

▼ The rotation cycle of the Wankel engine. The space between the eccentrically revolving rotor and its housing varies in volume, expanding and contracting twice during each rotation and so giving the effect of a piston moving up and down twice in a cylinder.

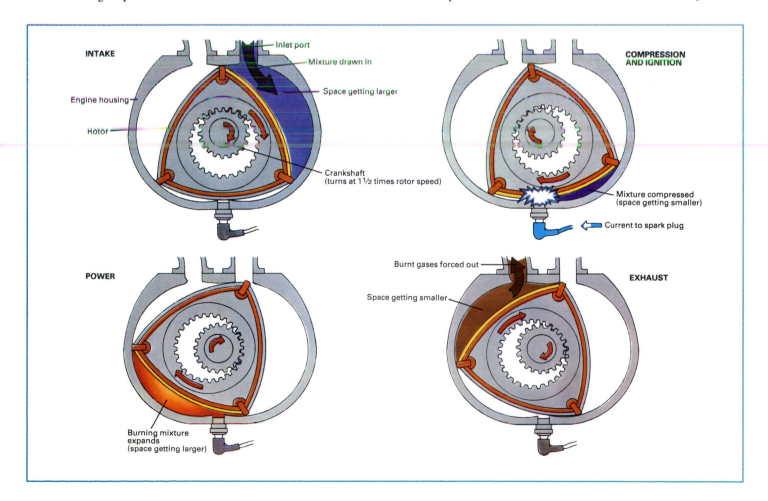

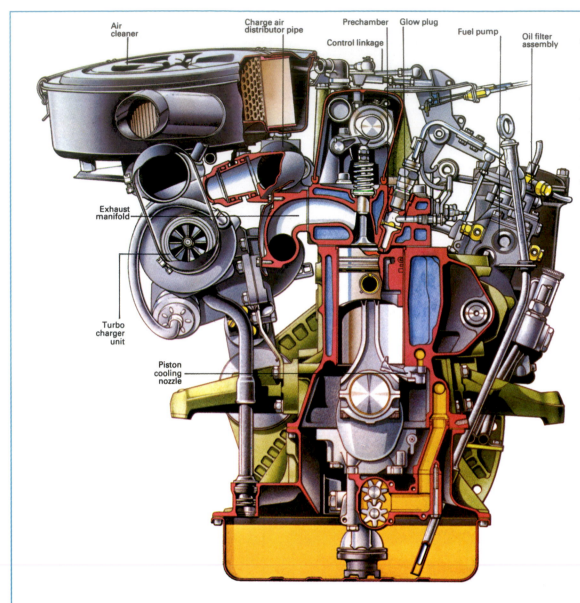

Air cleaner

Charge air distributor pipe

Prechamber

Glow plug

Control linkage

Fuel pump

Oil filter assembly

Exhaust manifold

Turbo charger unit

Piston cooling nozzle

TURBOCHARGER

Diesel engines respond well to turbocharging, and the Mercedes-Benz 300 SD was a sophisticated example of this technology. Turbocharged diesel engines were first used on heavy trucks in the 1950s. Turbodiesel manufacturers have since developed engines with reduced exhaust emissions and lower operating noise levels suitable for passenger cars. Benefits of turbocharging include improved fuel efficiency as well as better overall performance levels.

In all cases, the valves are operated against spring pressure; there are at least two valves for each cylinder (intake and exhaust), and the adjustment of the timing gear is vital to the performance of the engine. Some high-performance engines have four valves to a cylinder; some aero engines have sleeve valves, in which a tubular sleeve with holes in it covers and uncovers the ports.

The configuration of the internal combustion engine is determined by the number of cylinders, the length of the piston stroke, the compression ratio (the ratio of the size of combustion chamber to the volume displaced by the piston), and many other factors, all of which are design decisions affecting the theoretical efficiency of the engine and are made on the basis of the intended use of the engine. For example, lightweight parts can help the engine run better. The total weight for an internal combustion engine can range from a few pounds for lawn mower engines to more than 15 tons (13.5 tonnes).

Diesel engine

The diesel engine is named after its inventor, Rudolf Diesel, whose first working prototype ran in 1897 after many years of research work. Until the late 1920s, most of the development of diesel engines took place in Germany, and a great deal of experience was gained from the production of engines for submarines during World War I. The main companies involved at this time were MAN and Daimler-Benz.

The first successful diesel engines for road transportation appeared in 1922, although unsuccessful attempts had been made to produce such engines since as early as 1898. Diesel engines of this type during the 1920s were of two, four, or six cylinder designs producing about 40 to 50 horsepower. Power outputs increased steadily during the 1930s, and by the beginning of World War II diesel engines were in widespread use in road transport, rail locomotives, tractors and construction plants, and ships and boats and as an industrial power source (including electricity generating sets). Although diesel engines prevail in trains, trucks, and taxi cabs, more diesel automobiles and motorbikes are now being made. The reason is partly economic—diesel fuel is more energy efficient and gives better mileage per gallon than gasoline—but improvements in engine design have also made diesel engines less polluting than they used to be.

A diesel engine can be adapted to run on almost any fuel from vegetable oils to natural gas and high octane gasoline, but the most suitable and widely used diesel fuel is distilled from crude oil and is closely related to kerosene. It is much less volatile than gasoline, with a flash point (temperature at which a heated petroleum product gives off enough vapor to flash momentarily when a small flame is placed nearby) of around 168°F (75°C), whereas the flash point of gasoline, in contrast, is lower than ordinary atmospheric temperatures.

Wankel engine

The Wankel engine, named for its German inventor, Dr. Felix Wankel, is a rotary engine. Instead of oscillating to and fro in a straight line, as in the reciprocating engine, the power output member of the rotary engine moves in a continuous circular motion, giving the rotary engine a smoother operation than a piston engine, because it is perfectly balanced. Another advantage is that it has only two moving parts: the rotor and the crankshaft. As the rotor rotates, the gap between the flanks of the rotor and the walls of the housing fluctuates cyclically, expanding and contracting to give the four strokes of the normal Otto engine. There are three firing strokes per revolution of the rotor but only one per revolution of the crankshaft, since the rotor rotates at one-third the angular velocity of the crankshaft. Seals are

▲ A Suzuki Wankel engine. This model has two radiators, one for water-cooling the engine and one for the oil. The engine has a 497 cubic centimeter capacity and gives the bike a top speed of about 115 mph (185 km/h). A twin exhaust system sucks in fresh air to cool the exhaust gases and contributes to noise reduction. The rotor housing is plated with composite electrochemical materials for durability.

◄ Economy and durability make diesel-powered vehicles vital in serving isolated areas. Trucking across the deserted Australian outback, this road train provides a link between scattered centers of industry. Road trains usually pull three containers that can carry anything from coal to cattle.

provided at the tips of the rotor to separate the three chambers formed between the rotor and the housing, with another set of seals fitted between the rotor and housing end faces.

Because each flank of the rotor acts effectively as a piston in a reciprocating engine, it is only necessary to consider one flank to follow the sequence of operations. Consider first that the leading seal of one face has just passed the intake port in the housing. As the rotor moves on, the gap between the side of the rotor and the housing increases, and mixture is drawn in. When the trailing seal passes the port, the mixture is trapped in the space, and as the rotor continues, this gap becomes progressively smaller, compressing the mixture.

When the gap is at or near its minimum, corresponding to top dead center, the spark plug fires, and the mixture ignites and expands. Because the center of rotation of the rotor is eccentric to the center of the casing, the side of the rotor in question is pushed around and turns the small gear on the crankshaft. Finally, the leading seal passes the exhaust port, and the gases escape. No valve gear is needed because the movement of the rotor carried the combustion volume over the inlet and exhaust ports at the appropriate stages in the four-stroke cycle.

FACT FILE

- *In July 1984, at Silverstone, Britain, at a fuel economy competition, the Ford UFO vehicle, powered by a 15 cc motor, achieved the equivalent of 3,803 miles per gallon (1,346 km/l).*

- *The Terex Titan 33-19 is the world's largest dump truck. It is powered by a 16-cylinder engine that delivers 3,300 horsepower. Overall weight of the vehicle is 540 tons (485 tonnes), with a fuel capacity of 1,560 gallons (5,900 l).*

- *Experimental diesel engines with single cylinders were tested prior to World War I, mainly for submarine use. The Sulzer S100 had a single cylinder with a bore of 3 ft. (0.9 m) and a stroke of 3.6 ft. (1.1 m).*

Developments

The advantages of the gasoline engine as a power source for mobile applications like automobiles and power boats are such that, despite worries about declining oil resources, the gasoline engine is likely to remain dominant. However, considerable efforts have been applied toward achieving greater efficiency in the interests of fuel economy, while pollution considerations have similarly affected engine design.

The use of emission-control systems is one way of meeting pollution regulations, but a better approach lies in the design of more efficient engine-combustion processes, which generally also increase fuel efficiency. One such approach is the stratified-charge engine, where the carburation or fuel-injection system is designed to produce a fuel-rich mixture close to the spark plug with the rest of the combustion chamber containing a much weaker mixture. The rich mixture ignites readily and expands into the combustion chamber to ignite the rest of the mixture, while the excess of air in the weaker mixture ensures complete combustion and thus reduces emissions.

Another approach is lean burn, using weak mixtures that are finely atomized to give optimum fuel–air mixing, together with high-turbulence combustion-chamber designs to give complete combustion. Similarly the use of electronic engine management allows more precise control of the combustion process.

In diesels, common-rail fuel-injection systems provide high-pressure fuel at any point in the engine cycle, and thus help to lower emissions as well as aiding torque output at lower speeds.

▲ This Rover M74R turbo diesel engine uses Bosch's common-rail high-pressure injection technology to improve its performance. Common-rail systems work on the accumulator principle: a special high-pressure fuel rail is maintained at pressures of up to 19,000 psi (1,350 bar) by the injection pump. The four injectors in the engine can access this source of high-pressure fuel at any point, regardless of the position on the engine cycle or the speed of the engine.

SEE ALSO: AUTOMOBILE • AUTOMOBILE ELECTRONICS SYSTEM • BIOFUEL • ENGINE COOLING SYSTEMS • FUEL INJECTION • IGNITION SYSTEM, AUTOMOBILE • MOTORCYCLE • RACING CAR AND DRAGSTER • STEAM ENGINE • STIRLING ENGINE

Internet

The Internet is an enormous group of computers situated in all parts of the world and linked together either permanently or as required. Any person possessing or having access to a computer can link to and participate in the Internet. The Internet offers facilities so considerable that for many people, they have become essential. It allows a person to communicate quickly and cheaply with any other person in the world whose computer is connected to the Internet and who has an e-mail account. It enables transfer of large quantities of information—such as complete books—to anywhere in the world for the cost of a local phone call. It allows voice communication with people in any part of the world, also for the cost of a local call.

Once linked to the Internet, the user can shop from the comfort of his or her own home. He or she can do private or business banking, check the weather forecast in any area, get the latest news about anything, join discussion (chat) groups, or listen to radio broadcasts and music from many countries. Above all, the user has access to the biggest accessible volume of information in the world.

Many people are uncertain about the difference between the Internet and the World Wide Web. The Internet is the entire network structure to which personal and other computers can be linked for these and other purposes. The World Wide Web is an information highway that links an almost unlimited number of sources of information by hypertext transfer protocol (http) so that whenever a key word is underlined (a hypertext link), a click of the mouse will take the user to another site with more information.

The amount of information, good and bad, available on the World Wide Web is astonishing, and all of it is accessible from millions of other sites simply by clicking on any linked word.

▲ Internet cafés are an increasingly popular way for people without computers to access the Internet. For a small fee, users of these facilities can set up their own addresses to receive and send e-mails.

The early days

Back in the late 1960s, the U.S. government Defense Department was seriously concerned that communications between defense installations and control headquarters could be cut by an attack on the country with atomic weapons. So in 1969, a Department of Defense program called the Advance Research Projects Agency Network (ARPANET) was set up. This was a network set up initially between organizations concerned in defense research and was so organized with multiple linkages that full communication could be maintained even if many of the line links between units were destroyed.

ARPANET proved its point but was soon found to be intrinsically useful, and many more research scientists and academics began to use it for reasons of convenience. Meantime, the U.S. National Science Foundation had set up a similar network called the NSFNet to link several very large computers in various parts of the country. It took over the transmission control protocol/internet protocol (TCP/IP) that ARPANET had been using and built up a linked network of networks. NFSnet became the backbone of what was to become the Internet, and the National Science Foundation still has the central function of maintaining the main transmission part of the network. The development of the Internet is, however, now the responsibility of the Internet Architecture Board.

Various other networks had sprung up, initially independently and intended for limited educational and scientific purposes, but it was not long before these were linked into the common network, which in this way, continued to grow rapidly in size. The next major development in the Internet, the World Wide Web, was the advance that aroused massive public interest. It was originated by Tim Berners-Lee (see box) and associates working at the European Organization for Nuclear Research (CERN).

In 2001, more than one-third of the total populations of the United States and the United Kingdom used the Internet. Current developments in mobile computing make it likely that this figure will soon be greatly exceeded.

Development of the Internet

The account of the origins and evolution of the Internet illustrates how there are processes in society that, once started, become unstoppable. It is unlikely that anyone could have anticipated at the time that a set of links between computers, organized for purely military purposes, would evolve into a system that would revolutionize society. But this is what is currently happening, and it is a consequence of the human need to communicate with each other and to make use of every available means of communication and information. Experts believe that just as the industrial revolution in the 18th and 19th centuries transformed Europe and the United States, so the communication and information revolution of the 20th and 21st centuries will transform and enrich not only the Western world but, in time, all the nations of the world.

In 1985, when the Internet was in its early stages, users could communicate with only about 2,000 other computers. In the late 1980s, various commercial enterprises, known as Internet service providers (ISPs) began to offer the public various facilities on the Internet—such as e-mail, file-transfer facilities, and discussion groups.

TIM BERNERS-LEE

The man who created the World Wide Web, the Englishman Tim Berners-Lee (1955–), was the son of two computer scientists and from an early age was familiar with computers. He was also a creative boy who was able to make his own computer using electronic parts and an old TV set. In his late teens, he studied physics at Queen's College, Oxford University, and graduated with an honours degree in 1976. Four years later, after holding down various jobs in technology, he was appointed to a position as a developer of computer programs at the European Laboratory for Particle Physics in Geneva, part of CERN. One of the main problems he faced in maintaining good communication and information links between remote organizations was that the information concerned was held on a variety of computers with different hardware, different operating systems, and running different programs. Such diverse computers refused to recognize each other.

To solve this problem Berners-Lee developed a program using hypertext markup language. This program he called Enquire and it used hypertext links to connect files. The authorities at CERN took eight years to see the benefit of such a system and to encourage him to develop it. But in 1990 the system—which he called the World Wide Web—was up and running for CERN employees.

Berners-Lee was not interested in making a fortune and turned down many attractive commercial offers. Like the Finnish programmer and creator of the Linux operating system Linus Torvalds, Berners-Lee believes that software of such fundamental importance should be distributed freely at very low cost. In 1995 he became Director of the World Wide Web Consortium, which had just been set up at the MIT Laboratory for Computer Science.

```
HTML: Brown Partworks
<html>
 <head>
  <meta http-equiv="content-type" content="text/html;charset=iso-8859-1">
  <meta name="generator" content="Adobe GoLive 4">
  <title>Brown Partworks</title>
  <meta name="keywords" content="Book packager, Partworks, Brown Partworks, Continuity Series, Packager, Publish
  <meta name="description" content="Brown Partworks was set up in 1995. We are a packaging company: that is, we c
  <script language="JavaScript"></script>
  <!-- ImageReady Preload Script (rollover.psd) -->
  <script language="JavaScript"><!--
function newImage(arg) {
 if (document.images) {
  rslt = new Image();
  rslt.src = arg;
  return rslt;
 }
}

function changeImages() {
 if (document.images && (preloadFlag == true)) {
  for (var i=0; i<changeImages.arguments.length; i+=2) {
   document[changeImages.arguments[i]].src = changeImages.arguments[i+1];
  }
 }
}

var preloadFlag = false;
function preloadImages() {
 if (document.images) {
  index_01_over = newImage("images/index_01-over.gif");
  preloadFlag = true;
 }
}
// -->
  </script>
  <!-- End Preload Script -->
 </head>

 <body bgcolor="#001966" background="images/2000.gif" onload="preloadImages();">
  <table border="0" cellpadding="0" cellspacing="2" width="580" height="321">
   <tr height="40">
    <td width="100" height="40"></td>
    <td width="474" height="40"></td>
   </tr>
   <tr height="200">
    <td width="100" height="200"></td>
    <td width="474" height="200" align="right" valign="top">
     <div align="right">
      <a href="about.html" title="Enter..."><img height="122" width="346" src="images/logo.gif" border="0" alt="E
    </td>
   </tr>
   <tr height="70">
    <td width="100" height="70"></td>
    <td width="474" height="70"></td>
   </tr>
  </table>
  <a href="mailto:info@brownpartworks.co.uk"><font color="white">
  <table border="0" cellpadding="0" cellspacing="2" width="580">
   <tr>
    <td>
     <center>
```

◀ All web pages are created using hypertext markup language (HTML), a program that describes how the constituent parts of the page will appear on the screen. These are the instructions for the home page for Brown Partworks, the publishing company that revised this edition of *How it Works*. The instructions feature a number of meta tags that will bring up the company's Web site address if certain key words are typed into a search engine. Other commands describe the location of typefaces, colors, and images used on the page.

These services were offered for a monthly fee. As popularity rose, the cost dropped. But it was with the development of the World Wide Web that it became apparent to the public generally that the Internet might be an indispensable facility. E-mail also was a germinal feature. Both have now been fully assimilated into business life and play a growing part in private life. As a result, the Internet has become a personal necessity for millions and an essential business tool for almost all commercial enterprises. Its use confers so many benefits that many of those who have not adopted it can find themselves at a commercial or social disadvantage.

It is now impossible to enumerate with any accuracy how many machines are linked into the Internet. The figure runs into many tens of millions, and we are now approaching the point at which half the populations of the major Western industrialized nations have personal access to the Internet.

Structure of the Internet

Essentially, the Internet is just a very large collection of computers linked together. Every connected machine is called a host. The great majority of host machines are also called clients because they look for and use information stored on other machines. The term *client* is also applied to any program used to perform an online operation, such as reading e-mail, surfing the net, or transferring files. The machines that supply information to others are called servers. Servers are not necessarily very large machines. The machine used by any individual who has set up a Web site is a server.

But the real structure of the Internet resides in the way these machines achieve two-way communication with each other. Every machine on the net communicates with every other machine using the transmission control protocol/Internet protocol (TCP/IP). A protocol is an agreed-upon set of rules to which all communicating machines must conform. It includes an agreement on speed of transfer, how the sending machine will indicate that it has finished sending a message, the type of error checking and correction used, and how the receiving machine notifies the sender that it has received the message.

The TCP part of the protocol has a lot to do. In addition to error checking, it carries out a process called packet switching. It cuts up long messages into shorter lengths called packets each of which carries a note of its destination. Packets normally travel by different routes, and on arrival, they must be put together again in the right order. TCP sorts all this data.

The IP part of the protocol is used by special computers called routers that actually do the moving around of the packets, sending them out by the most convenient route. Each packet carries the IP address of the machine that sent it and the IP address of the machine it is going to. Thus, all computers on the Internet recognize each other by their unique IP addresses. This is a set of four numbers separated by dots. Fortunately for most Internet users, the IP address need never be known. They are set up in his or her machine by the Internet service provider (ISP), using the TCP/IP dial-up networking software incorporated into Windows programs and the Apple Mac operating system. These programs include a standard called Winsock (Windows socket) that allows a wide range of client programs (browsers) to run using TCP/IP. In most cases, the IP address is assigned by the ISP when the user logs on at the beginning of each Internet use and then is cancelled so that it can be used by some other machine. If a user were to check the IP address in the dial-up networking software while off-line, he or she would probably find a row of zeros.

Addresses

The addresses that most Internet users need to know about are different from the IP addresses. They are called domain names and are the familiar designations, ending in .com, .org, .edu, and so on, used to connect to Web sites.

These three-letter extensions after the dot are known as the top-level, or first-level, domain names. The second-level domain name is the name that identifies the organization. Domain names are assigned by registration services and have to be paid for, usually with an annual fee, to maintain the right to use the name.

To address a site on the Web, the domain name must be preceded by http://www. Browser software will, however, often put in the http:// part of the address for you. The whole address, including these preliminaries is called the URL

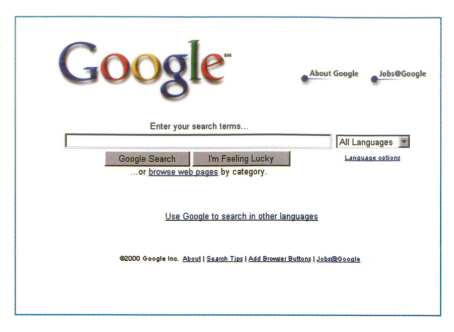

(uniform resource locator). The important part of the address is the bit that immediately follows http://www. This is the domain name.

E-mail addresses are different. The mail service provider must agree on the person's e-mail name (the user name) to ensure that no two people have exactly the same name. This name is the first part of the e-mail address. Then comes the symbol @ (read as "at"), then the host domain name—usually the company that provides the service. So a typical e-mail address might be "Yourname@Compuserve.com" with no spaces and no period at the end. You can always tell an e-mail address by the presence of the @.

Addresses may also include a two-letter country code tacked on at the end, such as .ca for Canada; .uk for Britain; .jp for Japan; .de for Germany (Deutschland); .es for Spain (España); and so on. If an address does not include a country code, it is likely to be in the United States.

Browsers

A Web browser is a program used to open and view Web pages on the Internet. Two programs, Microsoft Internet Explorer and Netscape, dominate the field, mainly because they are both excellent programs and are provided free of charge. Internet Explorer comes already installed in computers with the Windows 98, Windows 2000, and Windows ME operating systems. It is also to be found on every iMac and every Apple Mac running Mac operating system version 7.5.3, or later. With modern high-capacity hard disk-drives, there is plenty of room to install more than one browser, so both Internet Explorer and Netscape can exist on one machine. One of them, however, must be elected as the default browser so that it opens when required, and it can easily be changed.

▲ This is the homepage for Google, a search engine on the Internet. Search engines can save Internet users hours of trial and error in finding the Web site addresses by using meta tags incorporated into Web sites to find key words that relate to the user's enquiry.

Browsers like Internet Explorer are much more than the interface between the user and the Internet. They include a range of tools and offer excellent facilities for e-mail and a range of additional tools such as news programs, online radio, chat facilities, voice communication, media players, security levels to prevent children from accessing unsuitable material, automatic error correction in addresses, and so on.

Accessing a Web site with a browser simply involves typing in the domain name of the site. In many cases, even this step is unnecessary. Many educational programs, such as the major encyclopedias, have links in their articles that will take you at once, via your browser, to a site providing further information. Britannica, for instance, has over 125,000 verified and checked Web links.

Once a site has been found, you are likely to come across other hypertext/hypermedia links from which, with a click of the mouse, you will be taken to other relevant sites.

Search engines

The amount of material on the Internet is enormous and it is growing daily. To try to find anything without help brings to mind the old saying about a needle in a haystack. A search engine is a program on the Internet that solves this problem. Search engines, such as Yahoo, Alta Vista, Northern Light, HotBot, Deja.com, and Infoseek are readily accessible, and links to some of them are incorporated into the software provided by the ISP when the new Internet user signs up.

When these programs have been accessed, the user is presented with a box into which is typed a word or short phrase relating to what he or she wants to find. Plain-language entries will often succeed, but some understanding of how search engines work will help to refine the search and save time and trouble. Before typing in the search term, it is worth studying the home page of the search engine. The user is likely to find that information has been divided into various categories, such as art and humanities, science, business and economy, sport, reference, computers and Internet, government, and so on. Each of these headings will have a hypertext link to further narrower categories. Following all these links allows the user to get very detailed information.

There is also likely to be a link to an advanced search facility. This offers "intelligent searching," in which the program tries to interpret your needs, exact-match searching, Boolean search using AND (search on all words typed) or OR (search on any word typed), and searches limited as to dates. Much time and trouble can be saved by enclosing the phrase you enter in quotes so as

▼ The results of a search will usually bring up a list of hundreds of sites containing the key words entered by the user. The list contains the URLs (uniform resource locators) of all the Web sites so that simply by clicking on the address, the user will be taken to that page automatically by a hypertext link.

to ensure that it is treated as a unity and not as several words, each of which may be searched for separately. Using a search engine is something of an art and it is an art well worth mastering.

Search engines do not actually search the Internet; they search their own databases for key words that the authors of the millions of Web pages have hidden in the opening lines of their home pages. These key words are marked with symbols known as meta tags, which describe the contents of the Web site. Text within meta tags does not appear on the displayed Web page but is recognized by a program that the proprietors of the search engines use to find new sites and detect changes to those it has already entered into its databases.

Different search engines have different databases and some are better for certain purposes than others. Yahoo is one example, and a link to it is provided as part of the Compuserve software. In Compuserve you can access Yahoo simply by clicking on the GO button and typing Yahoo. You can then, if you wish, use Yahoo to find other search engines.

E-mail

E-mail (electronic mail) is a system of communication between individuals, whether for private or business purposes, in which text, graphics, and computer files of any kind, including programs, can be sent via the Internet to any part of the world for the cost of a local phone call. The convenience, speed, ease of use, and cheapness made e-mail one of the principal reasons for the remarkable growth of the Internet in the last year or two of the 20th century.

E-mail facilities may be provided by your ISP, by your browser program, or as a separate, stand-

◀ The Internet has revolutionized business and commerce. Online stock trading is gradually replacing the old trading floor stock exchanges, enabling stocks to be bought and sold anywhere in the world in an instant.

alone commercial program, such as Eudora. Both the Internet Explorer and Netscape offer excellent e-mail facilities, respectively called Outlook Express and Messenger. Compuserve also includes an efficient and easy-to-use e-mail resource.

E-mail messages can be composed off-line, checked and edited, and sent only when complete. Once on line, it takes only a few seconds for the message to be transmitted to the mailbox of the recipient or recipients. And it is of no concern whether the mail is addressed to the house next door or to the other side of the world, for the cost is that of a local phone call. The e-mail program will keep a copy of every letter you send and will file away every letter you receive. Your e-mail filing cabinet can be subdivided into as many categories as you wish so that different classes of correspondence may be kept separate.

When dealing with short and immediate correspondence, messages can be replied to immediately, while still on line, simply by clicking on a "reply" button, typing the response, and clicking on "send." In such cases, it is unnecessary to re-enter the address of the recipient. The addresses of new correspondents can be added automatically to the program's address book so that future correspondence can be addressed by starting to type the person's name. Any number of recipients can be addressed simultaneously.

E-mail attachments are complete files of any size or kind—books, spreadsheets, databases, programs, images, music—that are sent linked to an e-mail message. The message need be little more than a few words of introduction to indicate to the recipient that a file is attached.

Future of the Internet

All current predictions emphasize the importance that wireless will play in the future of the Internet. It is a natural evolution from the current almost universal use of mobile telephones and the rapid expansion of Internet access via mobile phones. Wireless transmission has to be broadband to be capable of carrying out all the functions that are predicted for it. The practical significance of bandwidth—which is measured in the number of binary digits (bits) that can be transmitted per second—is that a narrow bandwidth seriously increases the time taken to download material. Currently, conventional connections via analog telephone lines have narrow bandwidth and are slow. ISDN connections are purely digital and are faster. But truly wideband communication requires very-high-frequency bands and this means modulated light transmission via fiber-optic cables, or wireless transmission.

An Internet development that will allow a subscriber to use a range of application programs without first having to purchase the software, or even to have a hard drive, is the application service provider (ASP) concept. With a fast, broadband, and preferably wireless connection to a large mainframe computer that is running the desired application program, such as a sophisticated word processor, the user—who will need only a Web browser—will be able to proceed as if the program was present on his or her own machine. The latest version of the program will always be available, and the cost will be very low. The principal advantage of this development is that it will make possible truly mobile computing without restriction on the quality of the software. Developments in the design of computer hard disk drives have enormously increased their capacity, so large centralized machines offering ASP facilities will also be able to offer personalized safe storage for data and text, and so on.

The significance of this development is that it seems likely to radically reduce the power, size, and price of the personal machines needed to carry out all the computing tasks that have become so indispensable. The use of the Internet in this way will mean that such machines will need far less hardware—no hard disk or floppy disk drives, no CD-ROM drives, and no modem. They will run a much smaller and simpler operating system, and the only software required will be a simple browser with which to link to the application service provider.

SEE ALSO: CELLULAR TELEPHONE • COMPUTER • COMPUTER NETWORK • DATA STORAGE • MICROPROCESSOR • MODEM AND ISDN

Ion and Ionization

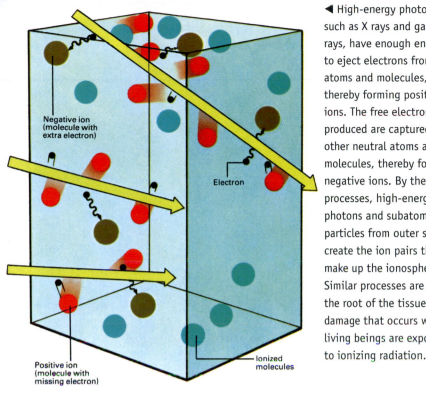

Negative ion
(molecule with
extra electron)

Electron

Positive ion
(molecule with
missing electron)

Ionized
molecules

◀ High-energy photons, such as X rays and gamma rays, have enough energy to eject electrons from atoms and molecules, thereby forming positive ions. The free electrons produced are captured by other neutral atoms and molecules, thereby forming negative ions. By these processes, high-energy photons and subatomic particles from outer space create the ion pairs that make up the ionosphere. Similar processes are at the root of the tissue damage that occurs when living beings are exposed to ionizing radiation.

An ion is an atom or molecule to which one or more electrons have been added or from which one or more electrons have been removed. Whereas atoms and molecules owe their lack of electrical charge to exactly balanced numbers of positively charged protons and negatively charged electrons, ions have electrical charges by virtue of imbalances in these numbers. An ion that has more electrons than protons is a negatively charged anion; an ion that has fewer electrons than protons is a positively charged cation.

In chemical notation, the chemical composition of an ion is accompanied by an indication of its charge: a plus or minus sign indicates a positive or negative charge equal in magnitude to the charge of an electron, and a number before the sign indicates a multiple charge. In this way, H^+ represents a hydrogen ion, which is simply a proton; Fe^{3+} represents an iron (III) ion, which has a positive charge of three; SO_4^{2-} represents a sulfate ion; and $C_5H_5^-$ represents a cyclopentadienyl ion. In an older form of notation, multiple signs were used instead of a number and a sign, so CO_3^{2-} would be written CO_3^{--}, for example.

Stable ions
The electrons in an atom occupy discrete collections of orbitals, called shells, that surround the nucleus. There is a characteristic limit to the number of electrons that each shell is able to accommodate, and particularly stable configurations occur when every shell is either empty or occupied to its capacity. Since all the electron shells of noble gas atoms obey this criterion, such a configuration is frequently referred to as a noble gas configuration.

Stable atomic ions frequently have noble gas configurations, so the type of ion most readily formed by an element can often be predicted by determining how many atoms must be added to or removed from an atom for it to acquire a noble gas configuration. Calcium (Ca) atoms have two electrons each in excess of a noble gas configuration, so they readily form calcium (II) (Ca^{2+}) ions. Chlorine (Cl) atoms, on the other hand, are one electron short of a noble gas configuration, so they form chloride (Cl^-) ions.

The charge of a polyatomic ion, such as sulfate (SO_4^{2-}) can be calculated by considering the noble gas configurations of each of its atoms. For example, sulfur has six electrons in its outer shell; it can achieve a noble gas configuration either by gaining two electrons or by losing six. In the case of a sulfate ion, the sulfur atom effectively loses six electrons. Although sulfur does not actually form an S^{6+} ion, it can be considered as doing so for the purposes of calculating the ionic charge. Similarly, each oxygen in the sulfate ion can be thought of as gaining two electrons to form O^{2-}.

The overall charge of the polyatomic ion can then be calculated by adding together the charges of the component theoretical atomic ions, so $S^{6+}(O^{2-})_4$ has a charge of $6 + (4 \times -2) = -2$. In fact, the covalent bonds that hold the molecule together neutralize some of the charges, and the net charge of -2 is spread between the four oxygens.

Chemical ionization
Ionization is any process that produces ions from uncharged atoms or molecules. Certain chemical reactions produce ions as a consequence of electron transfers. An example is the formation of sodium chloride, which consists of sodium and chloride ions, from metallic sodium and molecular chlorine (Cl_2). The processes that form sodium and chlorine atoms demand energy, as does the formation of sodium ions from atomic sodium. This energy demand is more than satisfied by the formation of chloride ions from atomic chlorine and the subsequent formation of sodium chloride, which is stabilized by strong electrostatic attractions between the opposite charges of the sodium and chloride ions. The excess energy is released as heat.

Other types of ionizations

The energy required to rip electrons from neutral atoms and molecules can be provided by sources other than the chemical energy of salt formation. High-energy photons (from high-frequency UV, through X rays, to gamma rays) possess enough energy to cause ionization. Also, fast-moving particles, such as accelerated electrons, possess enough kinetic energy to remove electrons from neutral species. Photons and particles that cause ionization are called ionizing radiation.

Ionization of a gas can be caused by using an electric field to accelerate electrons liberated from a hot metal by a process called thermionic emission. When the fast-moving electrons produced by such a process collide with neutral atoms or molecules they have a chance of producing positive ions and more free electrons, which can then cause further ionizations. The faster the electrons, the greater is their chance of causing ionization. Such ionizations are the source of the plasma ("gas" of ions and electrons) in a discharge lamp, such as a sodium-vapor street lamp. The source of light in such lamps is the energy released as electrons and positive ions recombine to form neutral species.

Ions and electromagnetic fields

Being charged, ions experience forces in electrical fields. In the case of an ionic solid, alternating positive and negative charges produce attractions that overwhelm an external electrical field, but in a dissolved ionic substance or an ionized gas, each type of ion is driven by a field in a direction that depends on its charge.

Electrolysis is an electrochemical process whereby an ionic liquid or solution is split into its components as a consequence of the electric field between two electrodes—the anode (which is positively charged and attracts anions) and the cathode (which is negatively charged and attracts cations). When an ion reaches an electrode with a charge opposite to its own, it tends to lose its charge by electron transfer. In this way, molten sodium chloride can be split into metallic sodium, which forms at the cathode, and molecular chlorine gas, which forms at the anode.

Once an ion is in motion, it has some of the characteristics of an electrical current, which consists of moving charges. As such, a moving ion can be deflected from its path by a magnetic field—a consequence of the same effect that makes a motor turn. This effect is used in a molecular-analysis technique called mass spectrometry. A molecular substance is first vaporized into a vacuum and then bombarded with electrons to form its positive ions. These ions are then accelerated

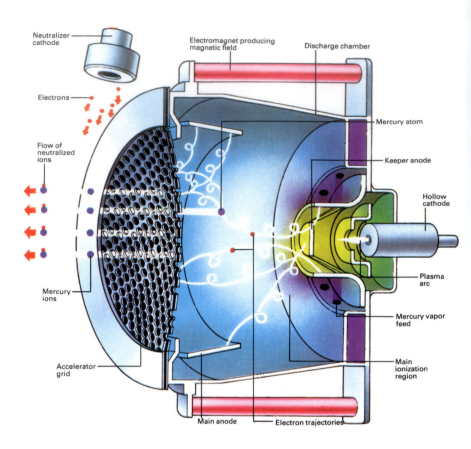

by an electrical field and deflected by a magnetic field. The path they follow depends on the ratio of charge to molecular mass, thus allowing the molecular mass to be determined with great precision. Also, the molecular ions tend to fragment, since they have lost one of the electrons that participate in the bonding system that holds them together. The masses of the ionic fragments so formed can provide a great deal of information about the structure of the original molecule.

Ions in the atmosphere

Rain showers, waterfalls, and crashing waves are natural sources of airborne negative ions; the presence of such ions in the atmosphere has been linked to a feeling of well-being. When airborne negative ions collide with particles such as dust or soot, they can lose their charge to the larger particles and thereby lose their beneficial properties.

In dust-laden industrial atmospheres, particularly where natural sources of negative ions are few, the air can become depleted in negative ions. This condition has been linked with unusually high incidences of headaches, fatigue, and allergic reactions, such as asthma. Devices called ionizers, which release streams of negative ions from needles at negative potentials of around 6,000 V, can help remedy the shortfall of negative ions.

▲ This diagram shows the components of an ionic propulsion unit, such as is used to drive deep-space probes. Mercury ions from a plasma source are accelerated through an electric field within the motor. Fast-moving mercury ions leave the motor through a grill at the rear of the craft, and the reaction to their acceleration drives the craft forward. At the same time, electrons stream from an external cathode to neutralize the ions and prevent the craft from developing an excess negative charge. Ionic drives provide gentle thrust for prolonged periods so that a craft with such propulsion can develop extremely high speeds over extended periods of time.

Labels in diagram: Neutralizer cathode · Electromagnet producing magnetic field · Discharge chamber · Electrons · Mercury atom · Flow of neutralized ions · Keeper anode · Hollow cathode · Mercury ions · Plasma arc · Accelerator grid · Mercury vapor feed · Main ionization region · Main anode · Electron trajectories

SEE ALSO: ATOMIC STRUCTURE · PARTICLE DETECTOR · ROCKET AND SPACE PROPULSION · SPACE PROBE

Iron and Steel

COTTON FABRICS   BROADWAY MFRS. SUPPLY CO.   COTTON FABRICS

Iron, chemical symbol Fe, is the most widely used of the metals. Its ores are abundant, and the metal can be extracted from them relatively easily. When mixed with other elements, notably carbon, iron forms alloys with a wide range of useful engineering properties. Iron containing up to 1.7 percent carbon is known as steel and when mixed with other metal elements it is known as alloy steel. Iron that contains more than 1.7 percent carbon is generally referred to as pig iron or cast iron.

Physical properties of iron

Iron is a hard gray metal with a density of 7.9 g/cm³. At temperatures below 1670°F (910°C), its crystal structure is body-centered cubic, between 1670 and 2570°F (910–1410°C), the stable structure is face-centered cubic, while above 2570°F (1410°C), the structure reverts to body-centered cubic. Iron melts at 2802°F (1539°C). The presence of these three types of structure, or allotropes as they are called (known as α, γ, and δ iron, respectively), contributes in a large measure to the astonishing range of mechanical properties

that can be obtained by heat treatment of steels and other alloys.

Iron, being one of the transition elements (metallic elements having incomplete inner electron shells), is not an especially good conductor of heat or electricity. The specific electric resistance (resistivity) of iron is about eight times that of silver, the best electrical conductor. It is, however, in common with cobalt and nickel, intrinsically magnetic. Small regions, or domains, of the natural metal are normally arranged in such a way that the magnetism cancels itself out, but it can easily be turned into a magnet by aligning the domains in the metal using an external magnetic field.

Occurrence

Next to aluminum, iron is the most common metal in Earth's crust. It is widely distributed, and some of the high-grade ores have an iron content that is in excess of 50 percent.

Ores can be classified by their appearance. Black ores are based on magnetite (Fe_3O_4), which, if pure, contains more than 70 percent iron. The

▲ In the 19th century, cast iron was often used for structural engineering purposes, as in this building in New York. It is rarely used for such purposes now because it is so brittle.

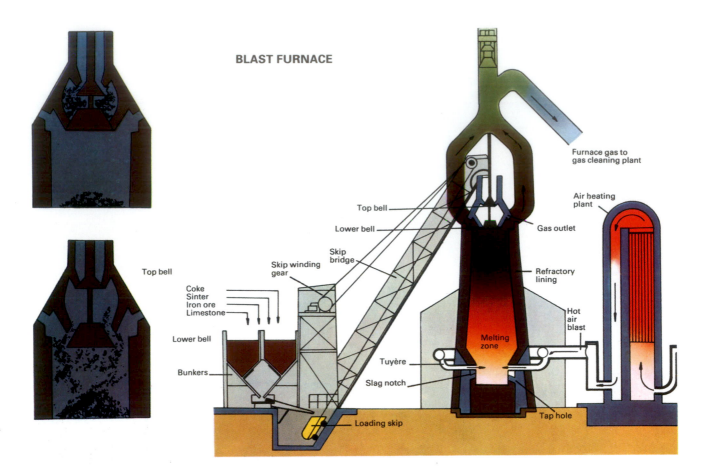

BLAST FURNACE

Furnace gas to gas cleaning plant

Air heating plant

Top bell

Lower bell

Gas outlet

Skip bridge

Skip winding gear

Coke
Sinter
Iron ore
Limestone

Refractory lining

Hot air blast

Top bell

Melting zone

Lower bell

Tuyère

Bunkers

Slag notch

Tap hole

Loading skip

red ores are mainly hematite (Fe_2O_3), and the brown ores are either limonite, which is hydrated hematite ($2Fe_2O_3 \cdot 3H_2O$), or siderite, which is mainly composed of iron carbonate, $FeCO_3$.

Alternatively, ores are sometimes referred to on the basis of the impurities they contain. For example, siliceous ores contain silicon impurities, and there are also calcareous ores (containing calcium carbonate), aluminous ores, and so on.

High-quality ores are found in workable quantities in Australia, Sweden, the United States, Russia, and Spain. The value of a deposit depends not only on the richness of the ore but also on the ease with which it can be won and its proximity to coal supplies and industrial centers. With improvements in bulk transportation methods, however, proximity to coal and industrial centers is becoming less important. For example, most Australian ore is now exported to Japan.

Blast furnace

The blast furnace has been the world's principal method of iron production for hundreds of years. Early versions were in use in the Middle Ages, using bellows to provide the air blast and carbon in the form of charcoal, but the major developments did not occur until the 18th century. In 1709, the English iron manufacturer Abraham Darby first used coke instead of charcoal, and in 1766, the English industrialist John Wilkinson introduced steam power to produce the air blast.

The idea of preheating the air used in the blast was developed in 1828 by the Scottish inventor James Neilson, and the use of the hot gases produced in the reduction process to help preheat the blast was first employed in Germany in 1831.

The reduction process reduces iron ore (usually iron oxide) to metallic iron containing about 4 percent carbon (pig iron) by heating the ore in the presence of coke. Burning the coke with superheated air provides heat and also produces carbon monoxide, which, after being oxidized to carbon dioxide, is the main factor in reducing the iron oxides to iron. As mentioned above, this is not pure iron, and it is the 4 percent or so of carbon in it that makes blast furnace operation possible.

Modern iron making

Today, considerable attention is paid to the preparation of the ore, coke, and limestone flux before it is charged into the top of the blast furnace. The flux is required to ensure that the earthy components of the ore form a liquid slag at the temperature of the molten iron. The ore is crushed to uniform lumps, between 1 and 2½ in. (2.5–6.25 cm) across, that are small enough to be easily reduced by the carbon monoxide in the furnace but not too small to impede the flow of gas up the stack. In practice, some of the ore will be too finely divided to be charged (placed in the furnace) directly. These fines, together with dust collected from the gas coming off the top of the

▲ The working principle of the blast furnace. A double bell arrangement (top left) is located at the top of the furnace to accept the charges of ore and coke without venting the gases and cooling the furnce. With the bottom bell closed, the top one is opened to accept the charge. Next, the top bell is closed (bottom left) and the bottom one opened, releasing the charge into the hot furnace.

furnace, are mixed with about 10 percent coke powder and fired to produce a coherent mass, or sinter, suitable for charging. Some furnaces operate using 100 percent sinter—all the ore being finely powdered at the outset. The result is an improvement in efficiency that is enhanced still further if the limestone flux is also incorporated into the sinter.

The charge is inserted into the furnace throat via a double-bell arrangement, which minimizes loss of the useful blast furnace gas and aids even distribution on top of the existing burden. As iron and slag are removed from the hearth, the burden gradually moves down the furnace stack against a countercurrent of gas that is mainly carbon monoxide and nitrogen. The carbon monoxide is formed by the interaction of the hot coke with preheated air that is injected through openings, called tuyeres, placed radially near the bottom of the furnace. The chemical reactions inside the blast furnace are complex, but the overall reaction may be represented simply as:

$$\underset{\text{hematite}}{Fe_2O_3} + \underset{\text{carbon monoxide}}{3CO} \rightarrow \underset{\text{iron}}{2Fe} + \underset{\text{carbon dioxide}}{3CO_2}$$

As the iron is released from its oxide form, it melts and drips down to the hearth. (The molten iron will have dissolved a few percent carbon, and several other impurities may also be present.) The limestone flux will also have done its job and combined with silica, alumina, and any other unreduced oxides to form molten droplets of slag, which fall to the hearth. Being lighter than iron, however, the slag floats on the surface.

It is current practice to improve the efficiency of blast furnace operations by running at a top pressure of about two atmospheres, thus enabling a greater mass of gas to be in contact with the burden at any one time. Further improvements in general efficiency as well as the ease with which the furnace can be controlled have been obtained by the practice of injecting both steam and oxygen into the air blast at the tuyeres.

Wrought and cast iron

Wrought iron has long been superseded by mild steel as the main material for structural engineering, although it is still produced in small quantities for certain applications. Wrought iron is made by holding pig iron in the molten state in an atmosphere of air. A large proportion of the carbon, silicon, phosphorus, and manganese impurities are removed as oxides. As the purity of iron increases, it gradually solidifies into a pasty mass that on completion is removed from the furnace and then mechanically worked with heavy-duty hammers or presses.

Cast iron can be made from iron with a silicon content of between 2 and 4 percent, called acid

◀ This blast furnace can produce 350 tons (315 tonnes) of pig iron per day. There are 48 ovens that produce coke for use in the blast furnace. The process of making coke from coal produces several tons of by-products, such as coal tar. A stream of molten iron is tapped from the bottom of the furnace. The carbon content of the iron lowers its melting point and makes the molten metal easier to handle.

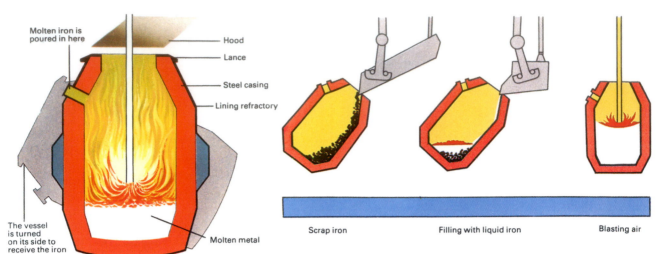

BASIC OXYGEN STEEL CONVERTER

Molten iron is poured in here

Hood

Lance

Steel casing

Lining refractory

The vessel is turned on its side to receive the iron

Molten metal

PROCESS FOR BASIC OXYGEN STEEL

Scrap iron

Filling with liquid iron

Blasting air

iron, or from iron made with a minimum of flux from ore that has a substantial manganese content, known as basic iron.

When cast, basic iron containing less that 1.5 percent silicon is hard and brittle because it contains 3 to 4 percent carbon, which is present as iron carbide—itself hard and brittle. When broken, the fracture surfaces have a bright appearance, and have led to this iron being called white cast iron. It cannot be easily machined and is only used in situations where abrasion resistance is of prime importance.

The 2 to 4 percent silicon in acid pig iron causes the carbon to be present as graphite flakes rather than iron carbide. It is readily machinable but brittle because the graphite flakes act rather as if they were small cracks. The graphite is also responsible for the dull appearance of the fracture surfaces, giving the metal its name, gray cast iron. It is very widely used for engine cylinder blocks, machine tool beds, foundry casting boxes, stove parts, flywheels, and so on.

Iron compounds

Although the importance of iron obviously lies in its value as a metal, there are several compounds of interest other than the naturally occurring ores. For example, it is an essential part of the respiratory pigment hemoglobin, which is found in the red blood cells and some muscles of all vertebrates and in the blood plasma of certain invertebrates—earthworms, for one. Hemoglobin has a great affinity for oxygen, so its job is to carry oxygen that is breathed in around the body in the form of oxyhemoglobin.

Because it is a transition element and therefore has variable valency, two series of iron compounds exist: the ferrous, Fe^{2+}, with a valency of 2 and the ferric, Fe^{3+}, with a valency of 3. Ferric

oxide, Fe_2O_3, the principal iron ore, is very hard and can be used as an abrasive in polishing. Its red coloration makes it useful as a pigment. In a hydrated form, $Fe_2O_3 \cdot H_2O$, iron oxide is familiar as rust. Ferric chloride, $FeCl_3$, has a widespread range of uses from the coagulation of sewage to etching. Oxidation of ferrous compounds to ferric ores is put to good use in writing inks, where ferrous sulfate is used.

Steel

Steel is the most widely used of all the manufactured metals. It is not easy to define because it can be made in many forms, each with its own characteristics. It can be defined broadly as an alloy (a substance composed of two or more chemical elements, one of which must be a metal) of iron and carbon, the carbon content being not more than 1.7 percent and usually only about 0.2 to 0.3 percent. Carbon content controls the hardness (strength) of steel. Other elements are added to confer hardenability or to produce specific properties, such as ease of machining, toughness, and the ability to resist wear or attack by heat, corrosion, or chemicals.

History of steel

The fact that carbon controls hardness has been known for thousands of years, but there was really no steel as we know it until 1740. In that year, the British inventor Benjamin Huntsman devised a method of melting wrought iron that had carbon diffused into it and so produced a reasonably consistent steel. Huntsman's steel could be made only in small batches, so its uses were limited.

It was the British inventor and manufacturer Sir Henry Bessemer who made bulk production of steel possible in 1856 with the invention of the Bessemer process. In 1857, the British industrialist

▲ An oxygen steel converter into which molten iron is poured. Oxygen is blown through the metal by means of a water-cooled lance and reacts to form iron oxide. The oxide mixes rapidly with the rest of the metal, and impurities are oxidized out.

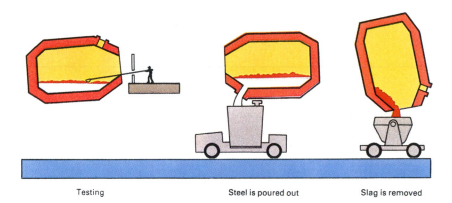

Testing   Steel is poured out   Slag is removed

Basic oxygen steel (BOS) process

The BOS process is fast, and because it is exothermic (the reaction produces heat), no fuel is needed. In BOS steel making, molten iron is poured into a large converter lined with refractory bricks. The vessel is so mounted that it can be turned on its side to receive the iron and turned to a vertical position for the next stage in the process. In that stage, a water-cooled tube, or lance, is lowered into the vessel until its tip is just above the molten metal, and oxygen is blown through it at high pressure. The force of the blast cuts through the slag on the top of the metal, and the oxygen rapidly reacts with the iron to form iron oxide. Turbulence caused by the force of the oxygen jet gives rapid mixing of the oxide with the rest of the metal so that the impurities are oxidized out.

A typical BOS vessel can hold 300 tons (270 tonnes) of molten iron, and steel making is completed in about 30 minutes. The exothermic reaction provides more than enough heat—in fact, a certain amount of cold scrap steel has to be charged to prevent the steel from getting too far above its melting temperature of about 2912°F (1600°C)—it varies a little according to the speci-

Sir William Siemens introduced another method of bulk steel manufacture, the open-hearth process. These two processes enabled steel to develop at the expense of wrought iron, which is now produced only in very small amounts. The first true alloy steel, containing 7 percent tungsten, was introduced by the English metallurgist R. F. Mushet in 1868, and many others have followed.

Carbon content of steel

Steel is generally made from pig iron (produced in a blast furnace), which is iron containing 3 to 5 percent carbon together with smaller percentages of other elements, mainly sulfur, phosphorus, silicon, and manganese. The required carbon content for steel is low—for example, around 0.25 percent for mild steel—and needs to be precisely controlled. Accordingly, the carbon has to be reduced to the required level—and in practice, this reduction is often carried out by removing the existing carbon completely and then adding the precise amount required to the molten steel. Removal of the carbon is achieved by oxidizing it to form carbon monoxide gas, which passes out of the molten metal.

The other elements are not specifically required—and because they can affect the properties of the steel, they are removed by the addition of fluxes, such as limestone, while the steel is being made to form a molten slag on top of the metal. Steel-making processes are known as acid or basic, according to the characteristics of the lining refractories (heat-resisting substances) that come in contact with the molten metal. The type of process used depends on the impurities that have to be removed from the iron—the basic process, for example, is capable of dealing with high levels of phosphorus and sulfur.

▶ An ingot of remelted metal produced in the vacuum arc remelting furnace in the background. This process resembles the electroslag refining process (ESR), but the arc is struck, in a vacuum, between the steel bar and some steel at the bottom of the mold, and no slag is used.

fication. This addition of scrap is useful because it provides a means of recycling old and worn-out steel articles and manufacturing scrap. Fluxing materials, particularly lime, are charged as required during the steel-making cycle.

Large quantities of carbon monoxide gas and fumes are evolved during oxygen blowing. These gases are collected by a hood above the vessel and drawn off by fans, the carbon monoxide being either used as a fuel gas in other parts of the works or burned at the top of a flare stack. The other gases are cleaned before discharge to the atmosphere. At the end of the process, the vessel is turned on its side to draw off the steel and finally inverted completely to dump the slag.

Electric furnace steel

Some bulk, or tonnage, steels and almost all alloy steels are made in electric furnaces, of which the most important is the electric arc furnace. This furnace is of cylindrical form, with a removable roof through which three electrodes project. Capacities can range from a few tons to 130 (118 tonnes) or more. A weighted charge of selected cold scrap, sometimes together with some cold cast iron, is deposited in the furnace. The roof is swung into place, and an arc is struck from the electrodes, generating enough intense heat to melt the charge rapidly. Fluxing materials are added by a charging machine through a door in the side of the furnace, and alloying materials are charged in the same way as required. Oxygen can be used, by means of a lance inserted through the door, to speed up the process.

Some of the more highly specialized alloy steels are often made in small batches in electric induction furnaces. They are similar in principle to an electric transformer, in which a primary alternating electric current induces a secondary one. In the induction furnace the secondary current is induced in the metal being melted, which is held in a refractory lined vessel. The furnace charge consists of cold metal and alloying materials in carefully weighed quantities to give the exact proportions of each element in the molten metal.

▲ A steel glove with iron mail finely decorated with silver and gilt, made in Jaipur, India, in the 18th century.

Casting

Steel, as made by any process, is a liquid when it leaves the furnace. Relatively small quantities are poured into molds to make steel castings, but most of it is made into forms that are suitable for further processing. Traditionally, forming was always done by teeming (pouring) the molten steel into heavy cast-iron molds where it solidified into ingots that could be forged or, more commonly, rolled into the shapes required, such as plates, sheets, beams, sections, or bars.

Refining

Although the BOS and electric-arc processes account for the major part of the world's steel production, there are certain steels that need further treatments to fit them for specialized purposes, such as use in the petrochemical industries. Such steels are usually made in the electric furnace and then refined to remove trapped gases and impurities.

Refining can be done in various ways. One is to remelt the steel in a vacuum. Gases released during melting are drawn off by the vacuum pumps, leaving a clean steel. An increasingly common method is electroslag refining (ESR). In this process an electric arc is struck from the end of a bar of the steel to be refined, which is submerged in a pool of specially prepared molten slag. The end of the bar melts into droplets, which pass through the slag and are washed clean of impurities. A water-cooled mold causes the molten metal to solidify into a bar that can then be processed as required.

FACT FILE

- At the beginning of the eighth century C.E., Catalonian iron workers developed the Catalonian forge, a hearth furnace into the bottom of which air was forced by water power. In five hours the forge could produce 350 lbs. (158 kg) of wrought iron.

- It is possible to ship iron ore on oceangoing tankers in slurry form. The 75 percent solids slurry is pumped aboard, allowed to settle, and then pumped almost dry, to about 92 percent solids, thus forming a stable cargo. High-pressure water hoses reslurry the ore for unloading.

SEE ALSO: ALLOY • CARBON • METAL • METALWORKING • OXYGEN

Irrigation Techniques

Irrigation is the artificial watering of crops so that they achieve their full potential growth. The first large irrigation schemes were developed in the Near and Far East in the ancient cultures of Egypt, Syria, Persia, India, Java, and Ceylon. In the West, elaborate schemes came later, about 2,000 years ago, in Mexico and Peru. Some ancient irrigation dams and canals are still used today and testify to the care and skill with which they were made. There is no country in the world that does not practice some form of irrigation. On a world scale, however, only about a quarter of all agricultural land is irrigated, even though most would benefit, including much of the temperate zones. In the United States, over 40 million acres (16 million ha) are irrigated, about 10 percent of the total cultivated area. Irrigation is most heavily concentrated in the western states, with irrigated land producing something like 80 percent of California's agricultural output.

One of the oldest methods of irrigation is basin flooding, which was the sole method used in the flat Nile valley until 100 years ago. It is recorded that 5,000 years ago King Menes of Egypt dammed the Nile with mud and stone to trap the annual excess water from the torrential tropical rains on the mountainous areas of Ethiopia where the river rises. After that, land near the river was divided into basins of between 1 and 40,000 acres (1–16,000 ha) surrounded by artificial banks. When the Nile flooded, the water entered the basins through short canals and sluices, flooding the land to a depth of 3 to 6 ft. (1–2 m). The water remained for 40 to 60 days and deposited a layer of rich silt when it drained away, so providing a fertilizing effect in addition to irrigation. However, with the construction of the Aswan High Dam, this practice ended, and the water of the Nile is now stored and released in a steady stream, allowing year-round irrigation and giving a considerably longer growing season. The loss of the fertility in the silt has been made up by the use of fertilizers, but a side effect has been a shortage of mud (originally provided by the silt) for traditional Egyptian brick production.

The best-known type of irrigation is that practiced in hot, humid climates where the commonest crop is rice, a plant that needs plenty of water to succeed. Most rice is grown in paddy fields that are flooded with about 6 in. (15 cm) of water during the growing season. This system is possible because there is no shortage of water in such areas, either because annual rainfall is high or because the rivers are large with reliable flows.

Irrigation of crops is a relatively simple matter if the level of the water source is higher than that of the land to be watered—the water is simply led through artificial channels, for example, canals and ditches, to the fields. Transferring water from a river through canals has been done since Babylonian times, and it is still one of the most common ways of bringing water to crops. If the river has a steep gradient, water is diverted into a canal some distance upstream and led along a contour so that it can flow into the fields by gravity. Alternatively, barrages with sluices are built at intervals in the river to raise its level so that water can be led upstream, away from the barrage. Canals are expensive to build if they are to be watertight; they also need to be dredged to keep them free from silt.

Similarly, dams can be built to impound large quantities of water in a reservoir for gradual release to irrigated areas. California, for example, has some 200 major reservoirs with a major system of canals to transport the water—the main Californian Aqueduct of the State Water Project has a length of over 800 miles (1,200 km), over three-quarters of which are artificial. A further source of water for irrigation is groundwater extracted from wells.

Raising water for irrigation

Often water must be raised from a lower level before it can be used for irrigation purposes. Early devices for raising water included the shaduf, in common use by 1000 B.C.E., which consisted of a pivoted pole with a bucket attached to one end and a stone counterweight on the other end. The Archimedes' screw was used in ancient Egyptian times to raise water for irrigation and is still in use today in some parts of the world. It can only, however, raise water up inclines of not more than 30 degrees. The saqiya, a wooden wheel with a number of clay pots attached to its rim, has also been used since ancient times for lifting water. A development of the saqiya is the Persian water wheel, which is driven by bullocks. It has pots suspended on an endless chain that fetch water up from wells and feed it into channels that lead across a field. Wells are the only source of water to be found in many arid regions of the world and have been used for irrigation for centuries.

Another ancient method of collecting water to irrigate arid regions is the qanaat. This consists of a tunnel that collects underground water from water-bearing strata at the foot of a mountain. Water flows along the gently sloping tunnel to the irrigated region by gravity, sometimes for as much as 30 miles (50 km). Every so often, vertical shafts extend from the tunnel to the surface and give workers access for repairs and for removing earth. Several thousand miles of qanaats exist in North Africa and Asia. A more modern version of this principle is the National Water Carrier, a 150 mile (240 km) pipeline that conducts water from Lake Tiberias in the north of Israel through an immense 9 ft. (2.74 m) concrete pipe to the arid regions of the Negev Desert in the south.

Today, water for irrigation is raised using mechanical pumps driven, for example, by internal combustion engines, electric motors, or wind power. Portable engine-pump units provide useful flexibility; they can lift water precisely when and where it is needed. They are widely used in hot countries for the irrigation of fields.

SALINITY PROBLEMS

Irrigating fields over a long period of time can lead to an increase of salts in the soil that can poison crops. Draining salt-contaminated water from fields requires an elaborate system of underground pipes sunk about 6 ft. (1.8 m) below the surface and 250 ft. (76 m) apart. Usually, the contaminated water lies out of harm's way below the roots of the growing plants. However, if the water table rises, the pipes drain off the water.

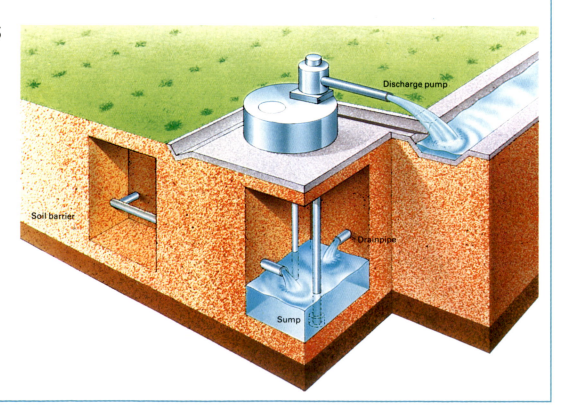

◄ In oil-rich Abu Dhabi, precious water is lavished on decorative plants by the freeway. Most of the freshwater supply in Abu Dhabi comes from huge desalination plants located on the coast.

Irrigation systems

There are a number of ways in which water can be applied to the land to be irrigated with the simplest (and oldest) being flooding. For this method to be effective the area to be flooded has to be as flat as possible, and in some cases, the land is artificially leveled using earthmovers. The recent introduction of laser-guided leveling systems allows very high-accuracy leveling to be achieved.

More efficient use of the water is achieved by furrow irrigation, where the water is distributed to the crop by means of a network of furrows that are supplied with water from a channel. Furrow irrigation can be applied to nonlevel fields, as some slope is necessary to ensure water flow. Underground irrigation systems use a network of perforated pipes to distribute water directly to the root zone, but this technique is limited by soil characteristics, with clogging of the pipes and disruption by root intrusion being major problems.

Sprinkler systems supply water to the plants as artificial rain, the water being supplied under pressure to perforated pipes or nozzles. Permanent sprinkler systems with fixed pipelines are used for applications such as vineyards, orchards and nurseries, while movable systems can be shifted from field to field according to requirements. Where appropriate, pest- and weed-control chemicals can be mixed with the water and sprayed on the crops. Similarly, fertilizer can be added—indeed, in some areas of the world, groundwater that is polluted with nitrates is being purposely used for irrigation so that the nitrates can be extracted from the water using the plants.

Water economy

The amount of water needed for irrigation can be considerably reduced by the adoption of trickle irrigation or drip irrigation, where the water is delivered slowly to the root area to create a wet region around the roots. A system of pipelines is used to supply the water, with fertilizers often being added. This technique can use less than half the water needed by furrow irrigation, for example. Recycling of irrigation water is also being practiced in some extremely dry areas, although the general problem of increasing salinization means that one quantity of water cannot be recycled indefinitely.

Another method used in very dry areas relies on the effects on vegetation of dew and fog, which in some parts of the world, like the coastline of Peru, are the only source of water for plants. Great advances in using this dew have been made by the Israelis in the Negev Desert, where the total annual rainfall, a mere 1 to 8 in. (2.5–20 cm), may

▶ Citrus trees are refreshed by a sprinkler system in Australia. Economical systems include drip irrigation, which supplies only the root zone of crop plants with a flow of water.

fall within ten days. However, there are many nights when dew forms. Sloping polyethylene sheeting with a gutter at the bottom edge leading to a pit in which seedlings are planted can collect enough dew to keep the seedlings alive until the rain comes again. As a result, there now stand in the Negev Desert avenues and woods of eucalyptus, Aleppo pine, and other trees.

Hydroponics

Hydroponics is the name given to a method of growing crops, such as tomatoes and cucumbers, in water without soil. The plants are grown in greenhouses in concrete troughs lined with a vinyl plastic. The roots of the plants are embedded in a material such as gravel, and water containing all the nutrients required for growth is pumped to the troughs through pipes. Similar methods use sand or a thin capillary matting as the growing medium. Humidity, temperature, and air circulation in the greenhouses are carefully controlled to ensure the best possible growth of the plants. Under such ideal conditions, the crops produced are of very high quality, and moreover, the yield per plant is greater than that achieved by conventional methods. For example, a mature tomato plant grown hydroponically can produce about 26 lbs. (12 kg) of fruit per year as compared with 20 lbs. (9 kg) by normal methods. Because the hydroponic system is carried out in greenhouses or under polyethylene, loss of water can be minimized, making the system especially suitable for use in hot, dry climates.

▲ The benefits of irrigation are shown on this satellite picture of one of the world's largest irrigated areas: California's Imperial Valley. The red dots clustered to the left are irrigated fields. The white area to the right is desert.

FACT FILE

■ *In modern Iran, there are over 20,000 conduit systems, with an overall length of more than 168,000 miles (270,000 km). Many of these are still in use, though they were constructed mostly in the third millennium B.C.E.*

■ *The world's largest artesian water supply is in Australia. The Great Artesian Basin stretches from the Gulf of Carpentaria in the north all the way to South Australia. The basin covers 676,250 sq. miles (1,753,000 km²) and supplies approximately 18,000 boreholes.*

■ *During the 18th-century, travelers to China brought back diagrams of human-powered treadmills used to raise irrigation water between levels. A rolling shaft moved an endless cable fitted with wooden paddles that forced the water up a wooden trough.*

SEE ALSO: AGRICULTURAL SCIENCE • AGRICULTURE, INTENSIVE • AGRICULTURE, ORGANIC • CANAL • DAM • DESALINATION • DRAINAGE • EROSION • FERTILIZER • FLOOD CONTROL • FORESTRY • HORTICULTURE • HYDROPONICS • SOIL RESEARCH

Jackhammer

Jackhammer is the popular term for a pneumatic road breaker. It is powered by compressed air, which imparts a hammer action to the tool enabling it to do a variety of jobs, such as breaking up road surfaces, demolishing buildings, and digging trenches. The jackhammer is able to do these different jobs by using several interchangeable tool bits.

The pneumatic breaker is a relatively modern invention, replacing other methods of breaking solid surfaces like the pickaxe or the hammer and wedge, which are both time consuming. The pneumatic breaker is a T-shaped machine ruggedly constructed in forged steel in a variety of weights to suit particular job requirements. Heavier machines weighing about 80 lbs. (36 kg) are used to break surfaces such as concrete sidewalks, while lighter hammers weighing less than 50 lbs. (23 kg) may be used to break floors and walls.

The main part of a jackhammer is a vertical cylinder with handles and throttle control across the top. Compressed air is fed in through a flexible hose from a compressor to the top of the cylinder below the handle and conducted alternately to each end of a sliding piston via a valve. As the compressed air released by the throttle lever first enters the upper cylinder, the piston is forced down onto a cylindrical sliding anvil, beneath which is the working tool.

The energy of the piston hitting the anvil forces it onto the tool, which is in turn struck down onto the working surface. After striking the anvil, the piston is driven back to the top of the cylinder by compressed air entering the lower end and forcing it upward. Following both the upward and downward movements, the compressed air is exhausted to the atmosphere in a downward direction.

In order to conduct the compressed air to the upper and lower parts of the cylinder, valves and ducts are built into the body, and since minimum wear on the moving anvil and piston is essential, the compressed air is normally lubricated by an oil valve in the throttle mechanism fed from a reservoir below the handle that holds enough oil for about eight hours' work. Further reduction in wear can be achieved by the design of air cushions at the top and bottom of the cylinder to prevent the piston from hitting the ends of the cylinder.

Pneumatic road breakers operate on compressed air at a pressure of about 85 psi (6 bar) and vary in consumption from 40 to 75 cu. ft. (1.1–2.1 m³) of air per minute, producing 1,100 to 1,500 blows per minute.

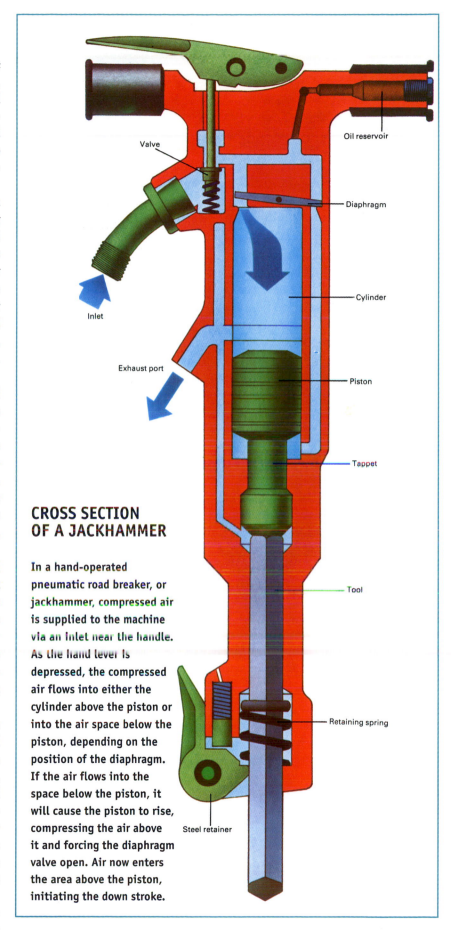

CROSS SECTION OF A JACKHAMMER

In a hand-operated pneumatic road breaker, or jackhammer, compressed air is supplied to the machine via an inlet near the handle. As the hand lever is depressed, the compressed air flows into either the cylinder above the piston or into the air space below the piston, depending on the position of the diaphragm. If the air flows into the space below the piston, it will cause the piston to rise, compressing the air above it and forcing the diaphragm valve open. Air now enters the area above the piston, initiating the down stroke.

SEE ALSO: PNEUMATIC TOOL • ROAD CONSTRUCTION

Jukebox

Although the precise origin of the word *jukebox* is unclear, it is probable that the word *juke* either comes from the West African word *joot*, meaning "to dance," or it derives from the African-American dialect of the southeast coast of the United States where *juke* means "disorderly" or "wicked." Initially, a juke joint was the sort of place where you would have expected to find a jukebox.

A jukebox is an automated record player, operated by inserting coins. Its antecedent was the coin-operated musical box. Early jukeboxes were called nickelodeons, because in the United States it cost a nickel to operate them. Nickelodeons played only one side of a 78 rpm record, and the stylus had to be replaced often because it was made of steel and wore down quickly.

During the early 1950s, a so-called battle of the speeds took place in the record industry, and for a while, records were widely available in three speeds and three sizes. Some jukeboxes were built that could play a mixed selection of records, but they were gradually superseded by jukeboxes that played only 7 in. (17 cm) records at 45 rpm, although some machines were made that play records at 33⅓ rpm as well.

Jukeboxes can be divided basically into two types of record-selecting mechanisms. The first type, typified by the Seeburg Selectomatic, has all the records standing vertically in a row, and the selector travels up and down the row. This design was also available in a conventional wooden cabinet for use in the home, playing full-sized LPs, or for continuous playing of background music in public places. The second type, used by Wurlitzer and others, has all the records in a magazine that revolves around the selecting device.

Credit cycle

When a coin is deposited, the mechanism decides what denomination it is by weighing it and measuring it. After the coin has been shunted into its respective channel according to its worth, it strikes a credit switch, normally two thin metal contacts touching together as the coin passes, closing a circuit to the credit unit.

The job of the credit unit is to establish the right number of plays for the coin deposited. This task is done in the majority of cases by a toothed wheel that steps around an appropriate number of teeth. As each selection is made, the credit unit cancels a credit by moving the wheel one tooth nearer to its rest position. When the last selection has been made, a lever attached to the wheel breaks contact with the selection circuit.

Selection mechanism

There are two ways of programming the selection mechanism. The pin selector has a bank of pins, one for each side of each record; when one of these pins is lifted or punched up by a small solenoid switch, the scanning device can find the selected record. The other type uses ferrite disks called toroids in a magnetic core memory unit, which is similar to that in a computer.

Each disk is shaped like a small washer and can exist in either of two magnetic states that can be called the "no," or off, state and the "yes," or on, state. Initially, all the disks are in the "no" state. When selecting a record, one and only one disk (corresponding to that record) will be addressed and in so doing its state will change to the "yes" condition. For the machine to discover which disk has been changed, each is scanned in turn—passing a current along a wire that passes through the center of each disk individually. This current will not affect any of the disks in the "no" state, but when passing through a disk in the "yes" state, it causes it to change back into a "no." This change in magnetic state induces a small pulse current in a sensing wire that passes through the

▲ Most jukeboxes are now made to play CDs rather than vinyl records and can therefore offer a much broader range of track options. DVD jukeboxes can also play promotional video clips.

center of every disk. The pulse is detected by a silicon-controlled rectifier (a semiconductor device that acts as a switch), which locks the mechanism to the associated record. This system is preferred because it has no moving parts. In some more modern designs, the selection sequence—and the credit cycle—are controlled by microprocessor systems, which allow more complicated operating sequences, such as repeated playing of a record or selection of records in a specific sequence.

From this point on the action is mainly mechanical. The record is pushed out of the rack into the selector by an arm and played vertically or lifted out of the magazine, placed on the turntable, and played horizontally. In the case of the mechanism that plays the record vertically, there is a stylus on each side of the tone arm for playing either side of the record, and stylus pressure is maintained by a spring. At the end of the record, the unit rejects automatically, as in a home record changer. During the mechanical operation, the pin or the toroid is restored to its rest position. With the older designs, if a record is selected twice before it is played, it will play only once; the records are played in the magazine sequence rather than the sequence in which they are selected.

Jukeboxes often use piezoelectric (ceramic) pickups because they can stand up to the difficult operating conditions—the jukebox has to keep playing despite heavy vibrations from dancers and accidental knocks—although magnetic cartridges are also widely used as pickups.

Remote selection

The remote selector, or wallbox, is used in places so small that the main jukebox must be located in a remote place or so large that there must be

▶ This classic Wurlitzer jukebox dating from the 1950s displays many of the design features typical of jukeboxes of this period, including a visible record-changing mechanism, revolving light columns, and a curved top. Many of these classic designs are now collected by jukebox enthusiasts.

more than one selection location for convenience. The wall box works much like a telephone dialing system. After credit is established in the normal way, a motor revolves, passing a wiper over a printed circuit board. The wiper sends a train of impulses to the main box, where they are received on a stepper that consists of two uniselectors, one for letters and one for numbers. Then the record playing unit is activated in the normal way.

◀ This selection device travels up and down the row of vertically standing records. The record is pushed out of the rack into the selector by an arm and then played vertically. The tone arm has a stylus on each side so it can play either side of the record, and stylus pressure is held by a spring.

CD jukebox

Today, jukeboxes that play vinyl records have largely been superseded by CD jukeboxes. These operate in much the same way as traditional jukeboxes, and many are designed in imitation of the classic jukeboxes of the 1940s and 1950s, with features such as visible CD changing mechanisms and bubble tubes. CD jukeboxes, however, include modern solid-state technology, digital displays, and much improved loudspeaker systems. Microprocessors enable the jukebox to play a random selection of tracks at regular predetermined intervals. This feature is useful in commercial environments as a means of encouraging people to use the jukebox.

SEE ALSO:	COMPACT DISC, AUDIO • DATA STORAGE • HI-FI SYSTEMS • PIEZOELECTRIC MATERIAL

Key-Cutting Machine

A key-cutting machine is essentially a rotary file that follows a template provided by the key being duplicated. The machine is fitted with two vises, one of which holds the key to be copied and the other the blank. The carriage has a profile follower at one end that follows the configuration of the key and a rotary filing wheel with a sharp cross section at the other end that removes metal from the key blank until it matches the profile of the key being copied. An adjustment is provided for raising or lowering the profile follower.

Electric and hand-cranked models are available. The vise jaws locate on the flute (longitudinal groove) on the side of the key; the key must be pushed in all the way up to its ear. Double-sided keys are copied by turning over both the key and the blank in the vise jaws, copying one side at a time. Care must be taken to ensure that the jaws locate on the corresponding flutes of the key and the blank, otherwise the notches that make up the profile of the key will be cut too deeply or not deeply enough.

Electric key-cutting machines are now fitted with a metal cover that encloses the device. The operator pushes the key and the blank into appropriate slots and flips a switch; the machine makes its traverse automatically, and the cover prevents the metal filings from flying into the eyes of any people standing nearby.

Key-cutting machines have been developed that cut keys by code without using an original key. A series of numbers is arrived at after decoding the number on the lock the key is required for. Each number corresponds to a depth of cut and these cuts are spaced correctly on the new key with the help of a space key. A dial is then set to each of the appropriate numbers, and the machine makes an accurate copy of the original key.

Some of the latest machines make high-security keys by using computers to control the cutting process. Another development is the replacement of rotary filing wheels with lasers that can cut with a high degree of precision.

▼ This type of key-cutting machine is about ten inches long. The feeler on the left follows the key being copied, using it as a template, and the rotary file on the right makes the duplicate. The machine comes with two rotary files, a rotary saw, washers, test blanks, and adjustment tools.

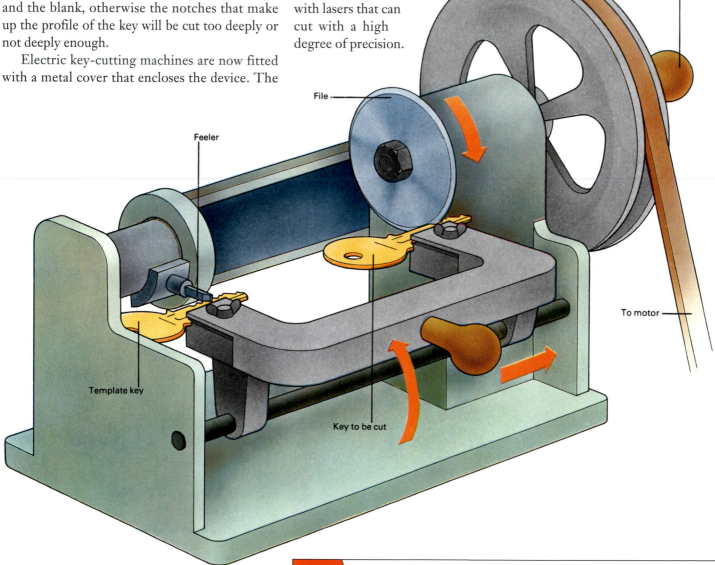

Handle for manual operation

File

Feeler

To motor

Template key

Key to be cut

SEE ALSO: ELECTRIC MOTOR • LOCK, SECURITY • MACHINE TOOL

Kiln

◀ Ceramic diffusion plates used in sewage treatment to introduce air efficiency into the activated sludge being fired in a gas-fired kiln. Such kilns are among the least mechanized and should be compared with the tunnel kiln and the continuous-chamber brick kiln. In the former, trucks loaded with wares pass along the heated tunnel. In the latter, the separated coal-burning grates are fired in succession around the kiln, hot air from the chambers' cooling down being used to help firing and hot air from those firing to preheat others.

Kilns vary in function from those that are used for drying, at comparatively low temperatures, commodities such as hops, corn, timber, or metal ores to those that produce physical and chemical changes in a substance and operate at much higher temperatures, such as when firing bricks. Here the temperatures range from 1650 to 2190°F (900–1200°C), and the kilns are really a type of furnace. The kilns themselves are usually made of firebrick or other refractories that can withstand the high operating temperatures necessary for firing.

Various fuels, including coal, oil, and natural and liquefied petroleum gases, are used to heat or fire kilns—the choice in most major industries, such as brick and china manufacture, depends on available sources. Many brick kilns of the chamber type have been fired successively by coal, oil, and gas over the past 25 years, and if pollution problems can be overcome could well revert to coal. Studio potters, however, have tended to favor small electric kilns, because they are easy to install and control and require little maintenance if properly treated.

In operation, kilns may work on an intermittent or a continuous basis. In the intermittent process, the kiln is loaded, brought up to the required temperature, which may need to be maintained for a certain period, then cooled, and the goods are removed. Continuous kilns, however, are designed so that they can work virtually nonstop.

Low-temperature kilns

Probably the most picturesque kiln is the oast, which is used for drying hops. Oasts are built of brick, and most are circular, about 20 ft. (6 m) in diameter, and are tapered at the top, which is covered by a hooded cowl to prevent any back draughts in windy weather. The hops are scattered on the porous kiln floors, and fans are used to assist the circulation of heated air, which must not exceed 149°F (65°C). The air is normally heated by means of steam-filled pipes. Hop kiln designs in the United States vary and may be of wood, brick, or concrete, but the principle of drying remains the same.

A timber kiln is a small heated building where the conditions of temperature, ventilation, and humidity are carefully controlled so that the green timber attains the correct moisture content. This forced method is much faster than seasoning timber by piling it outdoors, taking about one week as opposed to one year. It is, however, better suited for wood to be used indoors.

Continuous kilns

There are various types of continuous kiln; perhaps the most interesting one, designed by a German railway engineer named Hoffmann in 1858, introduced the biggest advances in conserving heat and increasing efficiency. The Hoffmann kiln is still used, with slight modifications, in brickmaking. Originally the kiln was a circular tunnel, but today it consists of a series of separate chambers, and the fire travels from one to another. The green bricks are stacked in a chamber, and cold air, which is needed for combustion, enters through the open doorway or wicket. The air passes through holes in the walls between chambers into areas containing cooling bricks, thus becoming heated. This hot air now passes to the zone where the fuel is burned, and the hot combustion products pass onward to heat and dry bricks set in successive chambers.

The tunnel is another type of continuous kiln that appeared some 50 years after the development of the Hoffmann kiln. Goods to be fired

► Electric insulators stacked in a kiln prior to firing. The introduction of a catalyst to the silicon incorporated into the clay causes it to crystallize out as it cools.

pass slowly through a tunnel, usually on cars using a hydraulic pusher system. The tunnel is divided into various zones; the goods are heated gently by hot air recirculated from the cooling zone, then they pass through the firing zone and finally enter the cooling zone.

The cement industry uses rotary kilns that are fired by powdered coal, oil, or gas at temperatures of about 2700°F (1500°C). The kiln is slightly inclined and revolves slowly as the raw materials, either chalk and clay in the form of a slurry or milled limestone and shale, are fed in and converted to clinker by the heat. Similar kilns are used to manufacture lime (calcium oxide). The carefully graded limestone ($CaCO_3$) is burned in the kiln, and the carbon dioxide gas that is given off is allowed to escape or is used as a by-product.

FACT FILE

- Greek red and black pottery depended for its color on the amount of oxygen in the kiln. Deep red resulted from a well-oxygenated kiln. Burning damp wood or closing air inlets reduced the oxygen in the air so that the heat took oxygen from the clay, producing a ferrous oxide that fired black.

- The Indian rural trench kiln, oval shaped, has a daily capacity of up to 28,000 bricks. The oval trench, 7 ft. (2.1 m) deep, is coal fed a section at a time. A number of 55 ft. (16 m) steel chimneys mounted on wheels can be moved to the requisite section. Ash is used to close the top.

- Chinese Chou dynasty (1155–255 B.C.E.) kilns were built on the sides of hills, with high enough temperatures at the bottom to fire stoneware (2190°F, 1200°C). Higher up in the kiln, lead-glazed earthenware could be fired at lower temperatures.

SEE ALSO: Beer and brewing • Brick manufacture • Ceramics • China and porcelain • Furnace • Iron and steel • Metalworking

Kinetics

The word *kinetics* derives from the Greek verb *kinein*, "to move." Kinetics is the study of objects in motion and particularly of the changes in the momentum of such objects. The objects in question vary in scale from atoms to planets, although different aspects of kinetics apply to the two extremes of scale. Together with kinematics—the study of equations of acceleration, displacement, and velocity of moving objects—kinetics forms a branch of mechanics called dynamics.

Classical kinetics

Classical kinetics applies to all but the smallest objects, such as atoms and molecules. The basis of classical mechanics is Newton's Second Law of Motion, which states that the net force that acts on an object is proportional to the mass of that object and its acceleration. Given an appropriate choice of units, the second law can be stated as the equation $F = ma$, where F is force in newtons (N), m is mass in kilograms (kg), and a is acceleration in meters per second squared (ms^{-2}), for example.

The second law can be expressed in terms of momentum changes by a mathematical process called integration with respect to time. Imagine a constant force acting on an object for a fixed amount of time, t. Since the constant force causes a constant acceleration, a, the change in velocity, Δv, is equal to the product of acceleration and time: $\Delta v = at$. (Note that Δ is the Greek letter *delta*, which signifies "change in.") Integration is the equivalent of this multiplication for cases where force and acceleration vary with the passage of time, such as in the case of space flight. In effect, integration divides time into intervals so small that the value of the acceleration does not change significantly within each interval of time. The mathematical products of acceleration and time are added together for all the intervals to give the total change in velocity. The operation is represented by $\Delta v = \int a.dt$, where $\int$ signifies "integral of" and $.dt$ signifies "with respect to time."

Changes in linear momentum

When the mass of an object is constant for the time that the force acts on it, the resulting change in momentum, Δp, is calculated by multiplying the mass of the object by the change in velocity, so $\Delta p = m\int a.dt$. If the mass of the object changes with time, as happens when a rocket burns its fuel, for example, then the product of mass and acceleration must be multiplied by time for each instant, and the operation becomes $\Delta p = \int ma.dt$. The expression $m\int a.dt$ is a special case of this equation.

Where m or a vary with time, they are replaced in the above integration by expressions that describe their values in terms of time—an equation such as $a = kt^3$ would be an example—and the integration is then done using standard mathematical procedures. Since momentum and acceleration are vector quantities—they have direction as well as size—separate calculations may be done for the change in momentum for each of the three dimensions of space.

Using these expressions it is possible to calculate changes in momentum of an object given a knowledge of how the force acting on a body varies as a function of time. Since the kinetic energy of an object that arises from its linear motion obeys the expression $K.E. = \frac{1}{2}mv^2$, changes in kinetic energy are also readily calculated from the changes in mass and velocity of a body. Such calculations have numerous applications in planning and understanding the motion of spacecraft, planets, projectiles, and earthbound objects.

Changes in angular momentum

A spinning object possesses angular momentum, which is the mathematical product of its moment of inertia and its angular velocity. The expressions for linear momentum are modified for angular motion by substituting torque for force, moment of inertia for mass, and angular acceleration and velocity for their linear counterparts.

▲ NASA's space shuttle *Discovery* lifts off from launch pad 39-B of the Kennedy Space Center, Florida, on May 27, 1999. The success of a space mission depends on its planners' familiarity with kinetics. The launch vehicle must be designed to have sufficient thrust to achieve escape velocity, for example, while smaller rocket motors must deliver accurate bursts of thrust to control the motion of the vehicle in space.

CHEMICAL REACTION KINETICS

In chemistry, the term *kinetics* refers to the rates at which chemical reactions occur, and in particular the study of the mechanisms by which reactions occur, and how they determine the reaction rates. The final equilibrium of a chemical reaction is determined by a balance between tendencies toward minimum energy and maximum entropy, or molecular randomness, which are expressed in the laws of thermodynamics. The concentrations of the different compounds at equilibrium are determined entirely by thermodynamics, but these laws in themselves are inadequate to determine whether a given reaction will reach equilibrium in a millisecond or only after thousands of years.

Chemical reaction rates can only be understood in terms of the individual chemical steps by which a reaction occurs. In a very simple reaction, the rate limiting step may be the collision of two molecules with just the right geometry and just enough kinetic energy to break some chemical bonds while others form. Even though a net amount of energy will be released when the reaction is completed, a certain minimum activation energy is required for the reaction to progress. The rate of the overall reaction will thus depend on the fraction of such molecular collisions that have the requisite activation energy.

In photochemical reactions, molecules acquire activation energy by absorbing photons. The energy, E, of a photon is related to its frequency, ν, by the equation

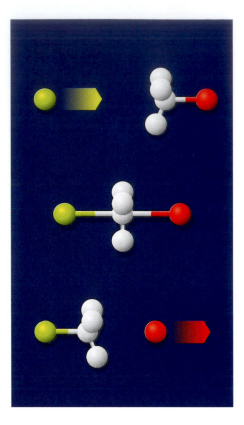

▲ The path of the reaction between chloride ions (Cl^-) and bromomethane (CH_3Br) is an example of a bimolecular nucleophilic substitution, or S_N2, mechanism. In such reactions, the attacking species—in this case, the chloride ion—is a nucleophile, an entity that has an affinity for positively charged sites—in this case, the carbon atom of bromomethane (top). For the reaction to occur, the reacting species must collide with the correct geometry and enough kinetic energy to form the transition state (center). The transition state forms chloromethane (CH_3Cl) by losing a bromide ion (Br^-, bottom).

$E = h\nu$, where h is Planck's constant. As such, the minimum frequency of light that can cause a photochemical reaction to occur is E_A/h. At this and higher light frequencies, the rate of reaction is governed by the rate at which molecules absorb photons and, hence, by the light intensity.

In the majority of chemical reactions, the energy required to form the transition state must come from the kinetic energy that molecules possess as a consequence of their thermal motion. Collisions between molecules are the events that cause the transfer of kinetic energy between molecules and allow transition states to form, provided the reacting molecules have a sufficient amount of thermal energy.

Laboratory experiments led to three basic observations about the rates of chemical reactions. First, reactions in which one or more components are solids proceed more rapidly when the solid matter is finely powdered rather than in the form of lumps, because reactions occur at the surface of a solid and powders have more surface area per unit mass than do large lumps. Second, reaction rates are greater for higher concentrations of reacting liquids and for higher pressures of reacting gases, because more densely packed reacting substances collide with greater frequencies. Third, there is an approximate twofold increase in the rate of a reaction for every 18°F (10°C) increase in temperature, because such an increase in temperature approximately doubles the number of molecules that have sufficient energy to react.

Elastic collisions

A more complete understanding of the changes of momentum of moving objects requires a consideration of what happens when two objects interact in a collision. In vehicular collisions, for example, some of the kinetic energy of the colliding vehicles is absorbed in the deformation of the vehicles. The exact amount of energy dissipated in this way is impossible to predict. This type of collision is described as inelastic.

Since the energy levels of atoms and molecules are quantized, most of the interactions between nonreacting atoms and molecules can be treated as perfectly elastic collisions, in which the kinetic energy of the molecules before the collision is redistributed among the same molecules afterward. Such collisions are similar to the collisions that occur between billiard balls, for example. For the very short duration of a collision between molecules, the effect of external forces like gravity can be ignored and the colliding molecules can be considered as an isolated system that is free of external influences. As such, the overall angular and linear momentums of the colliding objects must be unchanged by the collision. Thus, any change in either of these quantities for a given particle must be matched by an equal and opposite change in the other particles in the system so that the overall change is zero.

The linear interaction between colliding particles is the integral, with respect to time, of the force between the particles: $\int F.dt$. This quantity is called impulse, and the impulse experienced by a particle in collision is exactly equal to the change in its linear momentum that results from the collision. An equivalent angular quantity determines the change in angular momentum.

Maxwell–Boltzmann distribution

Quantum mechanics dictates that the kinetic energy of a moving particle may only assume certain values separated by distinct intervals. For large objects, these intervals are so small that they can be ignored. For atoms and molecules, however, the gaps between energy states become so significant as to influence the properties of gases and liquids, which are collections of enormous numbers of fast-moving molecules.

A major step in understanding the properties of matter was taken by the Austrian physicist Ludwig Boltzmann, who derived an expression to describe how the molecules in a gas share the available kinetic energy at any temperature. Boltzmann's work built on the earlier ideas of the British physicist James Clerk Maxwell concerning the distribution of molecular velocities in a sample of gas. Boltzmann obtained his result using statistical reasoning, assuming that the main effect of the collisions occurring in the gas was to make every alternative way of distributing the total kinetic energy among the gas molecules equally probable. This led to an exact expression for the fraction of molecules in a gas within any range of kinetic energy that depends only on the temperature. The energy distribution is easily converted into a distribution of molecular speeds when the molecular mass is taken into account.

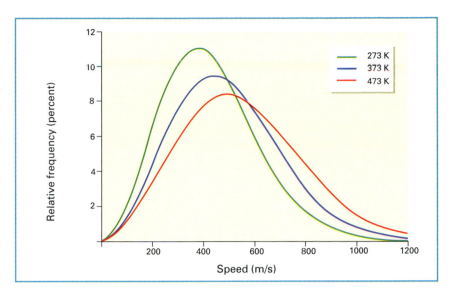

▲ The Maxwell–Boltzmann distribution of particle speeds in a gas at three temperatures: 212°F (100°C; green), 392°F (200°C; red), and 572°F (300°C; blue). The area under each line between two vertical lines (speed values) represents the number of molecules that have speeds within that range for the respective sample temperatures. Each value of speed corresponds to a distinct kinetic energy level, but the individual quantized energy levels are too closely spaced to be resolved in a graph of this small a scale.

A notable feature of the Maxwell–Boltzmann distribution is that the fraction of molecules possessing more kinetic energy than any set value increases as the temperature increases. Thus the number of molecules that have the activation energy to undergo any particular reaction increases markedly with temperature, and chemical reactions generally speed up as the temperature is increased. In addition to the kinetic energy of translational (back and forth) movement, molecules of more than one atom will have rotational and vibrational energy. Quantum effects become important in understanding the distribution of these forms of energy. The overall distribution of energy among translational, rotational, and vibrational modes is reflected in the heat capacity of the gas, the energy input required to produce a one unit increase in temperature. For gases and solids, though not yet for liquids, heat capacities can be calculated that match the experimental measurements very closely.

Kinetic theory of gases

The Maxwell–Boltzmann distribution provides a theoretical basis for the so-called gas laws, which interrelate the pressure, temperature, and volume of a sample of a gas. For a given number of gas molecules in a known volume of space at known temperature, the Maxwell–Boltzmann distribution can be used to calculate the rate and impulse with which molecules hit the walls of a container. This data can be used to calculate the pressure on the container walls. The relationship between this pressure and the temperature and volume of the sample is confirmed by the empirical gas laws.

FACT FILE

■ *Brownian motion is the jittery movement of fine grains in a liquid. It is caused by fast-moving liquid molecules colliding with much more massive solid particles and changing their momentum and, therefore, their direction of motion. In 1905, the German-born physicist Albert Einstein used kinetics to produce a mathematical description of the motion of molecules in a liquid by observing and measuring Brownian motion.*

SEE ALSO: BALLISTICS • CHEMISTRY, PHYSICAL • DYNAMICS • ENERGY, MASS, AND WEIGHT • GAS LAWS • INERTIA • MATTER, PROPERTIES OF • NEWTON'S LAWS • PRESSURE • QUANTUM THEORY

Lacquer and Varnish

◄ This elaborately decorated screen was made in China using the ancient art of lacquering. Pieces commonly have 30 layers of lacquer applied to a wooden surface before they are inlaid with other materials such as gold, mother-of-pearl, and ivory.

A varnish is a transparent liquid, a thin coating of which, when applied to a surface, solidifies—its solvent portion evaporates into the surrounding air and the remaining materials oxidize or polymerize to form a hard continuous, transparent film that protects the surface but does not obscure it. The usual constituents are a resin, a drying oil, driers, and thinners. The essential difference between a paint and a varnish is the absence of an opaque pigment (coloring matter) in the latter. Important types are oil or oleoresinous varnishes, spirit varnishes (solutions of resins in volatile solvents), and water varnishes (emulsion of resins in an aqueous solution).

Early varnishes were made from solutions of natural resins exuded from trees, such as copal, rosin, and dammar. The resin was heated with a natural oil and cooked for several hours until it reached the required viscosity, then diluted with turpentine. A disadvantage of such resins was a yellowing and cracking with age.

More stable varnishes began to be developed at the beginning of the 20th century with the introduction of synthetic resins, which can be manufactured in large quantities and chemically manipulated to alter characteristics such as hardness and viscosity. Alkyd resins are most commonly used in modern coatings, though phenolics, first introduced in the 1930s, are still used for marine and floor varnishes. Polyurethanes, vinyls, and epoxy resins are also used for specific purposes or effects.

Oils are used as the film-forming constituent and consist of natural triglycerides and unsaturated fatty acids. Oil contributes durability and flexibility. The commonest is linseed oil, but other types of slow-drying oils with isolated double bonds, such as fish, soybean, and tung (wood) oil may be used for greater resistance to water and mild chemicals. The resin, either natural or synthetic, such as alkyd or phenolic resins, improves the hardness, gloss, and adhesion to the substrate. Choice of resin can also affect properties like chemical resistance and electric insulation.

Thinners, usually a type of solvent, reduce the consistency of the oil-resin mixture to a suitable viscosity for the intended method of application. Turpentine is often used, while kerosene retards drying but gives better flow. Driers, added at low concentration, are typically salts of cobalt or manganese.

The terms varnish and lacquer are often used loosely and interchangeably. Strictly speaking, a lacquer dries by solvent evaporation only, whereas oxidation may also occur during the drying of a varnish. Varnishes are frequently described in terms of the resin-to-oil ratio, called the oil length. A ratio of 1:2 gives a short-oil varnish, 1:3 a medium-oil varnish, and 1:4 a long-oil varnish. Short-oil varnishes are characterized by fast-drying hard films with high gloss but poor flexibility. Long-oil varnishes are slower-drying, with high flexibility and good durability, suitable for use as media for exterior paints.

Manufacture

Varnish manufacture falls into five stages: dispersion, dilution, additions, tanking, and clarification. The procedure for initial dispersion of resin in oil depends on whether a natural or synthetic resin is being used. Natural fossil resins are not soluble in drying oils and require preliminary thermal decomposition, called gum running, during which some 25 percent by weight is lost as fume. Control of gum running is a skilled operation calling for extensive experience and was formerly something of a trade secret. Many synthetic resins, by contrast, are delivered ready to be dissolved by stirring into oil.

The next stage is oiling out until a drop on a glass plate is clear when cool. Driers are added and the cooled varnish is pumped to a bulk storage tank to allow any sparingly soluble portions to settle as foots. After maturing, the varnish is cleaned by straining, filtration, or centrifuging.

Typically, varnishes are used on surfaces that are to remain visible but need protection from wear and weather. Their uses are indicated by category—boat varnish, can lacquer, church oak varnish (for wooden benches), decorator's varnish, floor varnish, and furniture varnish. The coatings used on containers for food and drinks illustrate the types available and the constraints involved. Oleoresinous varnishes have a solids content, which makes them economical, and they are technically suitable for many foods. Alkyd-based coatings, however, impart too much taste to be used for interior lining and are confined to overprint varnishes for exterior decoration. Vinyl coatings are free from taste and odor, making it possible to can sensitive drinks such as beers and wines. Phenolic coatings have the important property of sulfur resistance, making them the natural choice for the interiors of meat and fish containers. They have recently been supplemented by epoxy-phenolic coatings, which show greater resistance to the preservatives often added to solid foods such as luncheon meat.

Another important group are the insulating varnishes used on electric windings. Impregnation protects other insulants from moisture, bonds the conductors, and promotes heat dissipation. Oleoresinous, epoxy, and silicone varnishes are all used.

Lacquer

Lacquer is an opaque type of varnish mainly used to decorate objects and surfaces to give them a highly colored and polished finish. The word *lacquer* is derived from a substance called lac, the purified and dehydrated sap of the lacquer tree, *Rhus vernicifera*, a species native to China. The technique of lacquering was developed in China and taken to Japan and Korea in the sixth century where it flourished until the 19th century. Lacquerwork began to be exported to Europe at the beginning of the 17th century, when the technique was taken up by European craftsmen, who never reached the heights of skill of the Chinese and Japanese artists.

Lacquer is usually applied to wood, although metal and porcelain have occasionally been used as base materials. The lacquer has to be specially prepared before it can be used. In its natural state, lacquer is a thick, syrupy liquid that darkens on exposure to air and becomes extremely hard. After tapping from the tree, lacquer undergoes purification and stirring to liquefy it. It is then heated and stored in an airtight container.

Lacquering is a long process, as the surface must be built up in layers to achieve a good finish. About 30 layers of differing type and quality are applied, each being left to dry before being rubbed down to take the next coat. The lacquer is left to dry in a very moist atmosphere to make it as hard as possible.

Minerals such as cinnabar can be added to the lacquer to give a range of colors, such as red, purple, black, brown, and green. The work is then further decorated by engraving or inlaying with gold, jade, mother-of-pearl, coral, or ivory. Finally, the piece of lacquerwork is polished to give a smooth and glossy surface.

▼ Varnishes are used on surfaces that are visible but need protection from wear and weather. Most varnishes consist of a resin, a drying oil, driers, and thinners. The oil is the film-forming constituent, the resin improves the hardness, gloss, and adhesion to the substrate, and the thinner or solvent reduces the consistency of the oil-resin mixture to a suitable viscosity for the intended method of application.

SEE ALSO:	Paint • Polymer and polymerization • Silicone • Water-repellent finish

Land Reclamation

◄ The Dutch Delta Project reclaimed land by constructing polders (the dark, square structures to the left of the picture). Planners of the project gave little consideration to its environmental impact. They were more concerned with economic issues, such as the future of the mussel and oyster beds whose salty water would become fresh. Now, economic issues must be reconciled with the need to conserve areas of outstanding beauty. These requirements demand an extensive knowledge of water movements and the ecology of the delta.

Land reclamation in various forms has been carried out for at least the last 5,000 years. Around 3100 B.C.E. the founder of the first dynasty in ancient Egypt, Menes, is reputed to have had a dam of mud and stone blocks built across the Nile in order to build the city of Memphis on the drained area, with the diverted river forming a perimeter defense.

The farmed areas along the Nile were divided into large flat basins by embankments of mud and stone several feet high. Canals and sluices admitted water from the river, which not only irrigated the ground but also deposited silt, thus improving the quality of the land. Other ancient civilizations depended for their existence and advancement on the regulation of rivers, notably the Babylonians in the Tigris–Euphrates valley and the Indians in the Indus valley. The Romans introduced land reclamation to Britain, constructing earth embankments and draining the enclosed areas for agriculture, especially in the east of Britain around the Wash.

The reclamation of land from below sea level, to create polders, was achieved in Holland in the second half of the 15th century following the development of the windmill. After the construction of an earth dam, the enclosed silt or peat was drained by pumping the water into neighboring land or into a drainage ditch. Since the windmills could raise water only about 5 ft. (1.5 m), double and triple lift systems were developed, in which the water was pumped into a storage basin between each of the windmills.

The use of windmills resulted in frequent flooding when there was little or no wind, but this problem was overcome in the late 18th century by the introduction of steam-driven pumps, followed by diesel or gasoline-engined pumps. Today, automatically controlled electric pumps are used.

A modern reclamation plan can be an extremely large and expensive project. The Delta Project, to the south of the Hook of Holland, has shortened 450 miles (724 km) of coastline to 15 miles (24 km), with dams up to 5 miles (8 km) long across estuaries as deep as 140 ft. (43 m).

Techniques

The first step in reclaiming land from the sea, river estuaries, or other submerged areas is to construct a bund, or dam, around the area to be reclaimed. This dam may be built in a number of ways, depending on the size and location of the site and the availability of suitable materials. The simplest method is to use clay or bags of sand, possibly lined with clay or polyethylene sheeting. The sand is prevented from being washed or blown away by the use of grass or fiber matting or steel mesh.

An alternative method is to use gabions, first used in the 16th century in the form of wicker baskets filled with soil. Modern gabions are formed from large plastic-coated steel wire mesh boxes, usually rectangular in shape and filled with stones. Large projects, particularly industrial plans, may involve the use of interlocking sections of steel, concrete, or timber called sheet piles that are driven into the ground, large concrete boxes called caissons that are sunk into the ground, or large, deeply embedded concrete structures reinforced with steel bars constructed in situ.

Once the dam has been formed, the confined area is ready for reclamation. The simplest method is to pump out the water and install a drainage system. Having done this, however, the risk of flooding remains, so the area may be raised above the level of the adjacent sea, river, swamp, or marsh. Raising can be done by using a suction dredger to pump in a slurry of sand and water, called a hydraulic fill, from outside the bund. The water is continuously drained off, and the level of the reclaimed land gradually rises. Another method is to fill in the reclamation with stones, rocks, hardcore, or any readily available material.

After the area has been filled, the ground will subside in time and become firm. This natural process can be speeded up; traditionally it was done, as in the case of Venice, by placing heavy layers of timber on the soil.

Stabilization is now achieved by a variety of techniques, including compaction with a vibrating roller, injecting cement dust into the ground, driving columns of rock into the ground, or the sinking of concrete piles into the ground. Surcharging is a method of compacting the ground using sand, soil, or water. The substance is contained inside polyethylene sheeting, which is placed on top of the area and removed at a later date, possibly as much as six months later, the weight of the surcharge forcing the water out of the soil and increasing its density. Another method uses fiber filter sheeting laid on the ground. Water is forced up through the sheeting, which allows water to pass but retains the soil.

Desert reclamation

Arid areas, where the annual rainfall is less than 20 in. (51 cm), can be farmed only at risk of crop failure unless irrigation water is provided. The

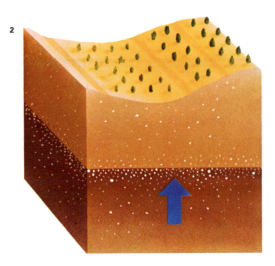

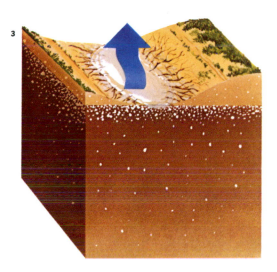

▲ Water that contains a salt level acceptable to living plants (1) can still lead to the creation of a desert if the problems of introducing an irrigation plan onto poorly drained land are not considered. The water gradually raises the water table (2) of the terrain: as the level rises, the salts come to the surface in increasing concentrations. The salts finally saturate the land, with the result that all vegetable life on it is destroyed. In the end, when all plant life has died, the land becomes a desert (3). Any future plans for reclamation must then wait for the water table to lower. Pure, fresh water can then be used to wash the salt deposits out of the soil. In this way, soils in arid land can again be productive.

soils in the drier lands are relatively unleached because of the low rainfall, that is, they are relatively rich in mineral salts as there is not enough water to wash them away.

In desert areas, the surface must be stabilized prior to irrigation. Stabilizing can be done in a number of ways, either naturally, by planting with a deep-rooting species combined with the construction of windbreaks, or by laying nylon matting or spraying a binding agent such as wax or resin onto the soil.

Landfill reclamation

Particularly in highly developed countries where space is scarce, landfill sites are being reclaimed for development. This process is problematic, because landfills produce both polluted leachate and explosive methane gas and, over time, are subject to subsidence.

Such problems are overcome by engineering—impermeable barriers are put in place to ensure that gases and leachates exit the landfill only at designated points, to be vented or treated as necessary. Foundations of buildings on such sites are designed so they do not intrude on the landfill beneath. To provide a stable base, piles, driven through the impermeable membrane, which is then resealed to prevent any escape of gas, can be used if the risk of subsidence is considered to be high.

Dutch land reclamation

The Netherlands has a rich history of land reclamation. As early as the 14th century, the first land areas were made dry and ready to inhabit. Over the following centuries, about 10 percent of what is currently Dutch territory was taken from the sea.

Land reclamation protects villages and towns from the sea and enables agricultural and urban expansion. The Netherlands has a coastline that is constantly being changed and eroded by wind and water. From its earliest colonization, the Dutch people have built primitive dikes around their settlements to keep out the sea.

With the development of windmills for water pumping in the 15th century, water could be drained effectively from fairly large areas, marking the beginning of the polder. Polders are formed by surrounding an area or lake with an earthen dike and then pumping the water out of the enclosed area into adjacent water bodies.

In the 20th century, the process of land reclamation was boosted by technology. The Dutch IJsselmeer polders were reclaimed from the IJsselmeer, a lake that used to be part of the former Zuider Zee (Southern Sea). The Zuider Zee was originally an estuary of the Rhine that had by natural erosion become a shallow inland sea, encroaching deep inland. Eventually it was eroded into an almost circular shape by wind and tide.

In 1920, work began on the Zuider Zee project. A 19-mile- (30 km) long dam, or dike, running northeast to connect the provinces of Noord-Holland and Friesland was finished in 1932. It sealed off the Zuider Zee from the Wadden Zee and the North Sea. In the IJsselmeer, or IJssel Lake, which was formed from the southern part of the Zuider Zee, four large polders with a total area of about 650 sq. miles (1,690 km^2) were constructed around a freshwater basin fed by the IJssel and other rivers. This system was linked to the sea by sluices and locks set into the barrier dam.

The first of five polders, the Wieringermeer, was diked directly from the sea, not from the IJsselmeer. This area was dry land two years before the Zuider Zee was closed off. The first two polders—the Wieringermeer and Noordoost (northeast) polders—were drained before and during World War II. They are used mostly for agriculture. The two polders reclaimed in the 1950s and 1960s—South Flevoland polder and East Flevoland polder—are used for housing, industry, and recreation. Among the cities built on this

▲ A giant mattress (center of photo) covered with stone ballast anchors a dike. Concrete and asphalt are then applied on top of it.

reclaimed land are Lelystad and Almere, the former being the capital of the new province of Flevoland, which was created in 1986 from the two Flevoland polders and Noordoost polder.

By 1968, the Dutch had transformed 770 sq. miles (2,000 km^2) of the Zuider Zee into polders.

The stages of development needed to turn sandy, unpromising reclaimed polder land into fertile soil begin with the polders being drained of water using pumps. Reeds are then allowed to grow naturally on the former sea bottom, and these help to dry out the soil. When the soil has dried, the reeds are cleared, and a crop called colza, which is related to cabbages and turnips, is planted. This crop is also cleared, and grain crops are planted in turn, creating an increasingly fertile soil structure.

In all, the polders are cultivated for up to five years before the land is ready for proper use. The polders are then leased to commercial farmers, or the reclaimed land is used for construction. Environmental monitoring researchers, conservation authorities, and departments of municipal affairs monitor changes in land cover for a number of reasons, including tax assessment and reconnaissance vegetation mapping. The Dutch government is also concerned with the general protection of national resources and becomes involved in publicly sensitive activities involving land-use conflicts.

SEE ALSO: CANAL • DAM • DESALINATION • DRAINAGE • EROSION • IRRIGATION TECHNIQUES • LOCK, CANAL • SOIL RESEARCH • WIND POWER

Laser and Maser

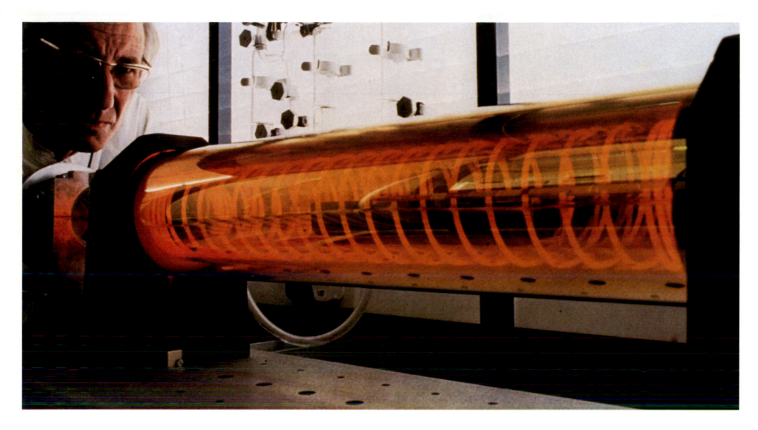

The term *laser* is an acronym of "*l*ight *a*mplification by *s*timulated *e*mission of *r*adiation"—a process that is capable of producing intense beams of coherent light in or near the visible range of the electromagnetic spectrum. Similarly, the term *maser* is an acronym of "*m*icrowave *a*mplification by *s*timulated *e*mission of *r*adiation." The acronyms *laser* and *maser* generally refer to the devices in which the respective stimulated-emission processes are induced.

Interactions of light and matter

As a consequence of the quantum behavior of matter, atoms and molecules can possess only certain values of energy. The permitted energy states may be considered as being rungs in an energy "ladder," and the spaces between the rungs are energy values that a given atom or molecule simply has no way of possessing. The permitted state with the least energy is the ground state; all other permitted energy levels are excited states.

The excited states of atoms correspond to electron configurations where electrons are at a greater average distance from the nucleus than they are in the ground state of the same atom. In the atomic-orbital model, they correspond to states in which one or more electrons have shifted from their ground-state atomic orbitals to higher-energy orbitals. Similar shifts, or transitions, occur between molecular electronic orbitals.

As well as possessing electronic energy—energy due to the motions of their electrons—molecules have rotational and vibrational energy. A linear molecule, such as hydrogen chloride (HCl), can spin end over end around a point along the central axis of the molecule and can vibrate as its bonds stretch and contract repeatedly. More complex molecules have several types, or modes, of rotation and vibration and each mode can be excited to distinct energy levels.

The two means by which atoms and molecules shift between energy states are by transfer of energy in collisions and by absorption or emission of photons. In the first case, the change in the total kinetic energy that occurs in the course of the collision accounts for the change in the energy level of the colliding bodies. In the second case, the energy of the absorbed or emitted photon accounts for the change in energy of the atom or molecule involved in the process.

The energy, E, of a photon is related to its frequency, v, by the equation $E = hv$ (h is called Planck's constant). Consequently, the frequency of light absorbed or emitted during a transition of an atom or molecule between two permitted states is determined by the difference in energy between the two states. A compex set of quantum mechanical selection rules determines whether a given transition is allowed or not (is forbidden). Even forbidden transitions occur at some rate, however,

▲ This cylindrical furnace is used to deposit films of reflective materials on the surfaces of crystals for use in solid-state lasers.

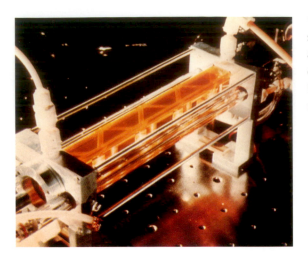

as the result of collisions or the coupling of different types of motion. The latter may involve electron spin, electron orbit, rotation, or vibration.

Spontaneous emission

If an atom or molecule in a given excited state is able to decay to a lower energy state by an allowed process, it will usually do so in a tiny fraction of a second, emitting a single photon. Such a decay is said to be spontaneous.

An example of spontaneous emission occurs in filament lamps. The passage of electrical current through the filament produces heat, and some of the metal atoms in the filament assume excited electronic states as a result of collisions between the rapidly vibrating atoms of the hot filament. Atoms excited in this way then decay to their ground states with the emission of photons, which constitute the light emitted by the lamp.

Stimulated emission

If an excited state cannot decay to any lower state by an allowed process, the state is termed metastable. Atoms and molecules can end up in metastable states as the result of collisions or following decays from higher excited states.

In 1917, the German-born physicist Albert Einstein realized that in addition to the spontaneous emission, the interaction of a photon of the right energy, with an atom in an excited energy level could act to stimulate the emission of a second photon. This type of process, called stimulated emission, is the basis of laser and maser action. When a suitable photon strikes an excited atom or molecule, it induces the emission of a second photon and decay to the ground state. The crucial feature of this process is that the emitted photon has exactly the same frequency and is exactly in phase with the stimulating photon. Consequently, the peaks and troughs of the electromagnetic oscillations coincide perfectly for the two photons.

◄ This apparatus uses a solution of an organic dye as a laser medium. Unlike other types of lasers, dye lasers can be tuned over a range of frequencies.

► A beam of incoherent light diverges, becoming more diffuse as the distance from its source increases. A beam of laser light, which is coherent, maintains its width and intensity over distance.

Population inversion

Stimulated emission is a reversible process: just as one photon can stimulate emission of a second photon from an excited state, a ground state can absorb two photons of the appropriate frequency and release the surplus photon.

In a sample that contains ground states and excited states of the same atom or molecule, both stimulated emission and absorption will occur. Laser or maser action requires a greater number of atoms or molecules to be in the excited state than in the ground state so that stimulated emissions outweigh absorptions. This condition is called population inversion, since it is the reverse of the normal condition, where the majority of atoms or molecules is in the ground state.

Pumping

There are a number of methods for achieving population inversion. One such method—optical pumping—uses a standard light source to promote ground state atoms or molecules to an excited state by an "allowed" transition. (Allowed transitions are those that occur by simple absorption or emission.) The initial excited state lies at a greater energy than the excited state that participates in laser action. Consequently, some of the atoms or molecules in the initial excited state decay to the laser state by spontaneous emission. There, they remain trapped until a suitable photon triggers their decay by stimulated emission.

Coherent radiation

As already explained, stimulated emission results in radiation whose photons are all exactly at the same frequency and exactly in phase. Such radiation is described as coherent, whereas radiation whose photons have differing frequencies or phases is described as incoherent.

Coherent radiation has distinctive properties. A beam of coherent radiation maintains its width over great distances, whereas a beam of incoher-

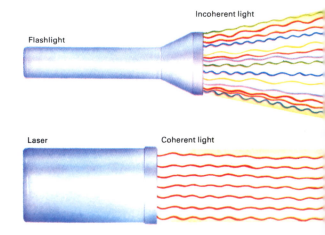

RUBY LASERS

The first laser was developed in 1960 by Theodore Maiman. While other physicists had banked on a gas or liquid being the working medium of the first practical working laser, Maiman concentrated on developing a solid-state device.

Maiman achieved success using ruby—a crystalline form of aluminum oxide (Al_2O_3) with around 0.05 percent by weight chromium (III) oxide (Cr_2O_3). The chromium (III) ions occupy crystal sites that would be occupied by aluminum ions in pure aluminum oxide. The presence of chromium gives ruby its characteristic deep red color and provides suitable excited states for laser action.

The crystal in a ruby laser has the form of a rod. Its end surfaces are polished to be flat and parallel to within one-third of the wavelength of the laser light. A thin film of silver is deposited on both ends by vapor condensation. One end of the rod is made totally reflective, whereas the other end is made partially reflective by applying less silver.

Maiman's laser was "pumped" to several excited states by bursts of light from a xenon flash tube wrapped around the rod in the form of a spiral. The initial excited states would then decay to partially stable excited states, forming the population inversion necessary for a burst of laser action and a pulse of laser light. Later developments of the ruby laser replaced the flash tube with an arc lamp to achieve continuous laser operation.

When a ruby crystal is optically pumped, many of the excited chromium ions lose their excitation energy through spontaneous decay to the ground state rather than by participating in laser

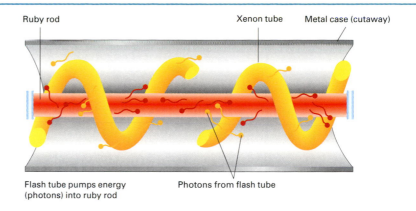

Ruby rod   Xenon tube   Metal case (cutaway)

Flash tube pumps energy (photons) into ruby rod   Photons from flash tube

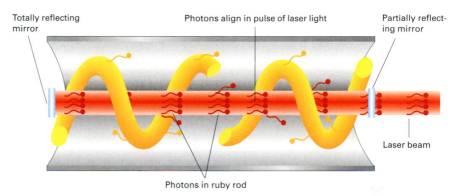

Totally reflecting mirror   Photons align in pulse of laser light   Partially reflecting mirror

Photons in ruby rod   Laser beam

▲ In a ruby laser, chromium atoms in the ruby crystal are excited by light from the xenon flash tube and some of them emit photons, stimulating further photon release (top). These are reflected back and forth and are finally emitted as a powerful beam (bottom).

action. They can do this because the quantum constraints that govern transitions in the gas phase are more relaxed in the solid state. The light from spontaneous emissions escapes through the sides of the rod.

Stimulated emission is initiated by the spontaneous emission of one or more photons along the axis of the crystal rod. The mirrored ends of the rod form the walls of a resonant cavity within the crystal, and the resonant cavity promotes

the stimulated emission of further photons. This phenomenon is sometimes described in terms of photons bouncing back and forth between the two ends of the rod, stimulating new emissions as they do so. The laser light escapes as a beam that passes through the partially silvered end of the crystal.

Only a small proportion of the energy input to the pumping lamp of a ruby laser becomes laser light. Some energy is lost as incoherent light, but the majority is lost as heat. Excessive heat development is a potential cause of damage in solid-state lasers. The possibility of damage by overheating makes the use of an efficient cooling system necessary and places a practical limit on the time of continuous operation of such devices.

ent light becomes broader with distance from the source. The spreading of incoherent light has the effect of diluting its intensity—power per unit area—as the distance from the source increases. Furthermore, the fact that all the photons in a coherent beam have peaks and troughs at the same time makes such a beam far more effective in delivering energy than an incoherent beam of the same intensity. These are the properties that make lasers and masers useful as research tools and in a number of practical applications.

Ammonia maser

The ammonia maser was the first device to use stimulated emission as a means of amplifying radiation. Invented in 1954 by a team led by the U.S. physicist Charles Townes, an ammonia maser uses one of the vibrational modes of ammonia as a basis for maser action.

An ammonia (NH_3) molecule has the form of a shallow tripod, with a nitrogen atom at its crown and three N–H bonds forming its "legs." In the excited state of the vibrational mode used for maser action, the ammonia molecule flips back and forth in a motion called inversion that resembles an umbrella being blown repeatedly inside out and back again in a strong wind.

Since the hydrogen atoms of an ammonia molecule have slight positive charges relative to the negatively charged nitrogen atom, ground-state molecules react to electric fields in a markedly different way than do molecules excited in the inversion mode of vibration. Townes used this difference to create a population by physically separating excited-state molecules from ground-state molecules. The separation occurred between four rod-shaped electrodes whose alternate positive and negative polarities created a quadrupolar electrical field. When ammonia gas was sprayed into one end of the electrode assembly, the ground-state molecules, repelled by the field, diffused through the gaps between the electrodes. At the same time, the field focused excited molecules into a metal resonance cavity.

The transition between the ground state and the excited state of the inversion mode of vibration has an energy that corresponds to a microwave frequency of 24 GHz. Townes found that, when he beamed this frequency of microwave radiation into the resonant cavity, the signal was amplified by excited-state molecules decaying to the ground state.

▼ In this experiment, two laser beams of different frequencies—and therefore different colors—are used to measure the temperature of a plasma. Standard thermometric devices, such as thermocouples, would be vaporized by the heat of the plasma.

Solid-state lasers

The 1960s saw the development of a variety of lasers—devices that use stimulated emission to amplify radiation in the infrared, visible, and ultraviolet ranges of the electromagnetic spectrum. The first class of lasers was the solid-state lasers, and the first of that class was the synthetic-ruby laser built in 1960 by the U.S. physicist Theodore Maiman (see the box on page 1211).

Solid-state lasers use the electronic transitions of ions embedded in solid matrices for laser action. In the case of the ruby laser, the active centers are chromium (III) ions in an aluminum oxide (Al_2O_3) matrix. Other active centers include ions of rare-earth elements, notably neodymium (Nd); other solid matrices include a mixed oxide of aluminum and yttrium called yttrium–aluminum garnet (YAG), glass (a form of silicon dioxide, SiO_2), and fluorite (CaF_2).

In all cases, population inversion is achieved by optical pumping using flash tubes or arc lamps. Electrons are first promoted to a highly excited state from which they spontaneously decay to the excited state for the laser action. The laser medium has two mirrored parallel faces that encourage light to resonate within the medium.

One of the most widely used solid-state lasers is the Nd–YAG laser, which produces coherent light at a wavelength of 1,064 nm, which is in the near-infrared range of the electromagnetic spectrum. The output of such lasers can be modified using frequency doublers—devices in which quartz crystals absorb pairs of photons and emit single photons with twice the energy of the input photons. In the case of the Nd–YAG laser, the output wavelength is halved to 532 nm, which falls in the green part of the visible spectrum.

The most severe limitation of solid-state lasers is that the heat generated by the pumping process can cause crystal distortions that detract from the quality of the output beam. For this reason, solid-state lasers generally operate in pulses and must be cooled by a flow of air or liquid. A typical Nd–YAG laser produces one 150-joule pulse per second. The pulse rate must be reduced for higher-powered pulses.

Gas lasers

Gas lasers have the advantage over solid-state lasers that they are less prone to damage by overheating, so they can be run continuously. The first gas laser—a helium–neon device—was invented in 1961 and is still the most widely used gas laser. Gas lasers share many of their operating features with discharge lamps: an electrical field first ionizes gaseous atoms or molecules to form a plasma, then a current of ions starts to flow.

Excited states are produced by collisions within the plasma, and these states form the basis of laser action. In the case of a helium–neon laser, helium atoms become excited first, then transfer their energy to neon atoms through collisions. The result is a population inversion of excited neon atoms. The laser medium occupies a resonant cavity whose walls are coated to make them reflect the required laser frequency.

Helium–neon lasers can be devised to emit laser light at a variety of wavelengths corresponding to different transitions: 543 nm (green), 594 nm (yellow), 610 nm (orange), 647 nm (red), and 1,150 nm (near infrared). The continuous power output of such lasers can be as great as 75 mW, but most devices produce less than 1 mW.

Noble gas ion lasers use laser media that consist of pure or mixed samples of the noble gases argon, krypton, neon, and xenon. The discharge currents are greater than those used in helium–neon lasers, causing the noble gas atoms to ionize. Some 35 laser frequencies are available from this type of laser, ranging from infrared through visible to ultraviolet light. Individual frequencies can be selected for laser action by adjusting a prism within the optical cavity, or all frequencies can be used at once. Water-cooled ion lasers can operate at up to 20 W.

By far the most powerful gas lasers use carbon dioxide (CO_2) as the laser medium and emit light in the far infrared range (between 9,000 and 11,000 nm). They owe their high power output capability to the fact that up to 30 percent of their pumping energy can be converted into laser light energy, compared with around 0.1 percent for a helium–neon laser. The most efficient gas mixtures include helium and nitrogen with carbon dioxide. As a result, an optimized carbon dioxide laser will generate less than $\frac{1}{2000}$ the amount of the heat generated by a helium–neon laser for the same power output. Continuous output powers of around 20 kW are readily achieved.

Excimer lasers

The word *excimer* is a contraction of the term *exci*ted di*mer*, which refers to unstable combinations of an argon, krypton, or xenon atom with a chlorine or fluorine atom. These species form when mixtures of the appropriate noble gases and halogens are subjected to electrical discharges or X rays. Their excited states are capable of laser action in the ultraviolet range, producing the shortest of all laser wavelengths: from 193 nm for argon fluoride to 351 nm for xenon fluoride.

The short wavelengths of excimer lasers correspond to high photon energies, which make excimer lasers useful for initiating photochemical

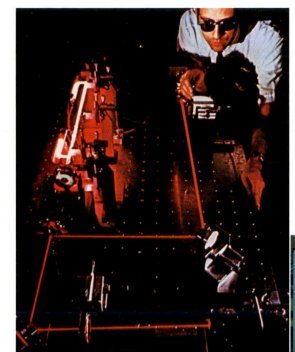

◀ This optical computer memory system uses a low-powered laser to record and retrieve information.

▼ A high-powered carbon dioxide laser can deliver sufficient power to cut through steel. Carbon dioxide lasers convert more pumping energy into light than do other lasers.

reactions and for pumping other types of lasers. The short wavelengths of ultraviolet photons allow them to form finer beams than are possible with other lasers, making excimer lasers useful in high-precision surgery, such as in the treatment of myopia.

Dye lasers

Certain organic dyes have a wide range of closely spaced excited states; therefore, their solutions can be used as tunable laser media. Rhodamine 6G, for example, has closely spaced transitions between 570 nm and 650 nm. A typical dye laser uses an argon-ion or excimer laser to excite Rhodamine 6G in solution and a prism to select the desired output frequency.

Semiconductor lasers

A semiconductor, or diode, laser has a bilayer of *n*-type and *p*-type semiconductor—typically gallium arsenide (GaAs). The junction between the two layers creates the structure of energy states necessary for laser action, and population inversion is induced by an electrical current.

Semiconductor lasers are small, low-power devices compared with other types of lasers. Their compactness and low production costs have earned them widespread use in laser-optical devices, such as compact disc players.

Lasers as machine tools

A laser beam can be focused onto a small area to give extremely high power densities. The heat delivered to a surface in this way can be used to make cuts by burning or vaporizing material where the laser strikes. Computer-guided lasers cut precise shapes in textiles, rubber, and other soft materials that tend to deform when cut using mechanical cutting tools. Lasers are also useful in cutting extremely hard objects, such as the diamond dies used in the drawing of wires.

By varying the rate of heat delivery, lasers can be used either to cut or to weld metals. They can also be used for localized heat treatment, such as in the spot hardening of metal components.

Lasers in medicine

One of the first medical uses of lasers was in eye surgery, where laser beams were used to weld detached retinas in place on the back of the eyeball. Excimer lasers are now widely used to treat vision disorders by reshaping the cornea.

Laser scalpels are useful for delicate operations, since they produce a fine cutting line while sealing off small blood vessels as the cut is made. Other applications include the cauterization, or heat sealing, of ulcers. In such cases, optical fibers guide the beam to the operation site.

Cosmetic surgery is another application of lasers. Green lasers, which are strongly absorbed by red tissues, are used to eradicate port wine stains and blemishes and to cauterize broken blood vessels in the surface of the skin. Lasers are used to treat skin disorders, to remove tattoos, to drill teeth prior to filling, and to resurface skin to reduce signs of aging.

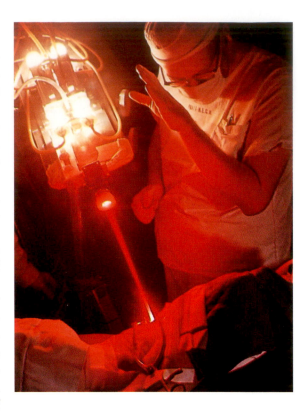

▲ Here, a laser is being used in surgery. The white lamps at the front of the apparatus are the "pumps" for the laser process.

Measurement and guidance

The fact that laser beams are perfectly straight makes them useful in the guidance of cutting and drilling equipment of all sizes—from wood saws to tunneling machines. In some cases, such as surveying, a laser beam is used simply to define a straight line; in others, light sensors on the remote equipment instruct its steering system if the equipment starts to stray from the beam.

Extremely small distances can be measured by interferometry, in which case distances are referred to the wavelength of the laser light in use. Measuring the Doppler shift of laser light reflected from a moving surface allows noncontact velocity or flow determinations.

Communications and data storage

Semiconductor lasers produce the light signals that carry data and telephone calls through fiber-optic networks. Using digital pulses, it is possible to transmit millions of signals on a single beam.

Semiconductor lasers are also used to read information from optical storage media, such as compact discs and DVDs. More powerful lasers store holographic images on film as an interference pattern formed by a reflected beam.

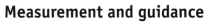

FACT FILE

- In May 1962, technicians at the Massachusetts Institute of Technology reflected a laser beam off the Moon for the first time. The laser was linked to a 48 in. (122 cm) telescope and produced a spot on the Moon 4 miles (6.4 km) in diameter.

- In 1997, a group of researchers—also at the Massachusetts Institute of Technology—announced that they had produced the first atom laser. Using temperatures within a few billionths of a degree of absolute zero, they formed a beam of Bose–Einstein condensate, a state of matter in which pairs of atoms behave as a coherent matter wave.

- The Nova system at the Lawrence Livermore National Laboratory, California, uses 10 coordinated neodymium-glass lasers to produce pulses of laser light. The intense heat and pressure generated when such a pulse vaporizes frozen hydrogen are intended to spark fusion reactions.

- X-ray and gamma-ray lasers are currently in development. They are likely to find uses in medicine and research. High-powered X-ray and gamma-ray lasers, pumped by atomic explosions, could be useful weapons.

SEE ALSO: COMPACT DISC, AUDIO • DATA STORAGE • ELECTROMAGNETIC RADIATION • FIBER OPTICS • FUSION • HOLOGRAPHY • SURGERY

Latitude and Longitude

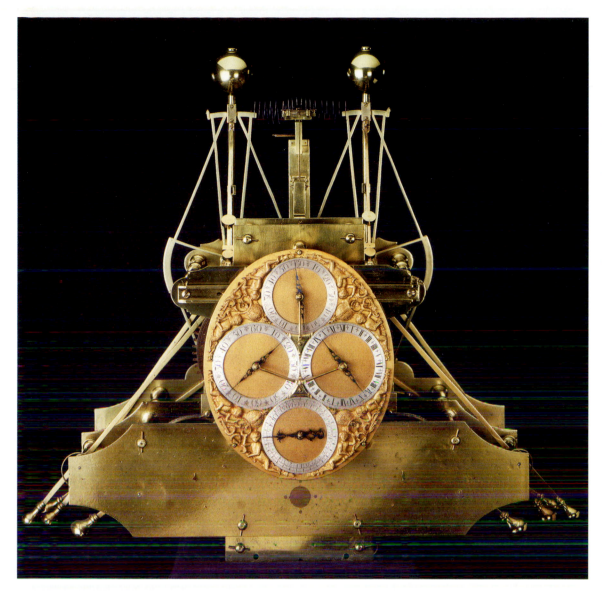

◄ The first marine chronometer, H1, designed by the British horologist John Harrison and constructed between 1730 and 1735. The complex system of linked balances ensures that the mechanism is unaffected by any changes of motion. This chronometer and the improved designs that followed solved the problem of finding longitude while at sea.

Latitude and longitude are the means by which any location on Earth's surface may be determined and described. Latitude describes the position of a point in relation to the equator, and longitude describes the position of a point in relation to the prime meridian, which passes through Greenwich, Britain (a meridian is any north–south line joining two poles). This meridian was designated zero by geographers who met in Washington, D.C., in 1884.

The globe is divided into 360 degrees along both the north–south and east–west circumferences, each degree being subdivided into 60 minutes ('), and each minute into 60 seconds (").

Latitude

Latitude is measured along a meridian. A point on the equator has a latitude of zero degrees (0 degrees) and the distance to each of the poles is 90 degrees: the North Pole has a latitude of 90 degrees north and the South Pole has a latitude of 90 degrees south. So 30 degrees N describes a point one-third the distance from the equator to the North Pole, and 10 degrees S, a point one-ninth the distance from the equator to the South Pole. All points with the same latitude lie on an imaginary line called a parallel. Because of the nonuniform curvature of Earth, however, the distance between two parallels one degree apart varies from from 68.7 miles (110.6 km) at the equator to 69.4 miles (111.7 km) at the poles.

Longitude

Longitude is measured along a parallel. It is measured both 180 degrees east and 180 degrees west of the prime meridian, the two together making the full 360 degrees of Earth's circumference and meeting at a meridian that runs through the Pacific Ocean, called the international date line. Technically, longitude is the amount of arc cre-

LONGITUDE AND TIME

Earth turns completely once every 24 hours. This means that all 360 degrees of Earth's circumference pass beneath the Sun once in every 24 hours. So, in one hour, $\frac{1}{24}$ of 360 degrees—15 degrees—passes beneath the Sun. Therefore:

24 hours of time = 360 degrees of longitude.

1 hour of time = 15 degrees of longitude.

4 minutes of time = 1 degree of longitude.

1 minute of time = 15' of longitude.

1 second of time = 15" of longitude.

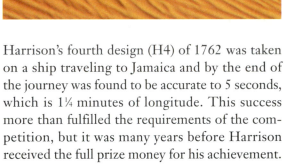

ated by drawing a line from the center of Earth to the intersection of the equator and the prime meridian and another line from the center of Earth to any point elsewhere on the equator. The number of miles per degree longitude is 69.17 (111.3 km) at the equator and 0 at the poles.

The combinations of meridians and parallels established a framework, or grid, by means of which an exact position at any point on the globe can be determined in reference to the prime meridian and the equator. For example, a position which is described to be 60 degrees N, 50 degrees W is located on the 60th parallel north of the equator and on the 50th meridian situated west of the prime meridian. New York City lies at a longitude of 74 degrees W.

Calculating longitude

Knowing the position of a ship at sea is essential for good navigation. Until the 18th century, however, no accurate method existed for determining longitude while at sea. In 1728, the British government offered £20,000—a vast fortune at that time—to anyone who could devise a means for calculating longitude with an accuracy of within half a degree over the course of a journey to the West Indies. Astronomers had attempted unsuccessfully to find ways of using the stars to determine position, but in 1735, the problem was solved by the British horologist John Harrison with the design of a marine chronometer (H1). The clock was set to the time in Greenwich in England and then tested by taking it on a journey to Lisbon. It was found to keep accurate time despite the pitching and rolling that would have prevented an ordinary pendulum clock from working. During the journey, the local time at noon was compared with the time on the clock and the difference calculated. Knowing that the world revolves 360 degrees in 24 hours, and therefore 15 degrees in one hour, the longitude could be determined by multiplying the time difference in hours by 15.

▶ Arid areas such as the Sahara Desert lie in a belt approximately 15 and 30 degrees north and south of the equator.

▼ If Earth were flat a simple Cartesian system, akin to street maps, would be quite satisfactory. Since Earth is a globe, however, each place is located by its latitude and longitude. The zero value for latitude, corresponding to its origin, is the equator.

Harrison's fourth design (H4) of 1762 was taken on a ship traveling to Jamaica and by the end of the journey was found to be accurate to 5 seconds, which is 1¼ minutes of longitude. This success more than fulfilled the requirements of the competition, but it was many years before Harrison received the full prize money for his achievement.

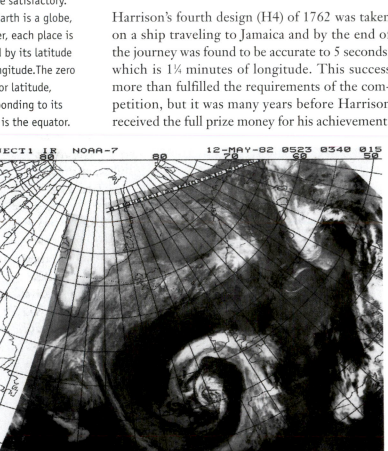

SEE ALSO: CLOCK • GEOPHYSICS • GLOBAL POSITIONING SYSTEM • GYROCOMPASS • NAVIGATION

Laundry

◀ Roller towels being pressed before being wound into bundles. Flat items such as these are easily automated and need no special attention during the laundering process.

At the turn of the century, apart from institutional laundries, for example, at hospitals, much commercial laundry was processed in homes by women who took in washing to supplement their income. The articles to be laundered were boiled up in a large pot, rinsed, put through a wringer, starched if necessary, and ironed. Today, the laundry industry has developed into an efficient service that has benefited from scientific research into washing and the continuing development of labeling machines, washing machines, and machines for ironing, pressing, and drying.

Marking, sorting, and washing

A vital first stage in the domestic commercial laundry process is the individual marking of every article in a customer's wash. Formerly, this tended to be done with a permanent marking system, requiring a large register to be kept and constant reorganization of the collection area as the finished work came off the process line. Today, marking machines are used to provide once-only labels. The mechanism enables a combination of letters and numbers to be selected for a customer, and each of his or her articles receives this mark. The labels are cut from a reel of tape as it is fed into the machine; heat, pressure, and solvent are applied to make the tape adhere to the article, and the mark is printed at the same time. One edge of the tape is free of adhesive, so a small tab is left on the label, enabling it to be removed before the laundry is finally dispatched. Color coding is also used, and various colored tapes are available.

The labeled articles are then sorted into bins, which are classified according to the wash process involved—for example, blankets, sheets, pillowcases, white shirts, rayons, silks, white coats, coloreds, towels, and so forth.

The washing machines used by the laundry industry range in capacity from 25 to 1,000 lbs. (11.3–454 kg) dry weight of washing, and generally have a tumbling motion—the internal cylinder rotates first in one direction and then the other throughout the wash and rinse cycles. Usually the operating conditions for a particular batch are preset. They include the amount of water to be used, the quantity of soap solution (the industry uses mainly soap rather than detergents) and alkali (sodium carbonate or sodium metasilicate), the number of wash and rinse cycles, and the quantity of steam that may be needed to raise the temperature.

There are, however, still large numbers of manually controlled machines where soap and alkali solutions and so forth are poured in by hand and the steam flow controlled by turning it on and off.

A development is the continuous-tunnel type of washing machine, which is about 20 ft. (6 m)

◀ Although totally mechanized systems are available in which laundry is rarely touched by human hand between delivery and dispatch, older, more manual systems exist, particularly in public hospitals. Here laundry from the delivery point passes along a conveyor, where it is sorted into large and small articles, towels, and so on. The loaded bins are then transferred to the washing machines.

long and open at both ends. The washing is introduced at one end and travels down the sloped tunnel assisted by internal ribs based on the Archimedes' screw principle. It washes using a tumbling action, and excess moisture is extracted by passing the articles through a mangle, although this is not as efficient as centrifugal spinning.

Normally at the end of the washing and rinsing cycle, the load is partially dried by spinning in a separate hydroextractor (a type of centrifuge), or in the washing machine itself, which is then designed to run at high speed. Other treatments may be included in the washing stage, such as bleaching and starching.

Finishing

At this stage articles are ready for finishing. Towels do not need ironing and are tumble dried in hot air. Flat work—a term that covers such items as sheets, tablecloths, and pillowcases—is fed into a mangle. The mangle is a machine that consists of smooth heated metal surfaces between which the articles are pressed. They are carried forward through the machine by means of rotating fabric-covered rollers. The articles are guided by a system of overlying tapes, which assist in carrying the work onward and also help to strip it from the final roller. The ironed articles are then folded, either by hand or machine.

A wide variety of presses have been developed for finishing shaped articles, but all consist basically of a heated, polished metal surface that is applied to the side of the article where finish is most important, the article itself being laid or arranged over a padded fabric surface. In some ways this is analogous to the heated surface of a hand iron being brought into contact with an article on a household ironing board, but in the case of presses, there is no sliding movement.

Although the demand for highly starched articles is rapidly diminishing, many launderers also provide this service. Because the machines used for finishing the article must also cook the starch, they must operate at temperatures higher than normal, usually about 450°F (232°C), and are therefore heated by electricity or gas. Generally the laundry steam pressure is from 100 to 150 psi (about 7 to 10 bar), giving temperatures of about 338 to 366°F (170–186°C).

Specialist laundry

There are some laundries that deal solely with industrial articles, such as those produced by industrial clothing rental firms and hospitals. A hospital laundry will have machines similar to those already described but may not need to use a labeling procedure as all articles are returned to a central storage point for redistribution. Eliminating infection, however, is important and is carried out by the application of heat. To achieve sterilization, at some stage in the wash a high temperature is maintained long enough to kill bacteria or viruses.

Other specialist procedures include those for handling very soiled (foul) work. It is stuffed into specially marked or colored plastic bags in the wards or operating rooms and kept separate from other laundry and handled carefully. The bags are sealed securely with alginate stitching, taken to the laundry, and tipped into the washing machine, where the alginate stitching dissolves, releasing the contents of the bag.

▼ Clean sheets emerge from the washing and wringing machines before being passed to the dryer.

SEE ALSO: DETERGENT MANUFACTURE • SOAP MANUFACTURE • WASHING MACHINE

Lead

Lead, a bluish-white metal, is the softest and the heaviest of the common metals, and it has been smelted for many thousands of years. In air, lead forms a protective oxide film and sometimes a patina. The Egyptians had prepared lead as early as 3000 B.C.E., although the Romans were probably the first to put it to practical use—to create their extensive drainage and water systems. The Latin name for lead, *plumbum*, is the source of the word *plumbing*.

The softness and ductility of lead make it unsuitable as a load-bearing material. It yields at a stress less than one ton/sq. in. (154 bar); the yield stress of mild steel is about 40 ton/sq. in. (6,178 bar). On the other hand, the ease with which lead can be worked is an advantage in applications that utilize its outstanding resistance to chemical corrosion. Lead is one of the five most commonly used metals; its world production is more than three million tons a year, about 40 percent of which is used in the United States.

Occurrence and extraction

Lead is not found uncombined in nature. Sulfate, chromate, carbonate, and molybdate ores are best known, but lead is extracted mostly from the sulfide ore (galena, PbS). The main sources of this ore are Australia, North and Central America, Spain, and Germany. Frequently, it is found in association with zinc sulfide (sphalerite, ZnS), the presence of which influences details of the extraction process. A large proportion (about 30 percent) of the lead used is reclaimed from scrap.

The first stage in the extraction of lead from crushed ore is concentration of the wet ore by gravity, which exploits the high density of galena. Further concentration is effected by separating the galena from any sphalerite present by the flotation process. Chemical compounds, such as xanthates, are added to an aqueous suspension of the crushed ore and selectively coat the galena particles, making them water-repellent. Small particles thus coated will float, especially if aided by the formation of a froth. Material collected from the top of flotation cells contains about 75 percent lead sulfide, whereas its concentration in the original ore may be less than 5 percent.

Lead sulfide is not easily reduced to lead by coke in a blast furnace. For this reason the sulfide is first roasted to convert it to lead oxide (PbO), which is much more readily reduced. The roasting is carried out under closely controlled conditions so that the oxide is formed as a sinter. The roasted and sintered material contains some free lead. The equation below shows the result of the reaction:

$$PbS \rightarrow 2PbO \rightarrow 3Pb + SO_2$$

lead sulfide   lead oxide   lead   sulfur
                 1740°F or above   dioxide

In fact, lead can be extracted from high-grade ores by roasting alone—the method used by the Roman metallurgists—but the process is difficult to control.

The blast furnace used to smelt the oxide sinter is much smaller than that used in iron making and is of rectangular cross-section. The principle is similar—carbon monoxide gas from the burning coke reduces the oxide to the metal. The sinter charge is mixed with iron ore, which, with limestone powder added prior to the roasting stage, acts as a flux. The flux ensures that silica in the ore forms a liquid slag that floats on top of the molten lead as it collects in the crucible below the furnace hearth. The lead tapped from the blast furnace is known as bullion.

Refining

The first stage of refining is called drossing. The molten bullion from the blast furnace is held at about 750°F (400°C), and impurities that form

◄ Samples of galena, or lead sulfide, the principal ore from which lead is extracted.

► A flotation process is used initially to separate lead sulfide ore from other minerals. The crushed ore is suspended in water to which chemicals are added. The chemicals selectively coat the galena and make it water repellent. The galena floats to the top of the flotation cells and is collected.

◀ Crushed lead ore, which usually occurs as lead sulfide, in a warehouse. It will be refined down to tens of thousands of tons of metallic lead.

insoluble oxides are removed from the melt surface as dross. Copper is removed at this stage by adding sulfur to the melt to form copper sulfide, which floats to the surface as a liquid matte. If there is a significant amount of arsenic, a second layer of iron arsenide, or speiss, forms between the melt and matte. The speiss is removed with the matte because it contains a significant proportion of the total copper impurity. The matte and speiss are treated to recover the copper, which is sold as a valuable by-product.

After drossing, the lead will still contain some 1.5 percent impurities, mainly arsenic, antimony, and tin, which are sufficient to render the metal unacceptably hard for many applications. A further purification step, known as softening, is employed in which the molten bullion is heated with added lead oxide (litharge) in the presence of air. The impurities are oxidized and form slags that are periodically skimmed from the liquid metal surface, or alternatively, removed by pumping the melt through molten caustic soda and sodium nitrate in the Harris process.

Silver is a common impurity remaining in drossed bullion and normally present in sufficient quantities to make its removal extremely worthwhile. Usually, it is extracted by the Parkes process. Zinc is added to the lead bullion and both metals (they do not mix in the liquid state) are held molten in a large kettle. The melt is agitated, and the silver, because of its much greater solubility in zinc, diffuses from the lead to the zinc until its concentration in the zinc is 300 times that in the lead. A silver–zinc alloy contaminated with lead forms as a crust on the zinc and is

scraped off for further separation. Desilvered lead contains about 0.5 percent zinc, which can be removed in several ways: by oxidation with steam or air, by treatment with chlorine gas, or by a vacuum technique.

As a result of these treatments, only bismuth remains in the lead. For mechanical properties, this impurity is of limited consequence. Its presence, however, in a concentration as low as 0.05 percent in basic lead carbonate paint pigments is sufficient to turn them from white to dirty gray. The demand for bismuth-free lead from the paint industry contributed to the popularity of the Betts electrolytic process. Here the bullion, after drossing, is cast into anodes and subsequent purification effected by electrodeposition in a cell containing a solution of lead fluorosilicate as the electrolyte. This process removes most impurities, including bismuth, but tin is deposited along with the lead. Another way of removing bismuth involves adding a calcium–magnesium alloy to the molten lead to form an insoluble compound with the bismuth.

A method has been perfected for the

▼ Lead is highly resistant to atmospheric corrosion, making it an ideal material for roofing. When it is freshly cut, lead first forms a surface film of oxide then, after weathering, a silver-gray patina of unreactive lead carbonate.

removal of bismuth after desilverization without recourse to electrolysis. It involves the addition of a calcium–magnesium alloy to the molten lead to form an insoluble compound with the bismuth, which is subsequently separated and collected.

Properties and uses of lead

The combination of high density (specific gravity 11.37) and comparative cheapness means that lead has traditionally been used for weights, counterbalances, and ballast. Its high density also renders it opaque to penetrating radiation, and it finds application in biological shields around nuclear reactors, X-ray generators, and sources of gamma rays.

Lead has excellent resistance to corrosion. This has been an important factor in its use for water pipes, roofing, and cable protection, although in these applications it has been largely superseded by plastics, which are lighter and more resistant to creep (slow deformation under stress, such as that owing to the weight of the lead itself). Lead, however, continues to remain in widespread use in the chemical industry owing to its outstanding resistance to attack by sulfuric acid.

The mechanical properties of lead can be improved by alloying. Antimony is the most common addition, being added in concentrations ranging from 1 percent in lead used for cable sheathing to 8 percent in plates for electricity storage batteries and to greater than 10 percent for some chemical plants. The superior mechanical properties of lead–antimony alloys are in part due to precipitation hardening, and accordingly, the full strength is not realized until after an aging period. Small additions of arsenic also improve hardness, and lead shot is made from an alloy consisting of 99.5 percent lead and 0.5 percent arsenic.

The low melting point of lead (620°F, 327°C) makes it a useful constituent of solder alloys, which can be made up to give particular melting temperatures and ranges of solidification. The fusible alloys have very low melting points (for example, Wood's metal melts in hot water at 154°F, 68°C) and are used for applications such as fire-sprinkler controls and for supporting tubes during bending. Lead is easy to cast, and the addition of about 15 percent antimony together with about 10 percent tin effectively counteracts the tendency to shrink on solidification.

Lead is also a major constituent of bearing alloys where it provides malleability to the bearing, allowing it to accommodate slight misalignment of the rotating member. Another alloy is pewter—tin with up to 25 percent lead—used for ornaments.

The use of lead as a gasoline additive has been banned in certain countries and is currently being reduced in many others, because of the dangers of lead accumulating in the environment. Research has indicated that children are especially susceptible to its harmful effects.

Lead compounds

About one-third of the lead produced is used in lead compounds, which are widely used as pigments for anticorrosive paints. Basic lead carbonate $(2PbCO_3 \cdot Pb(OH)_2)$ is white and made by dissolving the high-purity metal in acetic acid and subsequent precipitation by carbon dioxide. Red lead, Pb_3O_4, and yellow lead chromate, $PbCrO_4$, are also used as pigments, and red lead together with litharge, PbO, finds application in the coating of accumulator plates. When lead oxide is fused with silica, it forms a frit, which is incorporated into the lead glazes for pottery. Other compounds of interest include lead azide, PbN_6, which is explosive and used as an alternative to mercury fulminate as a detonator for TNT, and lead tetraethyl, $Pb(C_2H_5)_4$, the antiknock additive in gasoline. Most of these compounds, however, are poisonous, and in many cases their use is declining or has already stopped.

Lead legislation

Some uses of lead, such as for water pipes or solders used to join such pipes, and paints have been discontinued because of the metal's toxicity. The use of lead tetraethyl in gasoline has been halted in many countries, and laws have been passed in the United States and Europe to limit the amount discharged to the air or present in drinking water.

◀ Lead compounds are poisonous. Here an industrial hygienist monitors the lead content of the air near a factory. Lead is increasingly being replaced by less harmful compounds in many of its applications.

SEE ALSO: ALLOY • ELECTROLYSIS • METAL • PLUMBING • SILVER • TRANSITION ELEMENT • ZINC

Leather

◀ Pulling a wet hide through a splitting machine, which makes two or three layers from one hide. Five strong operators are needed for this process. The best split is the grain side.

The making of leather from animal skins is one of the oldest accomplishments of humankind, and its origins are lost in history.

Leather can be produced from the skin of many creatures and comes mostly from seven main groups: cattle and calves, sheep and lambs, goats and kids, equines such as horses and mules, buffaloes, pigs, and aquatic species such as seals and whales. Commercial leathers are also made from a wide variety of other animals, including elephants, kangaroos, turkeys, ostriches, camels, reptiles, fish, and even eels.

Preservation

Animal skin is made up of a network of protein fibers that give it its unique properties. Fresh hides contain between 60 and 70 percent water and 30 to 35 percent protein. About 85 percent of the protein is in the form of collagen fibers, which are held together by chemical bonds. Mammal hides are made up of three layers: the thin outer epidermis, the thick central corium, or dermis, and a subcutaneous fatty layer. The middle layer, the dermis, is used to make leather after the two layers surrounding it have been removed.

In life, skin remains flexible because it contains a watery liquid, suspended between the fibers. Off the animal, the skin becomes hard and rigid if allowed to dry, but if kept wet, it will be rapidly decomposed by the action of bacteria.

Since much leather is produced using skins that originate from distant countries, they must be preserved to ensure that they reach the tannery without decomposing. Controlled drying while stretching the skins out flat is common in developing countries. This method requires no

chemicals, so it is cheap and produces a material that is light in weight and convenient for transportation. When it reaches the tannery, however, skins produced in this way need to be well soaked before they can be processed.

The other common method of preservation involves the use of salt. Green, or uncured hides, are placed into large drums containing a salt solution combined with small amounts of preservative chemicals. If this process is carried out within one hour of the hide being removed from the animal, this treatment will prevent any deterioration in the quality of hide or skin, enabling transportation across long distances. Pickling—preservation in acid and salt—is also used as a preserving process, particularly for sheepskins such as those shipped in barrels from abroad.

Liming

During manufacture, fat and flesh must be removed from the skin, unless the hide is to be made into furs or wooled sheepskins. The chemical action of lime and sodium sulfide removes the hair and makes the skin swell, so that removing any surplus flesh is easy. Liming used to take place in pits, but today revolving wooden drums are used. Traditionally, the flesh used to be removed with a sharp knife, but now this step is done by machine. If the hair or wool is to be recovered, the chemicals are applied to the underside of the skins, which are piled until the hair or wool is loosened. After the lime is neutralized, the skin is bated (enzymes are used to remove nonfibrous protein to enhance colour and suppleness) before

▼ The hides are fed into a machine to remove the flesh, after the hair has been taken off.

the tanning process begins. The skins are also usually pickled to make them react better with the tanning chemicals and also to provide a final cleansing and softening.

Tanning

Traditional tanning methods, which impart a characteristic color to the skins and convert an otherwise perishable material into a stable and nonperishable hide, traditionally used vegetable tannins leached from the leaves of shrubs and trees, such as quebracho and sumac leaves, and the bark of oak to tan the skins. Modern processes use concentrated vegetable extracts instead. The process was discovered early in human history, probably when a raw skin was left soaking in a pool of water into which tannins had coincidentally leached from fallen leaves.

Vegetable tanning produces the tan color still seen in sole leather and some harness and industrial leathers, such as belting. Apart from these applications, vegetable tanning is not widely used as the principal tanning agent, except in countries such as India. The process is slow: heavy sole leather, for example, can take several weeks to tan as the hides move progressively through tan liquors of increasing strength.

The discovery of the chrome tanning process early in the 20th century revolutionized leather making by introducing a mineral tanning process that can tan leathers in hours. Most shoe upper leather is now tanned in this way, and the process can be recognized by the blue-green color of the undyed leather. Chrome-tanned leathers were found to be more heat resistant and easier to waterproof and, in some cases, could even be made fully washable.

Other mineral tanning salts include aluminum and zirconium, which produce white leather. Various synthetic tannins have also been produced. They can be used separately but are generally mixed with vegetable tannins to retan chrome-tanned leather in order to modify its character or dyeing properties. A wide range of synthetic tanning agents (or syntans) derived from phenols and hydrocarbons are also used.

Chamois leather, well-known for its water absorption and cleaning properties, is often marketed as full-oil chamois, because the tanning process uses fish oil instead of chrome or the other mineral salts. Originally, the oil was beaten into the skin in kickers or stocks, but the process now generally takes place in rotating drums where the temperature can be raised and controlled accurately. Beside its traditional uses, for instance for washing windows and glass in automobiles, chamois leather is also sometimes used as a clothing material.

Dyeing and fatliquoring

Methods have existed for many years to color leathers using natural plant dyes, but the range of colors is limited. Chrome tanning, however, developed with the modern dyestuff industry, which uses aniline dyes. These enabled the tanner to produce leathers in virtually any shade. One disadvantage of chrome tanning is that the resultant leather dries out hard and stiff, unlike vegetable tanning, unless treated with a softening agent. To soften the leather, soaps and natural oils are drummed into it so that the fibers remain separate and flexible even when dry. Today, natural fats can be treated with sulfuric acid to make them water soluble so that they are absorbed into the

◄ Hides suspended in tanks containing wattle tannage, which takes eight days to penetrate the hide fully and chemically react with it to make leather.

▲ A wide variety of tools are used for working leather, including awls, shapers, and special knives and cutting tools.

be glazed using heat and friction to a high gloss. Modern methods use synthetic products, such as acrylic and polyurethane resins, into which pigments can be incorporated. Patent leathers, once produced using linseed oil, are now made using polyurethanes. Suede leather is also chrome-tanned, but instead of the finish being applied on the grain side of the hide, a nap is produced by buffing the hide on the flesh side before dyeing.

Mechanical processes

Leather manufacture has benefited from the development of many specialized machines to replace the laborious hand processes that were once used. For instance, to ensure the thickness of the variable natural material is uniform, skins are split after tanning using a band-knife machine that is able to produce level thicknesses to an accuracy of less than 0.004 in. (0.1 mm).

Many repetitive, lengthy hand operations have been replaced by feed-through machines, notably those involved in staking or softening the leather. Automatic spraying machines apply controlled amounts of finish, and hydraulic presses can produce flat, smooth leather or emboss designs onto the finished hide. Modern technology enables a range of specialist leathers to be produced, from thin, silky leathers that can be used for clothing to water-repellent shoe leather and leather suitable to provide protection against extreme heat. Leathers can also now be treated to produce metallic finishes.

leather. The dyeing and fatliquoring processes were traditionally carried out at raised temperatures in rotating wooden drums, but increasingly stainless steel processing vessels with computerized controls are being used.

Drying

The next stage is to dry the leather to about 14 percent moisture. The method of drying depends on the type of leather and the use for which it is required. Some leathers are hung to dry slowly; others are suspended from poles or toggles and passed through heated tunnels. Leathers that are required to be flat may be stretched out on perforated frames using toggle clips or, less commonly, pasted onto glass or metal plates that are passed through drying tunnels. Leather can also be dried in a vacuum while held against a heated plate. The dried leather is then finished by reconditioning it using damp sawdust to achieve a uniform moisture content of 20 percent. The leather is then stretched and softened, and the grain surface is coated to give it extra resistance to abrasion and other conditions, such as heat and cold, that might otherwise damage it.

Finishing

Much of the attractive appearance of leather is due to the skill of the finisher. Aniline leathers, which use no pigments, show the natural grain to full advantage. Originally, proteins such as casein were used to give a protective coating that could

▶ Making a saddle by hand from pigskin and cowhide leathers. Saddlery is a specialized craft and it can take considerable time to make a saddle to a customer's specifications.

SEE ALSO: ALUMINUM • ANILINE AND AZO DYES • CHROMIUM • CLOTHING MANUFACTURE • DYEING PROCESS • SKIN • TAXIDERMY

Lens

A lens is a transparent object that modifies in a coordinated manner the path of light that passes through it. Lenses can be used to form magnified or diminished focused images or to concentrate light into narrow beams for localized illumination, for example. Refraction is the optical effect that underlies the function of any lens.

Refraction

Light travels through transparent materials at speeds slower than the speed of light in a vacuum. The amount by which light is slowed in a given medium is expressed as a refractive index value, which is defined as the speed of light in a vacuum divided by the speed of light in the medium. Since the speed of light in a vacuum is greater than the speed of light in any medium, refractive-index values are always greater than one.

When a beam of light passes from a low-refractive-index material—air, for example—to a high-refractive-index material, such as glass, its frequency is unchanged. Since the speed of light is less in the high-refractive-index material, the wavelength must therefore become shorter. In terms of the classical wave description of light, this corresponds to the wave fronts—lines that join peaks of light waves—becoming more closely spaced in the slower medium. The ratio of the wavelengths in the two media is the inverse of the ratio of the speeds of light in the two media and therefore equal to the ratio of refractive indices.

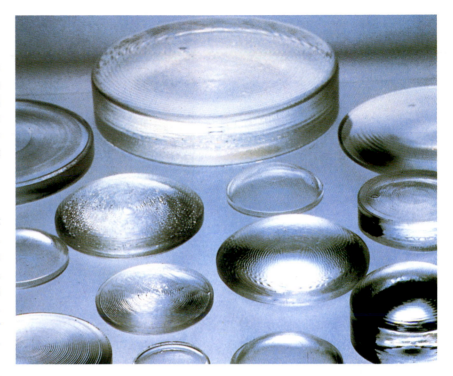

▲ A selection of surface-modified glass lenses. These lenses have been treated using ion exchange to alter the surface composition of the glass. Such treatment increases the durability of lenses.

When light stikes the surface between one medium and another, making an angle θ_i, measured with respect to a line perpendicular to the surface, it emerges in the other medium making a different angle θ_r, with respect to the same line. The angles are related to the wavelengths and refractive indices of the media by the expression

$$\frac{sin\ \theta_i}{sin\ \theta_r} = \frac{\lambda_i}{\lambda_r} = \frac{n_2}{n_1}$$

where λ_i and λ_r are the wavelengths of the incident and refracted light, respectively, and n_1 and n_2 are the refractive indices of the first and second media through which the light passes. This relationship is called Snell's law.

Basic lens types

Simple lenses are cylindrically symmetrical about an imaginary line—the principal axis—that passes through the centers of the two refracting surfaces of a lens. A typical refracting surface is a section of a sphere, with a constant radius of curvature originating from a single point.

Light that follows the principal axis of a lens passes through the lens without deviating from its path, because it strikes both refracting surfaces at right angles. Light that strikes a lens parallel to its axis, but at a distance from the center of the lens, is refracted. The extent of refraction increases along the radius of a lens, since the angle of incidence increases with increasing distance from the central axis of the lens.

Convex lenses—lenses thickest at the principal axis—cause parallel incident light rays to converge at a point on the opposite side of a lens to

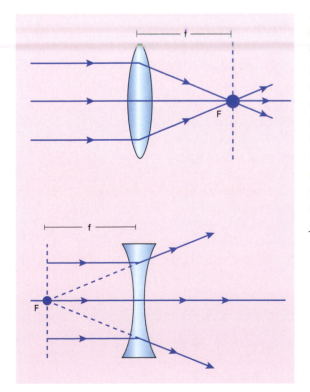

◀ Ray diagrams showing the passage of light through a convex lens (top) and a concave lens (bottom). The convex lens causes light to converge on a focal point, F, beyond the lens. With the concave lens, light appears to originate from a focal point behind the lens. In either case, the distance f is the focal length.

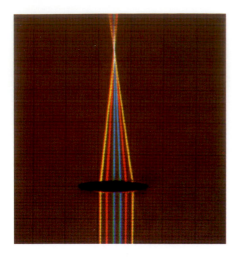 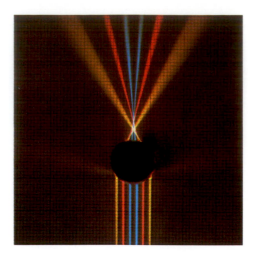 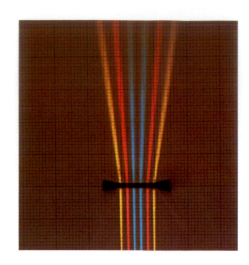

the source of light. One of the applications of convex lenses is in projecting magnified images onto screens. Planoconvex lenses have an out-ward-curved surface and a flat surface, while convex meniscus lenses have two curved surfaces.

Concave lenses—lenses thinnest at the principal axis—cause parallel rays of incident light to diverge, such that they appear to originate from a point on the same side of the lens as the light source. One of the applications of concave lenses is in magnifying glasses, which allow an enlarged virtual image to be viewed through the lens. Planoconcave lenses have an inward-curved sur-face and a flat surface, while concave meniscus lenses have two curved surfaces. Compound lenses consist of two or more simple lenses fitted to-gether to correct aberrations in one of the lenses.

Focal length

The main defining characteristic of a lens is its focal length—the distance along the principal axis between an image of an object located at infinity from the lens and the center of a lens. In practical terms, "infinity" means a sufficiently large dis-tance for the rays of light from an object to be essentially parallel to the principal axis when they strike a lens—an approximate minimum distance that depends on the diameter of the lens.

In the case of a convex lens, focal length is the distance between the center of the lens and the point where parallel incident rays converge after refraction by the lens. In this case, focal length is stated as a positive value, which is why convex lenses are sometimes called positive lenses.

For a concave lens, focal length is the distance between the center of the lens and the point from which parallel rays appear to originate after pass-ing through the lens. Since this point is behind the lens for an observer, focal lengths of concave lenses are stated as negative values, and concave lenses are sometimes called negative lenses. The stronger the effect of a lens, the shorter will be its

focal length. For this reason, lens power is stated in terms of the reciprocal of focal length. Values of lens power in diopters are equal to the recipro-cal of focal length in meters. Accordingly, a lens with a focal length of 4 in. (10.2 cm) has a lens power of 9.8 (= $\frac{1}{0.102}$) diopters.

Lens equation

The lens equation interrelates the focal length and the positions of the object and its image in the following way:

$$\frac{1}{\text{focal length}} = \frac{1}{\text{image distance}} + \frac{1}{\text{object distance}}$$

This equation is valid for thin lenses only, but with careful interpretation of negative values, it may be used for both concave and convex lenses.

Concave lenses have negative focal lengths, so the lens equation always gives a negative value of image distance that is smaller in magnitude than the object distance. The negative sign of the image distance implies that the image is virtual—it appears to be behind the lens. The smaller mag-nitude of the image distance implies that the image appears to be closer than the object.

For convex lenses, the sign of the image dis-tance depends on whether the object distance is greater than or less than the focal length of the lens. If the object is closer than the focal length, the reciprocal of object distance is greater than that of the focal length. Consequently, the image distance is negative, implying a virtual image.

If an object is beyond the focal length of a lens, the image distance has a positive value, which implies a real image—one that can be focused onto a screen placed at the image dis-tance. If the object distance increases, the distance at which the image is in focus becomes smaller.

The lens equation is an approximate expres-sion, and as lens thickness increases, its inherent inaccuracies become more apparent, particularly where the object distance is small. Calculations of

▲ In these photographs, rays of colored light demonstrate the actions of some simple lenses. A convex lens (left) causes rays of light to converge. A convex lens of greater curvature (center) causes light to converge closer to the lens surface. A concave lens (right) causes rays of light to diverge.

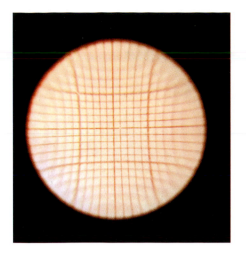 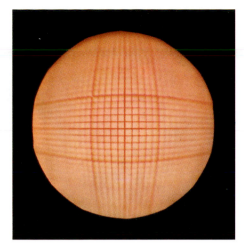 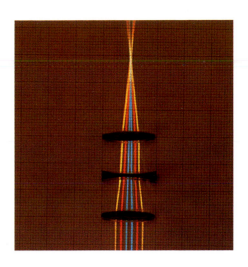

▲ Spherical aberration effects include pincushion distortion (left) and barrel distortion (center), seen here in images of graph paper. Spherical aberration occurs because rays that pass through the edge of a lens focus at a different point from rays that pass through the center of the lens. Compound lenses can reduce the effects of spherical aberration. In the right-hand image, all the rays pass through a single focal point.

image distances for thick lenses call for the inclusion of a more complex expression for focal length in the lens equation.

Magnification

The magnification of an image relative to an object can be calculated from image and object distances using the following expression:

$$\text{magnification} = \frac{-(\text{image distance})}{\text{object distance}}$$

In this expression, a negative value of magnification implies an image inverted from top to bottom and from side to side. A fractional value implies an image that is smaller than the object.

Since object distances are always positive, this expression shows that real images, which have positive image distances, are always inverted by lenses. Virtual images, on the other hand, always appear with the same orientation as the object.

Focal ratio

The focal ratio of a lens is its focal length divided by its diameter in a plane perpendicular to the principal axis. The focal ratio is expressed as f numbers, so a lens whose diameter is half its focal length is described as f-2 (read as "f two").

While the amount of light that passes through a lens increases in proportion to lens area, the image size—and the dilution of the light that forms it—increases for greater focal lengths. Consequently, a lens of large diameter and small focal length—and hence a small f number—forms brighter images than lenses with larger f numbers.

In photography, the amount of light that falls on a light-sensitive film during an exposure can be controlled by adjusting the size of a variable aperture in the light path. Partially closing the aperture reduces the effective diameter of the lens, thereby increasing its f number.

The pupil of an eye functions in a similar way to the aperture of a camera, a reflex reducing the effective diameter of the lens in response to increasing light intensity. The human eye functions in a range from f-3 (bright daylight) to f-10 (night, low-light intensities).

Reducing the f number of a lens increases its resolving power—the ability of a lens to give a finely detailed image. Image resolution is the smallest separation at which two points in an image can be seen to be distinct, and larger lens diameters reduce the necessary separation.

Increasing the f number of a lens increases the depth of field of images. Therefore, a smaller lens diameter increases the range of object distances that appear to be in focus, even though the resolution is poorer than that obtained with a larger-diameter lens.

The effects of decreased resolution and increased depth of field can be observed by looking through a pinhole. The tiny diameter of a pinhole increases the effective f number of the eye, thereby causing blurring while allowing distant objects to be seen more clearly.

In photography, a high f number produces photographs with a great depth of field, so that objects in the foreground and background of a scene are in focus and reasonably resolved. Low f numbers produce images in which only those objects that are within a narrow range of distances from the camera are in focus; the resolution of those objects is superior to that obtained with high f numbers, so a low f number is useful in highlighting selected objects within a scene.

Spherical aberration

Spherical aberration is an image defect that arises because the constant radius of curvature of the refractive surfaces of simple lenses does not result in a single focal length for all parts of the lens. For a convex lens, rays that strike near the edge of the lens are focused at a shorter focal length than rays that strike near the principal axis. Thus, the periphery of an image is out of focus when the

CAMERA LENSES

The camera industry is one of the greatest users of lenses, and its terminology has entered common usage. For example, film sizes and focal lengths of camera lenses are almost always quoted in millimeters.

Camera lenses are classed as standard, wide-angle, or telephoto (long focus), depending on whether their focal length is, respectively, equal to, less than, or greater than the diagonal of the film with which they are intended to be used. However, the popular combination of 35-mm film and a 50-mm lens is not strictly standard, since the diagonal measurement of a 35-mm frame is 43.3 mm (1.7 in.).

Wide-angle lenses produce images at lower magnification than achieved with a standard lens, so a broader view fits into a given frame size. In technical terms, such a lens is described as having a wide angle of acceptance. The shorter the focal length of the lens, the greater is its angle of acceptance. Images taken with wide-angle

lenses tend to exhibit spherical aberration, which at its extreme is used as a form of special effect called fisheye.

Focal lengths greater than standard for a given film size produce highly magnified images and are useful for taking detailed photographs of distant objects. Telephoto lenses, rather like telescopes, tend to suffer from chromatic aberration.

Lenses with variable focal lengths were first introduced for television and film cameras, which they enabled to zoom in for close-up detail and zoom out for wider views. This action earned such lenses the colloquial name "zoom lens." Zoom lenses are complex assemblies of many components. All the traditional

▲ A photograph taken with a fisheye lens, a type of lens that has an extremely short focal length. The distortion evident in this image is a consequence of spherical aberration.

problems of lens design are therefore compounded, and the quality of images can suffer—a particular problem in still photography, where the viewer has time to study the image and quality.

Mechanized zoom lenses are popular with photographers who want to be able to make quick and easy shifts in focal lengths. However, because of size and weight limitations, zoom lenses for still photography have smaller zooming ranges than those for moving pictures.

▼ A typical telephoto lens of 250 mm focal length is made up of three lenses at the front that form an image 10 in. (250 mm) away. The group of lenses at the rear reduces this distance to more manageable proportions, making the telephoto lens body shorter, lighter, and easier to handle.

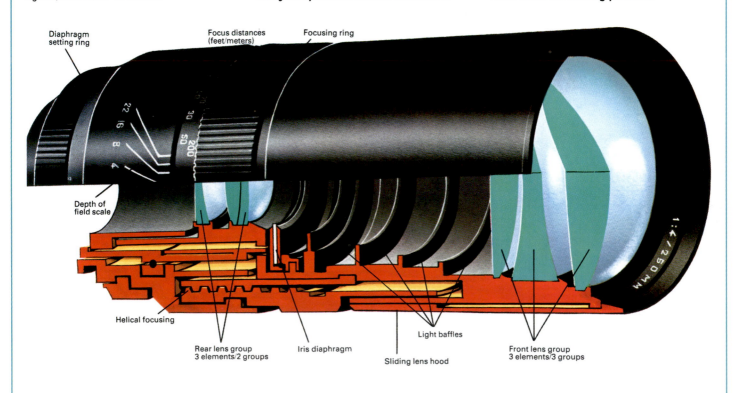

Diaphragm setting ring

Focus distances (feet/meters)

Focusing ring

Depth of field scale

Helical focusing

Rear lens group 3 elements/2 groups

Iris diaphragm

Sliding lens hood

Light baffles

Front lens group 3 elements/3 groups

center of the image is focused, and vice versa. Images with spherical aberration appear to curve out of the plane of the central part of the image, as can be observed with a magnifying glass.

Spherical aberration can be avoided by the use of aspherical lenses, whose surfaces are designed specifically to produce a constant focal length over the whole lens. The manufacture of such lenses is much more complicated than that of spherically ground lenses, which makes their production costs prohibitively high for all but the most demanding of applications.

In practice, spherical aberration can be minimized by combining two simple lenses in a so-called doublet. With an appropriate choice of lenses, the spherical aberration of one lens counteracts that of the second, and the two standard lenses are cheaper than a single aspherical lens. Alternatively, the two surfaces of a single lens can be ground so that one surface largely compensates for the spherical aberration of the other.

◄ This machine polishes ophthalmic lenses for use in spectacles. Such lenses are designed to transmit all frequencies of visible light while blocking potentially harmful ultraviolet light.

Coma

Coma is a form of aberration that causes points of light, such as stars, to acquire outward-pointing "tails" of light away from the principal axis. An appropriate choice of lens doublet can eliminate the coma effect, but the best choice of lenses for this purpose is inappropriate for reducing spherical aberration. As such, lenses must be chosen to give the best compromise of coma and spherical aberration for a given application.

Chromatic aberration

Chromatic aberration is a form of image defect that arises because a given lens has different focal lengths for different wavelengths of light. The effect is a consequence of dispersion, which arises from the variation of refractive index with wavelength. Short-wavelength blue light focuses differently from long-wavelength red light, which leads to a white object on a black background acquiring a red fringe to one side and a blue fringe to the other, depending on its position in an image.

Combinations of lenses made from different materials can reduce chromatic aberration, but the choice of lens can conflict with the reduction of other forms of aberration. A cheap and simple alternative is to use lens coatings that interact with light over narrow frequency ranges, altering its refracting charateristic accordingly. A number of such coatings must be used to ensure that all frequencies have the same focal length.

The complexity of overcoming chromatic aberration depends on the range of frequencies that must be taken into consideration. Early photographic film used with refracting telescopes was sensitive only to blue light, so chromatic aberration could essentially be ignored. Modern photographic techniques can extend from the visible range to the infrared, in which case the correction of chromatic aberration is more complex. The lens system of a general-purpose camera caters for chromatic aberration in the visible range only.

Lens materials

The power of a lens depends on the curvature of its surfaces: the greater the curvature of its two faces, the greater the power of the lens. Lens curvature is often limited by practical considerations, since strongly curved refracting surfaces imply thick lenses, which would be inconvenient for use in compact cameras, for example. In such cases, it is desirable to make lenses using materials that have large refractive indices, which require less curvature to achieve the same power as a lens made with a more weakly refracting material.

A thinner lens is not necessarily lighter than a thicker equivalent lens, since the refractive index of a material is closely related to its density. A comparison of borosilicate glass and dense flint glass is instructive: borosilicate glass has a refractive index of 1.52 and a relative density of 2.51, whereas dense flint glass has a refractive index of 1.81 and a relative density of 5.18.

For applications where it is desirable to keep weight to a minimum—for use in spectacles, for example—optical grade polycarbonate (refractive index 1.58, relative density 1.2) is a good choice of lens material. Polycarbonate is less than half as dense as an equivalent optical glass and has the advantage of high impact resistance.

Blooming

Numerous forms of aberration can be overcome simultaneously by combining several lenses in a single system. The drawback of such combinations is that the loss of light at each lens can cause unacceptable reductions in image intensity.

One of the main causes of light loss in lens systems is reflection from the surfaces of component lenses. Blooming is a low-reflectance coating that reduces such losses, thereby extending the potential of compound lens systems. Blooming appears as a faint surface coloration when a treated lens is viewed at an oblique angle.

Fresnel lens

Fresnel lenses are used to focus light from point sources into parallel beams. They result in lighter, smaller optics than would be possible using conventional types of lenses.

In principle, light from a filament or arc lamp could be focused into a parallel beam by placing the light source at the focus of a convex lens. In practice, the curvature necessary to produce such a beam would require a lens thickness and weight greater than acceptable for many applications.

In the early 19th century, the French engineer Augustin Fresnel realized that a great reduction in both weight and thickness would be achieved by removing cylindrical sections from a convex lens in such a way that the curvature of the refractive surfaces were unchanged. Since the curved surfaces are the only parts of a lens that participate in focusing light, such a modification makes little difference to the optical properties of the lens. Viewed from such a distance that the surfaces parallel to the principal axis are invisible to an observer, a Fresnel lens is indistinguishable from a conventional convex lens.

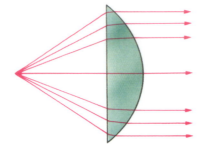 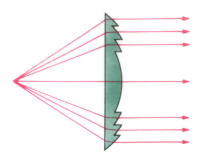

Fresnel lenses are used to focus light in stage lamps, lighthouse beacons, projectors, and stop lights. In many cases, the surface next to the light source is dimpled so as to prevent an image of the lamp filament from forming.

A form of Fresnel lens is sometimes stuck to the rear windows of buses. Viewed through the rear-view mirror, the compact lens provides the driver with a wide-angle view of the road behind.

Zone plates

Using a theory of interference that he had developed in 1815, Fresnel developed a type of lens that uses interference rather than refraction as the basis for focusing radiation. A zone plate is a sphere whose surface has been divided into circular zones such that each zone is half a wavelength farther from the intended focal point than the previous zone. Alternate zones are blacked out by an opaque material. Light from the transparent zones then converges on the focal point, where its intensity is reinforced by constructive interference in a way that the zone pattern allows at no other point. Zone plates can be tuned for other forms of electromagnetic radiation by using suitable transparent and opaque materials and a zone pattern that suits the wavelength of radiation that it is intended to focus.

▲ For many applications, a thick convex lens (left) can be substituted by a Fresnel lens (right) with a significant saving in both space and weight.

FACT FILE

■ *In 1959, the Rolls Royce company produced a 27 ton (24 tonne) camera. It had a 63 in. (1.6 m) f-15 Cooke Apochromatic lens in a case 8.8 ft. (2.7 m) high, 8.3 ft. (2.5 m) wide, and 35 ft. (10.7 m) long.*

■ *The Nimslo 3-D camera has four lenses and produces a single-print image that needs no special viewing apparatus. The optical glass lenses, positioned 0.4 in. (10 mm) apart, produce four simultaneous images, which a computer in the printing process converts into a three-dimensional picture.*

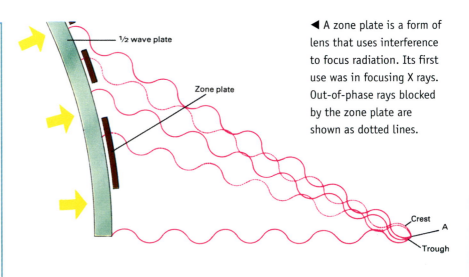

◀ A zone plate is a form of lens that uses interference to focus radiation. Its first use was in focusing X rays. Out-of-phase rays blocked by the zone plate are shown as dotted lines.

SEE ALSO: Binoculars • Camera • Eye • Light and optics • Mirror • Movie camera • Spectacles • Telescope, optical

Lever

EFFORT AND LOAD IN LEVERS

A beam pivoted on a fulcrum shows the principle of the lever. The farther the load from the fulcrum, the greater effort that must be applied to the other end. When load and effort are on the same side of the fulcrum, mechanical advantage increases the nearer the load is to the fulcrum. In many machines, levers are used to provide amplification of force, movement, or velocity and often a combination of these. One early example of a lever is a shaduf— a system invented by the ancient Egyptians and still in use for moving water to irrigate land.

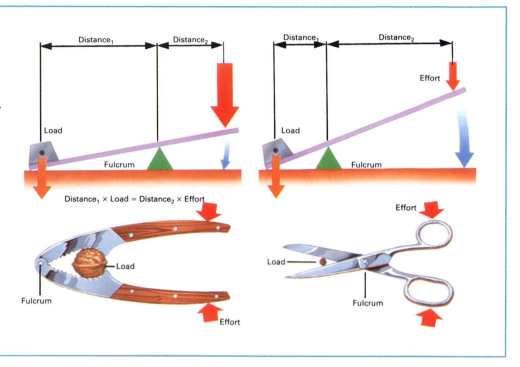

$$Distance_1 \times Load = Distance_2 \times Effort$$

The invention of the lever, one of the simplest machines, was of great importance to the development of human society, comparable in importance to the invention of the wheel. The lever allowed a person to amplify his or her strength to a level capable of lifting very large and heavy objects. The lever amplifies force, movement, and velocity.

Force

The simple lever consists of a pivoted beam, the pivot point being the fulcrum. The applied force, or effort, is brought to bear upon one end of the beam, preferably as far from the fulcrum as possible. An amplification of the effort is achieved when the load to be raised is nearer to the fulcrum than is the effort.

The amount of amplification of the effort, known as the mechanical advantage, is the ratio of the load to the effort. It is also the ratio of the distance of the effort from the fulcrum and the distance of the load from the fulcrum.

A small effort acting at a large distance from the fulcrum exerts the same leverage or moment as a large effort acting closer to the fulcrum. The moment is the product of a force and its distance from the fulcrum, so for a simple lever arrangement, the moment exerted by the effort equals that exerted by the load in order to balance it and exceeds it in order to lift the load.

The load and effort may be either on opposite sides of the fulcrum or on the same side. A pair of scissors, for example, which can be thought of as two levers acting in opposite directions through the same pivot, has the load at one side of the pivot and the effort is applied at the other.

In contrast, a common design of nutcracker is an example of the type of lever in which load and effort are on the same side of the fulcrum, and in order to crack a nut with minimum effort, it should be placed as near the fulcrum as possible.

Movement

Levers have numerous applications in which they are used to amplify an effort or force, but another important feature of the lever is that it amplifies movement. In the case of a simple lever with the fulcrum at the center, such as a seesaw, if one end moves a certain distance the other moves the same distance. If the fulcrum is nearer one end than the other, however, the two ends move through different distances; the ratio of the distances is the ratio of the lengths from each end to the fulcrum.

Velocity

The two ends of an unequal seesaw move through different distances during the same time interval, so they are traveling at different velocities, the ratio of these velocities being the same as the ratio of the distances traveled.

 SEE ALSO: PEN • PULLEY • TYPEWRITER

Life

The scale of life is enormous, ranging from simple single-celled organisms to human beings and from microscopic organisms to the blue whale. Theories of life have to account for the processes that these diverse organisms have in common. Life is found in a hugely diverse selection of environments, from the lowest depths of the ocean to the stratosphere. For example, the alga *Cyanidium caldarium* will grow in concentrated sulfuric acid solutions. Bacteria can thrive in acidic solutions having a pH of 0, as well as strong alkali solutions with a pH approaching 13.

Extremes of temperature can be tolerated, too. Pools in the Yellowstone National Park contain bacteria that live at temperatures of more than 190°F (90°C). At the opposite end of the scale, there is a kind of microflora that will metabolize at temperatures down to –9°F (–23°C). Some enzymes are more active below freezing point than they are above. Most forms of life seem to need to drink water, but there are some exceptions. Some desert animals, such as the kangaroo rat, do not drink at all; they absorb water from the plants they eat.

Many scientific disciplines have addressed the question of life, but scientists have difficulty in even agreeing on what is being studied. The medical profession needs a practical rather than a theoretical definition of life—is the patient still alive? A dead patient is not just a failure of medical science and a victory for disease, accident, damage, or old age but also a possible source of transplantation material.

Medical definitions

The medical profession sees life in a practical way—simply as what amounts to absence of death. It does not trouble itself with theoretical definitions of life: it is something to be preserved. Traditionally, a patient was deemed alive if the heart was beating, but if the heart stopped, the patient was dead.

In more recent years, the medical profession has changed its definition of death to that of brain death. Once the patient's neural activity has ceased, he or she has died. The heart may still be beating, but the motion is merely a mechanical reflex response that will keep transplantation organs fresh for use.

Definitions

Originating definitions is an important part of science, and definitions of life are almost as numerous as the scientific disciplines that are

interested in the subject. One of the most enduring definitions of life comes from physiology. Life is looked upon as a system capable of performing a certain number of specialized tasks. These are eating, metabolizing, excreting, breathing, moving, growing, reproducing, and interacting with the outside world.

The physiological definition has one great weakness—some machines fulfill these criteria, and no one would wish to classify machines as alive. Some skeptics have argued that even something as common as the automobile can be classified as being alive by these criteria.

Conversely, there are some organisms, such as bacteria, that need to be classified as alive, which are excluded by this definition. Clearly, a definition of life needs to be able to encompass organisms that do not breathe in the conventional way.

Metabolic definition

Biologists have tended to favor the metabolic definition. Again, the living system is the basis, but this time the defining factors are a definite boundary and an ability to exchange some of its materials with its environment. The system is not allowed to alter its general properties while doing so.

The definition runs into problems when trying to classify some seeds and spores. Some of them remain dormant for thousands of years, with no sign of metabolic activity, but can spring into life if they are exposed to the correct environmental conditions. Flames are equally problematic for this definition. Consider a candle flame. It has a definite boundary and is maintained by a metabolism consisting of the combi-

▲ The giant tortoises of the Galapagos Islands can live longer than any other creature on Earth. One specimen in an Australian zoo is known to have celebrated its 170th birthday in 2000, because zoo records noted the date of its arrival as a baby. Some of the very big Galapagos tortoises in the wild are believed to be more than 200 years old.

nation of organic waxes with oxygen, producing carbon dioxide and water. To further bolster the claim that flames are alive by this definition, flames have a capacity for growth.

Biochemical definition

Biochemists and molecular biologists have a different view of life. Living systems are those that have reproducible hereditary information, coded in nucleic acid molecules. The systems themselves metabolize by controlling the rate of certain chemical reactions within the organism—those that use enzymes.

Although generally more acceptable than the physiological and metabolic definitions of life, there are still a number of problems with the definition. Certain viruses seem to have no nucleic acid information, but conclusive evidence for this observation is still to be found.

Genetic definition

The genetic definition of life uses the discoveries of geneticists to construct a model for life. Hereditary information is carried by combinations of nucleic acids, known as genes. As organisms reproduce, so do the genes—the process is known as replication. Replication is not always straightforward, because hereditary information can become mutated or altered, affecting the instructions given for certain characteristics.

Mutations may be an advantage to the organism or may prove to be a disaster. The mutated organisms that have favorable characteristics will have a definite advantage over the ones that have unfavorable characteristics. Mutations that are unfavorable tend to lead to death, but favorable mutations give a heightened chance of survival. The model that has been constructed owes a great deal to Charles Darwin's theory of natural selection, and it is this quality that the genetic theory says systems need to achieve if they are to be classified as being alive.

This definition of life has the advantage that it is defined in purely functional terms. It accommodates theoretical mechanical systems that could replicate themselves from small building blocks, because it says that, if such a machine could work within this kind of system, it must be very complex, and it must have all the characteristics attributable to living systems.

Thermodynamic definition

The discipline of thermodynamics looks at open and closed systems. An open system exchanges light, heat, and matter with its environment. A closed system, on the other hand, does not and is isolated from its environment.

The Second Law of Thermodynamics states that, in a closed system, no event can occur that decreases the net entropy—degree of disorder—or increases the net order of the system. But living systems, which at first appear to be closed systems, present a challenge to the Second Law of Thermodynamics: the processes involved increase the organisms' order at the expense of the outside world.

In fact, thermodynamically, life is an open system. Most life forms have some dependence on sunlight—it is used for making large molecules from smaller ones. Scientists, in fact, see life as a specialized form of the carbon cycle. Carbon dioxide from the atmosphere is converted into carbon by plants and made into carbohydrates by photosynthesis. Such carbohydrates are oxidized by plants and animals, a process that extracts energy for use by living systems.

Since these kinds of cycles exist without the intervention of life, biological cycles are considered just as a special type of thermodynamic cycle. Whether thermodynamic systems are capable of producing the complexities of life remains to be seen, but thermodynamic systems are used by all living things.

Life on Earth

A general picture of what life on Earth consists of can be drawn from these definitions. Life consists of many cells and is often a complex and highly developed collection of cells. The amount of information present in a living organism can be appreciated from the estimate that a single cell contains the equivalent of 10^{12} bits of information, and a human being contains about 10^{14} cells. The information in cells is carried by their nucleic acids, which carry the blueprints needed for making more of the cells and hence more of the organisms that are made up of the cells.

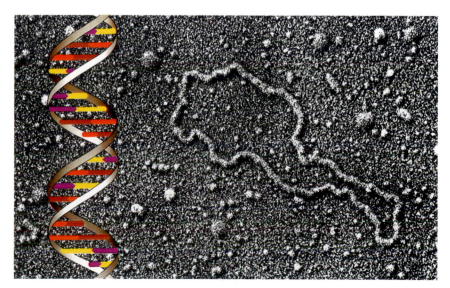

▼ Left: Every cell in a person's body contains all the information needed in the form of a code to build a perfect copy of the whole body. This code is carried in the structure of an acid found in the nucleus of each cell— deoxyribonucleic acid, or DNA, for short. The characteristic double helix structure of the DNA molecule is shown here. Right: a strand of DNA in the nucleus of an *E. coli* bacterium cell.

Biochemists have looked into the question of energy storage in great detail and have discovered the chains of chemical reactions that are used by living organisms to store energy. All life forms seem to rely on a chemical called adenosine triphosphate (ATP), or a related compound, to store energy. Similarly, metabolic systems that typify life forms have been investigated in great depth.

How life began

Debate continues about the origin of living organisms on Earth. There are scientists who argue that bacteria and other simple organisms are spread around the Universe by comets, and organic molecules have been found in clouds of interstellar gas. The distribution and abundance of elements throughout the Universe implies a common chemistry, but how quite basic compounds progress into complicated life forms and what conditions are necessary for them to do this is still a matter for conjecture.

Scientists realized in the 1920s that the present oxygen-rich atmosphere on Earth would not be conducive to the abiological production of organic molecules. However, a strongly reducing atmosphere would favor the synthesis of organic chemicals. To test this theory, experiments were carried out in 1953 by the U.S. chemist Harold Urey using a mixture of methane, water vapor, ammonia, and hydrogen that was continuously sparked by a corona discharge to simulate lightning flashes. After a few days, the mixture changed color and analysis revealed a number of amino and hydroxy acids common to present day life. Further experiments by the U.S. astrophysicist Carl Sagan using ultraviolet light as the energy source and hydrogen sulfide among the chemicals also created a large number of biologically abundant amino acids.

The pathways by which these amino acids became built up, first into sugars and porphyrins, then into nucleotide bases, and from there proteins, carbohydrates, and nucleic acids are less clearly understood, but all have been found to be possible under the conditions of a primitive reducing atmosphere.

◀ The fact that apes and humans share many brachiating characteristics—such as flexible shoulder joints—suggests they may have shared a brachiating ancestor. There is much disagreement among scientists, however, about the time we split from those ape predecessors. Theories based on the fossil record place the split anywhere between 20 million and 3.75 million years ago, but recently, biochemists, using the protein analysis method, have suggested that it occurred about 5 million years ago.

Living organisms

How organic molecules became transformed into living cells is not understood clearly, but it is known that some polyamino acids can form into small spherical objects that have properties similar to those of cell membranes. It is thought that cells developed as a response to increasing amounts of oxygen in the atmosphere—which is poisonous to some biological processes—and as a protection against ultraviolet radiation. The first organisms were probably prokaryotes, such as bacteria, with no defined nucleus to the cell. To get to the next stage, eukaryotes, with their separate nucleus, mitochondria, and chloroplast structure must have taken millions of years.

Studies of fossils indicate that many of the earliest forms of life must have lived in deep oceans as a way of shielding themselves from ultraviolet radiation. Colonization of the land some 425 million years ago would have been possible only when atmospheric oxygen and ozone had reached sufficient levels to start blocking ultraviolet light. From there, life-forms developed ways of exploiting niche environments and evolved slowly over millions of years into the range of plants and animals we know today.

Extraterrestrial life

Knowing the appearance of life on Earth, modern scientists are following the lead of tradition and looking to the stars. A new science, called exobiology (also called astrobiology), speculates on the existence of life on other planets and on the possible distribution of life throughout the Universe.

The central idea behind exobiology is that it is highly probable that life has evolved not only on Earth but on other planets, too. At present, science has found no firm evidence that life exists elsewhere in the Universe, but evidence from many different scientific disciplines indicates that its existence is more than just highly likely.

Astrophysics confirms that planets are the rule rather than the exception. Some estimates place the number of planets in our galaxy alone in the hundreds of millions. Some proportion of these planets, it is argued, must present similar conditions to those of Earth. If this is the case, theories of evolution predict that life will begin. Given a long enough timescale of stability, the simple life forms should evolve into some kind of higher life form, with intelligence. Some exobiologists inevitably have to conclude that somewhere in the Universe there are civilizations as advanced as—or even more advanced than—those present on Earth.

Investigating the conditions for life elsewhere is the focus of a new NASA research program. By studying hostile or unexplored environments,

such as Lake Vostok in the Antarctic, or life around boiling-hot fumaroles at the bottom of the ocean, scientists hope to be able to gain insights on how life can survive on Earth that they can relate to similar worlds in space. In fact, plans to extract samples from Lake Vostok, which has remained hidden 2½ miles (4 km) beneath the Antarctic ice for millions of years, are being used as a basis for the future exploration of Mars and two satellites of Jupiter, Europa and Ganymede, which are believed to have large quantities of water lying below their surfaces.

Mars has long been the subject of speculation on whether life may once have existed there. Examination of Martian meteorites that have landed on Earth has revealed bacterialike structures in the rock that may be fossils. Fossilized microbes recently found on Earth in ancient undersea springs suggest they lived on methane and other simple chemicals and were capable of surviving extremely harsh and changing conditions. Scientists believe that the early Mars may have been similar to Earth, with active volcanoes and water, making the Martian environment warmer and wetter and capable of supporting life-forms like the fossils found on Earth.

▲ Ganymede is one of several of Jupiter's moons that will be investigated for possible signs of life. Scientists have detected a number of organic compounds on the moon's surface, together with water-bearing minerals, water ice, and sulfur dioxide. Ganymede is also believed to have a large underground lake of water, similar to Lake Vostok in the Antarctic.

SEE ALSO: CELL BIOLOGY • ENZYME • EVOLUTION • GENETIC ENGINEERING • GENETICS • MICROBIOLOGY • MOLECULAR BIOLOGY • PHOTOSYNTHESIS • REPRODUCTION • THERMODYNAMICS

Light and Optics

◀ The "perfect mirror" reflecting the three researchers who created it (Y. Fink, E. L. Thomas, and J. D. Joannopoulos). This mirror is dielectric—made of transparent materials that do not conduct electricity—which allows it to reflect light much more efficiently than a conventional mirror.

The phenomenon of light, the explanation of what it is and of why objects are visible at all, is not easily understood even today. The earliest known explanation of vision was given in the sixth century B.C.E. by the Greek philosopher Pythagoras, who hypothesized that an object is visible because light rays travel outward from the eye to touch it. This theory failed to explain why we cannot see in the dark, and so a century later, the idea was elaborated on by Plato, who required in addition "emanations" from the Sun and from the object observed. Within the following couple of centuries, however, the true explanation (that light is emitted from luminous bodies like the Sun or a flame and is reflected off other objects into our eyes) had been widely accepted.

The nature of light rays was not satisfactorily explained until the 20th century. At the time of the British scientist Sir Isaac Newton (17th to 18th century), there was heated controversy between those who (like Newton) believed light to consist of rapidly moving particles (or corpuscles) and the followers of the Dutch physicist Christiaan Huygens, who regarded light as being a series of waves. The latter theory was strongly supported by the diffraction experiments in 1801 of the British physicist Thomas Young, whose results could not be explained in terms of the corpuscular theory. The theory was also supported by the theoretical prediction proposed by the Scottish physicist James Maxwell of electromagnetic radiation (consisting of oscillating electric and magnetic fields moving as a wave), whose properties were identical to those of light. This radiation was thought to require a special all-pervading medium, the ether, in which to propagate.

In 1905, the German-born physicist Albert Einstein modified the quantum theory put forward by the German physicist Max Planck in 1900. Einstein showed that when light is emitted or absorbed it behaves like a particle (known as a photon). The energy of a photon depends inversely on the wavelength of the associated electromagnetic wave—that is, short wavelengths are most energetic, and long wavelengths the least. The real nature of light is not easy to imagine, and it is simplest to regard it as a wave–particle duality, with the two aspects being important in different circumstances. Einstein's Special Theory of Relativity also did away with the necessity for an ether to transmit the radiation.

Light of only one wavelength is termed monochromatic, and it is usually incoherent; that is, the light consists of short wave trains, or strings of waves, each lasting about one-hundred-millionth of a second, with the peaks and troughs of each wave train occurring randomly relative to every other wave train. The light of a laser owes its intensity partly to the fact that the peaks of all the wave trains are in phase: it is coherent.

Most of the objects we see are not self-luminous but are only visible by reflected light. If the surface has irregularities larger than the wavelength of light, the reflection is diffuse, the light being scattered back in all directions. At a very smooth surface, however, light is reflected specularly. It is reflected back in such a way that the angle the ray makes with the perpendicular to the surface is equal to that made by the incident ray. These conditions make possible the formation of images.

If the body does not strongly absorb or reflect light, but is transparent, the light will pass through it. The velocity of light is different in different media, and consequently, the ray changes direction at the surface. This phenomenon, refraction, affects each wavelength to a different extent, and so the incident light is spread out according to wavelength.

Wavelengths

White light comprises a large number of colors, which constitute the spectrum. Newton demonstrated the constituent colors of white light by passing it through a prism. He produced the colors of the rainbow, stretching from red at one end to violet at the other—the wavelength of red light is about 7.5×10^{-7} m, and the wavelength of violet light is about 4×10^{-7} m.

These wavelengths are the extremes of the visible spectrum, but there is the complete range of possible colors arranged seamlessly between the extremes (the order of the colors is red, orange,

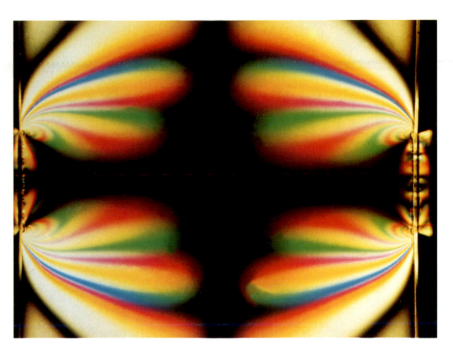

▲ Photoelastic stress analysis is a method of monitoring the forces within a structure under load. A model of the structure is made from clear plastic and loads are applied to it. When viewed in polarized light (light in which the waves vibrate in the same plane), patterns are produced to highlight the areas of stress. The brightest areas of the pattern are those where the stress within the model is at a maximum.

yellow, green, blue, indigo, violet). Physicists use devices called interferometers and spectrometers to measure light wavelengths accurately.

When physicists look at the light from a radiating source, they may be interested in a number of parameters. The spectral radiancy of the source is the rate at which energy from light of a particular range of wavelengths is radiated per unit area of the surface of the source. Physicists may also be interested simply in the radiancy of the source, which is the total amount of energy being emitted per unit area of the source. In the case of radiancy, the energy of all the wavelengths being emitted by the source has to be considered.

Every material has a family of spectral radiancy curves, obtained by plotting the spectral radiancy against wavelength. The shape of the curve varies according to the temperature of the light source. Spectral radiancy curves are often compared with that of a theoretical ideal, the cavity radiator. The light-emitting properties of such a radiator are independent of material and vary in a simple way with temperature. Max Planck's work on cavity radiation in 1900 was important in laying the foundations of quantum physics.

Beyond the visible spectrum

An enormous range of wavelengths that cannot be detected by the human visual system lies on either side of the visible spectrum. Strictly speaking, light is just a small part of the complete range of electromagnetic radiation.

Below the longest red wavelengths is a range known as infrared with wavelengths from about 7.5×10^{-7} m to about 0.001 m. They are sometimes called—a little misleadingly—heat rays. Past the violet wavelengths is the ultraviolet

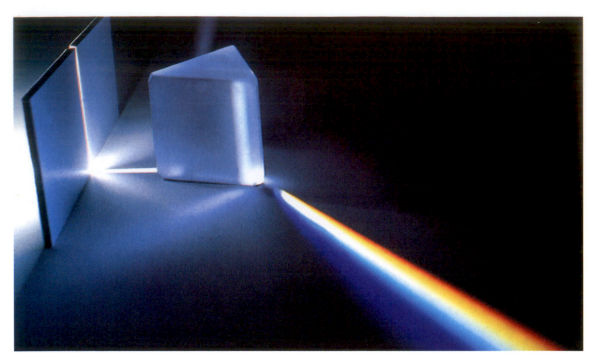

◀ Newton's famous experiment with a single beam of light and a transparent prism. The refractive qualities of the glass splits white light into its constituent colors, from violet through yellow and green to red.

range, with wavelengths of between 4×10^{-7} and 0.01×10^{-7} m. These wavelengths are the ones that cause suntans and, in extreme circumstances, may cause sunburn.

The complete range of electromagnetic radiation is enormous. Gamma rays have the shortest wavelengths—less than 1×10^{-11} m, while radio waves may be up to 6 miles (10 km) long.

Diffraction

If a beam of light passes through a wide slit and falls onto a screen, a sharp-edged path of light is obtained. As the slit is narrowed, however, the light spreads into the shadow region. This bending of light, known as diffraction, becomes more pronounced as the slit width decreases and is a maximum when the width is of the same order of size as the wavelength of the light used. The effect can be explained by considering that any point on a wave front can itself act as a source of waves. Thus, the slit behaves as a secondary source from which light is transmitted or radiated in all directions.

Interference

Two light waves that coincide at a point can interfere with each other. If the crests of one wave coincide with the crests of the other, they are said to be in phase and they reinforce each other, resulting in an area of brightness. If the crests of one coincide with the troughs of the other, they are out of phase and tend to cancel each other, leaving an area of darkness. These conditions define constructive and destructive interference, and between these extremes, the waves partly reinforce or cancel each other, depending on their phase relationship. An essential condition

for interference is that the sources must be coherent, that is, they must have the same frequency and exhibit the same changes of phase. In practice, this condition is most easily realized when an incident light wave interacts with its reflection.

This is the process responsible for the colors observable in soap bubbles and in thin oil films. Interference patterns produced under controlled conditions can be used as an accurate means of measuring the wavelength of light. An example is the Newton's rings interference pattern in which a path difference is produced when light passes across a wedge-shaped air gap.

Reflection and refraction

The formation of sharp-edged shadows by solid objects placed in the path of a beam of light shows that light can travel in straight lines. The velocity at which it travels through any material is a constant for that material and the maximum value is for light traveling through a vacuum—that is, 186,282.4 miles per second (299,792.5 km/s). When a light beam is traveling in a homogeneous (continuous) medium, it travels in a straight line. When, however a ray of light strikes the interface between two different transparent media, such as glass and air, it generally separates into two

◀ This apparent bending of a straight stick in water is caused by light refraction.

weaker rays. One is reflected back into the first medium, and the other is refracted: that is, it enters the second medium but changes velocity and consequently changes its direction whenever it enters at an angle.

The direction of travel of a ray is specified by the angle it makes with the perpendicular, or normal, at the point where the ray strikes the interface, the point of incidence. The incoming ray and this normal together define a plane, the plane of incidence. On reflection, the reflected ray lies in the plane of incidence, and the angle of reflection is equal to the angle of incidence. For refraction, the refracted ray lies in the plane of incidence, and its direction of travel is determined by the refractive index of the material under consideration. The index of refraction for any material is the ratio of the velocity of light in the material to the velocity of light in a vacuum or, for most practical purposes, in air. This index (*n*) can be calculated by the following equation:

$$n = c/v$$

In 1621, the Dutch scientist W. Snell discovered that refractive indices could be related to the angles of incidence and refraction (Snell's law) in the following way:

$$n_1 \, sin(\theta_1) = n_2 \, sin(\theta_2)$$

When light travels from a dense into a less-dense medium, for example, from glass to air, for angles of incidence greater than a certain limiting value—the critical angle—the refracted ray disappears and all the light is reflected. This condition is termed total internal reflection and is of considerable importance as the principle governing the use of prisms in optical instruments, such as binoculars, and in the behavior of glass fibers in fiber-optic devices.

Polarization

The vibrations of the electric and magnetic fields of light rays are at right angles to the direction the light is traveling—its direction of propagation. Around the direction of the light are an infinite number of possible directions that are at right angles to it. Therefore, the vibrations associated with light are almost certainly going to be random.

If light passes through a crystalline medium, the situation changes. The crystal will only allow through light waves with one or two directions. Passing through a second suitably cut crystal, the emergent light will have only one direction of vibration—the light has been polarized.

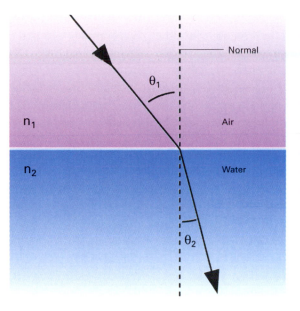

◀ When light moves from one medium to another, it changes speed and therefore direction. Every transparent material causes light to change speed and direction in a specific way. The sine of θ_1 and θ_2 and the indices of refraction n_1 and n_2 are related by Snell's law.

Synthetically produced polarizing sheet is a material that renders light polarized in one plane. It consists of a parallel arrangement of crystals that resolves the direction of the incident vibrations into two directions mutually at right angles and then absorbs one of these components and transmits the other. If two similar sheets of material are placed with their crystal row directions at right angles to each other, light is totally obscured.

In many crystals, such as quartz and calcite, the two perpendicular components of the light vibration are transmitted at different velocities and so travel in different directions through the crystal. These directions are specified by two different refractive indices. The numerical difference between these indices is called the birefringence of the crystal, and such behavior is termed double refraction.

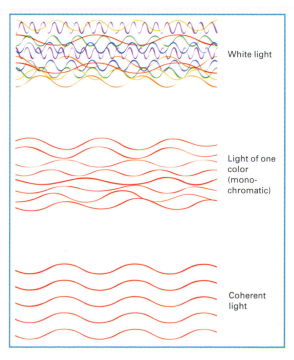

◀ White light is incoherent—the peaks and troughs of each wave occur randomly and the wavelengths vary. Monochromatic light is all of the same wavelength but the waves are not in phase. The light of a laser is coherent—the wavelengths are the same and the peaks and troughs are in phase.

Vision

When light reaches the eye, it is focused onto the retina, the sensitive screen at the back of the eye, mainly by refraction at the front of the transparent window at the front of the eye (the cornea). Adjustments to the focusing, in order to accommodate objects at different distances, are made by changing the shape of the crystalline lens by means of the ciliary muscles. The iris controls the amount of light entering the eye by altering the size of the pupil—from 0.08 in. (2 mm) in bright sunlight to 0.3 in. (8 mm) at night. The spaces between the cornea and lens and between the lens and the retina are filled with viscous liquids, the aqueous and vitreous humors, respectively.

The light-sensitive nerve cells in the retina are of two types: the rods, which detect only the light intensity, and the cones, which also respond to wavelength (color). The most sensitive part of the retina (the fovea) contains only cones, while there is a small region where the nerves and blood vessels pass through the back of the eyeball that has no receptor cells at all and is known as the blind spot.

Velocity of light

The velocity at which light travels in a vacuum is fundamental to modern physics. According to relativity theory, it is identical for all observers, whatever their own velocity, and it is also the limiting speed at which any material object can travel. The first measurement of the velocity of light (usually denoted c) was made in 1676 by the Danish astronomer Olaus Roemer, who observed that the movements of the satellites of Jupiter differ from the predictions, because the time taken for light to reach Earth varies as Jupiter and the Earth move around their orbits.

Until the development of electronics after World War II, the most accurate measurements of c were made by timing a light ray over an accurately measured distance, as the method devised by the French physicist Armand Fizeau first demonstrated in 1849. At the far end, a mirror reflected the light back to the observer, who measured the short time taken by means of a rapidly rotating toothed wheel. The outgoing light is chopped into bursts by the teeth, and at a critical wheel-rotation velocity, the teeth will have advanced far enough to cut off these bursts when they are reflected back. At this wheel velocity, the reflected light is seen to become dim, and the time taken for the light to make the return journey can be calculated from the rotation velocity of the wheel and the number of teeth on it. Later and more accurate experiments, by the U.S. physicists Albert Michelson and Edward Morley, used revolving mirrors instead of toothed wheels and enclosed the entire light path in a vacuum chamber to minimize the effects of air.

The most accurate measurements of c have been made recently using radar techniques to

◀ The colors in these iridescent cirrus clouds are caused by the refraction of light through tiny ice particles in a process called irisation. This rare phenomenon accounts for the color seen on clouds around midnight (noctilucent clouds) in latitudes greater than about 50 degrees—the ice particles refract light that has been reflected from below the horizon. Irisation also accounts for the mother-of-pearl coloration seen on nacreous clouds.

measure separately the frequency and the wavelength of microwaves, another form of electromagnetic radiation, and give the result $c = 186,282$ miles per second (299,792 km/s).

Optics

Optics, the branch of physics that deals with the properties of light, may be conveniently divided into three main categories. These are geometric, physical, and quantum optics.

Geometric optics deals primarily with rays of light. The laws of reflection and refraction of light are the rules on which the study of geometric optics is based and provide all the information required for predicting and locating the images formed by optic systems involving plane (flat) and curved mirrors and lenses.

Physical optics is concerned with the nature of light and its consequent properties and deals with light in terms of waves. Many optical effects cannot be explained by a single geometric approach, and such phenomena as diffraction, interference, and polarization can be understood only by considering that light is radiated as a series of waves.

Quantum optics deals with the interaction of light with the atomic entities of matter. The wave theory of light is unable to provide an explanation of interactions of light and matter on an atomic scale, and associated phenomena remained inexplicable until Albert Einstein postulated in 1905 that a light wave consists of small, highly localized packets, or bundles, of energy called light quanta, or photons. Subsequent work by Neils Bohr and others confirmed the existence of photons, and the experimental evidence in support of the theoretical concept soon became conclusive.

The Compton Effect and the Photoelectric Effect are two phenomena that require the concept of photons for complete explanation. When radiation is incident upon an atom, its direction is changed and its frequency decreased. This is the Compton Effect, and it is explained by considering an elastic collision between particles, namely an incident photon and an electron in the atom, like a collision between two billiard balls. The Photoelectric Effect, in which light striking a metal surface causes electrons to be released, results from photons in the incident beam providing energy to the bombarded electrons, enabling them to escape from the metal.

Emission of light energy by the processes of fluorescence and phosphorescence relies on the increase of the energy of electrons within the atom—atomic excitation. The electrons associated with an atom occupy a limited number of discrete energy levels and can move to higher energy levels only by the provision of discrete

UNCORRECTED LENSES

When light shines through an uncorrected lens, aberrations occur and show up as imperfections in the refracted image. In the case of eyesight, problems such as these can be rectified by the wearing of glasses.

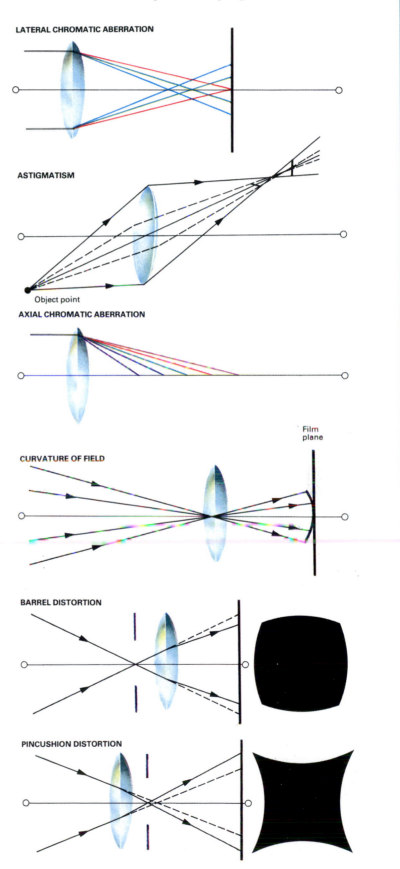

LATERAL CHROMATIC ABERRATION

ASTIGMATISM

Object point

AXIAL CHROMATIC ABERRATION

Film plane

CURVATURE OF FIELD

BARREL DISTORTION

PINCUSHION DISTORTION

bundles of energy provided by photons of the incident light beam.

The relatively modern development of quantum optics has resulted in a much fuller understanding of optical phenomena and has already led to the development of new technologies, such as those associated with the laser.

Optics production

Methods of producing optical components, such as lenses, mirrors, and prisms, have hardly changed in principle since the 17th century. The main requirements are that the optical surface should be polished to a highly accurate shape or figure—part of a sphere for lenses and some mirrors, flat for plane mirrors and prisms. The accuracy required is extremely high by normal standards, because the surfaces have to be smoother than the size of the waves they are to reflect or refract.

These measurements are so small that they are referred to in terms of the wavelength of light, usually the yellow sodium or green mercury spectral lines from discharge tubes, with wavelengths of about 0.00002 in. (0.5 µm). Thus, a surface with a half-wave error would be true to one-hundred-thousandth of an inch (0.25 µm). Because reflection bends light through twice the angle of incidence, mirrors need finer surfaces than lenses.

The principle that has always been used to produce both curved and flat surfaces is that if

▲ A solar halo with two bright spots on either side of the sun, known as sundogs. Both of these phenomena are caused by light refracting through hexagonal ice crystals in cirrostratus clouds. The hexagonal structure of the crystals refracts the light in such a way that the angle between the sun, the observer, and the halo is always 22 degrees. On rare occasions, a secondary halo and attendant sundogs can form at 46 degrees.

two disks of material are rubbed together with an abrasive material between them, their irregularities will eventually be smoothed out. If the rubbing motion is back and forth, it might be thought that the result would be a flat surface on both disks. In fact, both become curved, the lower stationary one becoming convex (bulging upward) and the upper moving one becoming concave (with a hollowed-out center). To ensure a completely symmetrical surface, the lower disk is usually rotated while the upper one is both moved across it and rotated in the opposite direction. A machine can perform both these operations. The curve that results from this process will be nearly spherical. Most optical work relies on this principle even if the components are to be made deliberately nonspherical (aspheric) later on.

Cutting the glass

The raw glass is sawed to outline with a smooth circular saw (or bandsaw) impregnated with diamonds, cooled by a water-soluble oil, which cuts glass quickly. Although a delicate material, glass can be machined almost in the same way as metal, using diamond tools. It can be turned in a lathe, have holes drilled in it, or have rough figuring generated on it with a milling machine.

Components thus machined need only one or two successively finer abrasives (usually aluminum oxide powder or garnet with water) to produce a surface smooth enough for polishing. The smoothing operation can be done by machine with a number of components stuck (blocked) with wax or pitch to a jig of the right curve. This block is then worked on an iron tool that has been previously trued up on a keeper of opposite form (that is, a convex tool has a concave keeper, and vice versa). The resulting spherical curve can be checked by optical means or by a spherometer—an instrument that measures the depth of the curve across the lens.

Polishing

Precision polishing is usually done on a preformed polisher made of pitch (refined from wood or coal) using cerium oxide as a polishing agent. Low-quality components may be polished on felt pads instead of pitch, and some optics require special polishing agents. Pitch is a viscous liquid that conforms slowly to any components worked on it. Some of the skill of optical work is concerned with choosing the correct hardness of pitch, because the flowing action of the polisher, changing shape as the work progresses, is critical.

Other problems are flexure of the glass and the heat produced by friction during work. The glass cools more readily at the edge than the cen-

◀ Drops of water in the atmosphere can split white light into a spectrum of colors, forming a rainbow in the same way as does a glass prism.

FACT FILE

- *Eyeglasses developed in the United States emit light from diodes etched into the glass. Designed for the deaf, the diodes are linked to a minicomputer that interprets sounds as visual cues to aid lip reading.*

- *The mercury bulbs at the top of the Empire State Building each have a rating of 450 million candlepower. The lights are visible from 80 miles (130 km) away on land and 300 miles (480 km) away from the air.*

- *The shortest pulse of light ever achieved was reported by the Massachusetts Institute of Technology in May 1984. The pulse of eight wavelengths lasted for just 15 femtoseconds, that is, 15×10^{-15} seconds.*

- *Scientists at the Massachusetts Institute of Technology (MIT) have invented a "perfect mirror." Unlike conventional mirrors, made of glass and a thin layer of reflecting metal, the perfect mirror is a form of dielectric mirror, made of layers of transparent materials that do not conduct electricity. Because dielectric mirrors do not conduct electricity, they absorb fewer electromagnetic waves than conventional mirrors and are thus capable of reflecting light more efficiently. Most dielectric mirrors reflect light only within certain specific wavelengths and within certain angles of incidence. The perfect mirror, however, is capable of reflecting all wavelengths of light from all angles with almost no loss of strength. Scientists hope this mirror will find applications in areas such as improved coaxial cables and thermoelectric devices.*

- *Lasers are used to produce individual light-scatter identity patterns for valuable diamonds. Subjected to laser light, no two gems produce the same pattern. The patterns are recorded by instant picture photography and filed for identification in theft cases. The gem-print method has been successful in several cases and is used by many police forces, as well as by the FBI.*

ter and thus introduces an important variable in high-quality work. This problem has been partly alleviated by the development of glass and ceramics having a zero coefficient of expansion over a wide range of temperatures. This glass, however, is suitable only for reflecting components, rather than lenses, because of its crystalline structure.

After testing, the components are unblocked and the reverse sides smoothed and polished if required. Prisms, which have flat faces, are held in metal jigs or plaster blocks in a similar way. Prism angles are checked optically in an angle dekkor, which compares the job with a master prism of known angle. Correction of the angle is often made by hand (by putting more pressure on one end or the other), and accuracies of half a second of arc can be achieved.

Larger optics—say, above 4 in. (10 cm) diameter—highly curved, or best-quality components have to be worked singly, making them relatively expensive. Aspherics of any quality are made partly by machine but finished by hand.

Testing

There are a number of ways in which the various types of optical components can be tested. The most common is to place the surface under test against a reference surface of the shape and accuracy required. As long as the two are approximately the same, Newton's rings (concentric interference fringes) will be seen. If the two surfaces are exactly the same, no fringes will be observed.

For nonstandard surfaces and for producing the reference surfaces, other optical tests are used, the simplest being the Foucault test. It uses a knife edge to cut off rays coming from the component that do not go exactly to the focus required.

Another test involves the interferometry of light when comparing an image with a copy of the object, a ground-glass scatter plate, that produced the image. This test shows up the size of errors in the image, rather than on the optical surface.

SEE ALSO: DIFFRACTION • ELECTROMAGNETIC RADIATION • GLASS • LENS • MIRROR • POLARIZATION • PRISM • REFLECTOR • WAVE MOTION

Lightbulb

If sufficient electric current can be passed through a conducting filament, the electrons in the filament become excited and the filament becomes hot and eventually glows. This is the principle of the lightbulb (more correctly, an incandescent filament lamp).

After many experiments with incandescent, metallic filaments in the mid 1800s, the first lightbulbs to show signs of becoming practical light sources were devised independently by Thomas Edison in the United States and Sir Joseph Swan in Britain in 1878. Swan's first lamp comprised a carbon filament made from vegetable fiber sealed in a glass envelope with platinum wire leads. The envelope was evacuated to quite a high vacuum, but oxygen trapped in the filament material was liberated during operation and, together with the nonuniform cross section of the filament, led to a short life.

By 1905, however, filaments were being made from a cellulose solution extruded through dies and then carbonized. Lamps using these filaments were commercially available and achieved a light output of about 2 to 3 lumens for every watt of electric energy supplied to the bulb (usually written as lm/W). A lumen is the amount of light falling per second on a unit area placed at unit distance from a small light source with an output of one candela. Attention was soon turned to the use of metal filaments in an attempt to improve efficiency. In 1909, the practical problems of drawing tungsten into a fine wire were solved, and because it has a melting point of 6120°F (3382°C), it could be operated at temperatures considerably higher than previously possible, with resulting benefits in light output.

Gas-filled bulbs

The life of the filament bulb depends upon the rate at which the metal filament evaporates, which in turn depends upon the temperature at which it operates. In 1913, it was discovered that filling the evacuated bulb with an inert gas, such as nitrogen, retarded the rate of evaporation, thus prolonging the useful life. Filling with gas, however, had the disadvantage that convection currents in the gas reduced the filament temperature and hence the light output. It was not until 1918 that forming the filament into a fine coil was introduced.

Coiling the filament and later coiling the coil (1934) maintained the filament temperature and is the basis of the bulbs used today. The standard

▲ Three 100 W lightbulbs (from left to right): halogen, pearl envelope, and clear envelope. The halogen bulb has a tungsten filament surrounded by low-pressure iodine gas and a quartz glass inner envelope. The other bulbs are conventional domestic bulbs, with a tungsten filament surrounded by an inert mixture of nitrogen and argon. They operate at lower temperatures than halogen bulbs, giving a warmer color.

pear-shaped bulb is known as a General Lighting Service (GLS) bulb and is available in a range of wattages from 5 to 1,000 W with efficiencies ranging from 8 lm/W to nearly 19 lm/W, depending upon wattage.

Types of filament bulb

Most mass-produced filament bulbs are of the GLS type, but the range of other types runs into many thousands. They include bulbs smaller than a grain of rice devised for medical instruments, bulbs larger than a basketball found in lighthouses, reflector bulbs with sufficient energy at the focus to light a cigar, and reflector bulbs designed to let most of the heat escape from the back of the bulbs, long-life bulbs that last 5 to 10 times as long as ordinary incandescent bulbs, as well as decorative bulbs of dozens of different shapes and several colors and ratings. One particular type is of special interest because it represents the most significant advance in the technological development of filament bulbs since 1934.

Tungsten halogen lamps

Originally called quartz iodine bulbs because of the materials used in early examples, the tungsten halogen bulb is conspicuous for its small physical size, unlike GLS bulbs of similar ratings.

The principle of the bulb's construction involves introducing a halogen, such as iodine (although bromine and fluorine are also used), into the gas filling, which combines with tungsten evaporated from the filament to form tungsten iodide. The evaporated tungsten is prevented from condensing on the lamp envelope and blackening it. The tungsten-iodide vapor is circulated within the bulb by convection until it approaches the filament, where at a temperature of more than 3632°F (2000°C) the vapor breaks down and some of the tungsten is redeposited on the filament; the iodine is then available for further combination. Because this cycle will function only at temperatures above 480°F (250°C), the bulb must be kept small to reduce its heat loss. This means that the filament is much closer to the lamp envelope, which is therefore much hotter than the glass on an ordinary incandescent bulb.

The main advantages of tungsten halogen bulbs are that the light output is maintained throughout the life of the bulb and that the filament can be run at a higher temperature, giving 20 to 22 lm/W and a much whiter light. Also, because evaporation is reduced, a life of more than 4,000 hours is readily achieved. The small physical size lends itself to precise optical control, and sizes currently in general use range from 50 to 55 W, for shop spotlights and automobile aux-

iliary lighting, to 10 kW bulbs for floodlighting. It has been suggested that even lower wattage bulbs enclosed in a diffusing bulb of normal size could be the domestic bulb of the future, but present costs of materials make this unlikely.

Fluorescent bulbs

A different replacement for the conventional lightbulb is provided by various types of fluorescent tube. The tube is folded into a compact shape and combined with a starter to give a direct plug-in replacement for the filament bulb.

Unlike conventional incandescent bulbs, fluorescent bulbs do not have a filament. Instead, the bulb contains mercury vapor and argon through which a stream of electrons is passed. The electrons cause the mercury vapor and argon mixture to become ionized and emit ultraviolet light. The inner surface of the glass tube is coated with a layer of phosphors, such as magnesium tungstate or zinc silicate, which absorb ultraviolet radiation and reemit this energy by fluorescing, giving off visible light. In tungsten filament bulbs, much energy is used in heating the filament in order to make it glow white hot and give off visible light. Fluorescent bulbs, however, do not emit light as a result of heating and therefore operate at lower temperatures than incandescent bulbs and use considerably less energy.

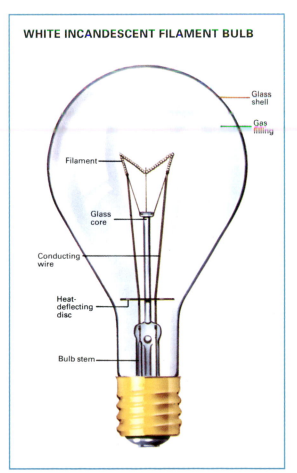

WHITE INCANDESCENT FILAMENT BULB

Glass shell

Gas filling

Filament

Glass core

Conducting wire

Heat-deflecting disc

Bulb stem

◄ An incandescent filament bulb is blown automatically from a continuous stream of a special high-purity glass. The tungsten wire for the filament is drawn from a coherent ductile rod. The filament of this bulb is a coil that is itself coiled.

Manufacture

The GLS bulbs of domestic size are made on automatic machines at a rate of up to 5,000 per hour. A specialized high-purity glass is fed in a continuous stream to the bulb-making machine, which first thickens the glass at regular intervals and then blows this thickened portion into a mold to form the bulb shape. The bulbs then move to a cooler, where they are cut off from the ribbon and drop onto a conveyor belt.

The tungsten wire for the filament is drawn from a coherent ductile rod made by subjecting tungsten powder to great pressure. The diameter of the filament wire is about 0.0006 in. (0.014 mm) for a 15 W bulb or 0.0017 in. (0.042 mm) for the 100 W. Because of the difficulty of measurement, the correctness of the filament is checked by weighing measured lengths, and the maximum variation is about 2 percent or, for the 15 W bulb, a tolerance of only 0.000006 in. (0.00014 mm) or a quarter of the mean wavelength of visible light. The filament is then wound around a mandrel to form the coil and then around another mandrel if it is to be a coiled coil. After annealing, the mandrels are dissolved in acid, and the filaments are reannealed and examined.

Automatic machines mount the filament to the stem assembly, clamping the ends to the lead-out wires. The mounted stem is fed into the neck of the glass bulb and fused to ensure a good seal. The bulb is then evacuated and flushed with gas until the residual oxygen is no more than 5 to 10 parts per million. The cap is then cemented to the bulb and the lead-out wires soldered to the contacts.

▲ Lightbulb manufacture is highly mechanized. These European bulbs are being filled with an argon and nitrogen gas mixture.

SEE ALSO:	Discharge tube • Glass • Halogen • Light and optics • Lighthouse and lightship • Noble gas • Vacuum

Lighthouse and Lightship

Until the introduction of lighthouses, the usual way to mark the entrance to harbors or the presence of rocks or sandbanks was with a beacon made up of a pile of stones or wooden spars. These are still used in small harbors, and more elaborate masts and pillars are widely used.

The first lighthouse of which there is any record was the Pharos of Alexandria, Egypt, a huge structure built by Ptolemy in the third century B.C.E. It has been estimated that the tower was built on a base 100 ft. (30.5 m) square and was 450 ft. (137 m) high. The Pharos survived until about 1200 C.E., when it was destroyed by an earthquake; it gave its name to pharology, the science of lighthouse building.

The Romans built many notable lighthouses, such as that at Ostia (the chief port for Rome) and others in Spain, France, and Britain. Following the fall of the Roman Empire, navigational aids fell into disuse. Once again it was left to individual ports to set up and maintain their own lights.

From about the 11th century, the increase in sea trading led to a revival of interest in lighthouses. Progress was slow, but in Europe from about 1600, there was an increase in lighthouse building, culminating in the great era of lighthouse construction in the 18th and 19th centuries.

Lights

The most important feature of a lighthouse is its light, and the efficiency of the lights has increased as technology has advanced. The first lights burned wood, which burns too quickly. Coal and candles were also used, but coal gave off so much smoke that soot collected on the lantern panes and blocked the light. Candles could not produce a satisfactory level of illumination no matter how many were used.

Lighthouse illumination did not become really efficient until the early 1780s, when the Swiss engineer Aimé Argand invented the type of oil burner that bears his name. It used a circular wick surrounded by a glass chimney, which created a central, upward draught of air to assist the burning. This lamp produced a steady smokeless flame of high intensity, and it remained the principal source of light for over 100 years.

The Argand burner was adapted for use in domestic gas lighting, and it was gas lighting technology that contributed to the next major advance in oil burners for lighthouses. The Argand lamp used a wick from which the oil vaporized for burning, but in 1901, Arthur Kitson produced a burner in which the oil was vaporized

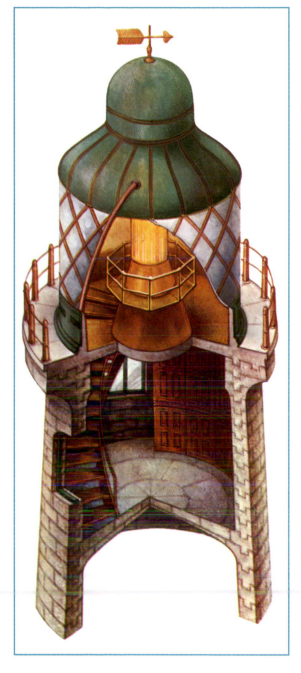

◀ A cross section of an offshore lighthouse built of interlocking stone blocks. This type of construction gives a strong, stable structure that can withstand the action of the strongest winds and of high, breaking seas.

in a copper tube placed above the mantle (adapted from a gas mantle). The vapor passed from the coiled tube to be burned in the mantle, like gas. The oil was vaporized by the heat from the mantle, with a blow lamp being used to heat the coil to light the lamp. The Kitson design was improved by David Hood in 1921, and this type of burner is still widely used where electric lighting is impractical. Many unattended lights burn acetylene gas.

Electric lighting was first tried in the South Foreland light on the Kent coast, England, in 1858, using a carbon arc lamp. In 1862, the installation of arc lamps at the Dungeness light, also in Kent, followed. Arc lamps did not, however, prove to be satisfactory in lighthouses.

The first electric filament lamps were also used at the South Foreland light, in 1922, and many lighthouses now use electric lights—high-powered filament lamps of several thousand watts or high-pressure xenon and mercury-arc lamps. It is possible to see the light up to 30 miles (50 km) away.

Optical systems

The development of efficient light sources led to the development of reflector systems, because without some form of beam projection much of the intensity of the light is wasted. The three main groups of optical systems used in lighthouses are the catoptric (reflective), the dioptric (refractive), and the catadioptric (reflective and refractive).

The first parabolic reflector, designed in 1752 by William Hutchinson, was made up of small squares of mirrored glass set in plaster of paris. The parabolic reflector is placed behind the light source, and the rays of light are reflected parallel to the axis of the reflector and emerge as a beam of light. Reflectors made from a hand-beaten composition of copper and silver soon replaced the heavy glass reflectors, and by 1800, they were standard equipment.

The use of a reflector increased the power of the light by about 350 times, and with the problem of beam projection overcome, the question of individual light characteristics for each lighthouse could be addressed. This question arose because shipowners often complained that although lighthouses were useful, it was difficult to tell them apart; they all emitted the same signal. This problem was solved by arranging reflectors in different positions on a frame and revolving it, producing groups of flashes (two or three in quick succession, followed by a period of darkness, then the flashes again).

The most important development in lighthouse engineering was the Fresnel lens, invented by Augustin Fresnel in 1822. This is a dioptric lens, with a central bullseye lens surrounded by concentric rings of prismatic glass, each ring projecting a little way beyond the previous one. The overall effect of this arrangement is to refract (bend) into a horizontal beam most of the rays of light from a central lamp. Further reflecting elements may be placed above and below the refracting prisms to form a catadioptric arrangement.

Sometimes two lenses are placed one above the other with a light at the center of each; and this is called a biform optic. Many refinements have been made to Fresnel's original design, but the basic principle is essentially the same today.

Improved methods of producing and finishing glass and the development of plastics have made it possible to reduce the size and weight of optical systems. This advance, together with the improvement in light sources, has enabled more efficient and compact apparatus to be produced.

Construction

Most lighthouses are built of stone or precast concrete, and some are many miles offshore. The Eddystone light, for example, stands on a rock in the English Channel some 13 miles (21 km) from Plymouth, England. The present structure is the fourth to be built on the site and was completed in 1881. The original was a wooden tower, built in 1698 by the English engineer Henry Winstanley, who was at the light in 1703 when it was washed away during a severe storm. The second one, also of wood, was built by John Rudyerd in 1708 and survived until 1755, when it burned down.

The third and most famous Eddystone light was designed by John Smeaton and completed in 1759, using a hydraulic cement he had invented, with the stone blocks dovetailed together for strength. Erosion of the rock on which it was built necessitated its replacement by the present light, which was built nearby, using an even more complex dovetailing arrangement than Smeaton's.

Where a suitable rock foundation is unavailable, for instance, if the hazard is a sandbank or coral reef, the light can be built on steel piles or concrete-filled caisson foundations.

Lighthouses are usually equipped with some form of siren or horn, which is sounded in foggy or misty weather and may be controlled by an automatic electronic fog detector. Radar responder beacons are also used for identification, transmitting only in response to an interrogation signal from a ship's radar.

Many lighthouses are now automated—all of the lighthouses in Britain are unattended, largely

▼ A view of part of the lens system of the Oigh Sgeir lighthouse on the coast of Cana, one of the Hebridean islands off the coast of Scotland. Oigh Sgeir warns shipping of the many dangerous rocks in the vicinity. Even in the stormiest weather, the light can be seen from many miles away.

AUTOMATED LIGHTSHIPS

In some locations, several LANBYs are monitored from one master control station, as here. Spaced along the Atlantic coast, they are controlled from Cape May, two directly by line-of-sight UHF and two, sited beyond horizon range, by radio to an automatic shore facility that then relays the information by a conventional land line. These unmanned stations can function for nearly a year before their generators have to be resupplied with fuel.

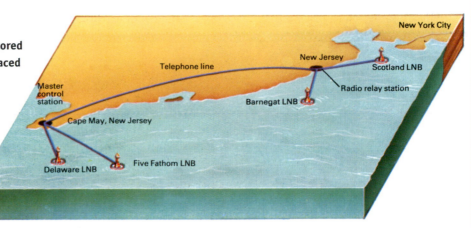

owing to advances in remote-control technology and the installation of helipads, which allow technicians to access the lights rapidly and easily.

Light vessels

The first light vessel (lightship) to go into service was moored near the Nore buoy in the Thames Estuary, England, in 1731, and was found to be of great benefit by shipowners, who willingly subscribed to her upkeep. The lighting consisted of two ship's lanterns mounted 12 ft. (3.7 m) apart on a cross beam on the single mast.

The light vessel was put on station by Robert Hamblin, who thought that navigation found it hard to distinguish one lighthouse from another and felt that light vessels should be moored at dangerous points around the coast, using different arrangements of lanterns to enable each station to be easily identified.

King George II granted a patent for the light vessel to run for 14 years from July 1730. Following the immediate success of the Nore vessel, the English lighthouse authority, Trinity House, became worried that light vessels would become so numerous as to upset the lighthouse system and eventually persuaded the king to revoke the patent in May 1732. The vessel had proved such a success, however, that it was impossible to remove it. Trinity House therefore obtained a patent in perpetuity and granted a lease for 61 years to Hamblin. After this breakthrough, light vessels became accepted as valuable aids to navigation, but no other country tried them until 1800, with the first used in the United States going on station in 1820.

In Britain, light vessels have no means of propulsion and are towed to and from stations. Each one remains on station for a three-year period before being put into dry dock and overhauled. Many other countries use self-propelled light vessels, including the United States and Germany.

The invention of the parabolic reflector made light vessel identification much easier, but the main problem was keeping the light steady. The solution was to mount the optic above a set of gimbal bearings and counterbalance it with a weight so that the optic would remain upright.

The lighting system now used in light vessels is multicatoptric, consisting of eight parabolic reflectors mounted in pairs, one above the other, with an electric filament lamp in each. These reflectors are mounted on a frame that is rotated by a small electric motor. By varying the angular position of the reflectors and the speed of rotation of the frame, it is possible to achieve single, double, triple, and quadruple flashing lights.

Many hundreds of lightships are in use around the world today. Some are manned, but there is an increasing trend toward automation. A typical automatic unit is the LANBY (large navigational buoy). These units have a disk-shaped hull 40 ft. (12 m) in diameter by 7½ ft. (2.3 m) deep and carry an electric light on a tower 40 ft. (12 m) above sea level. Diesel generators inside the hull provide power for the light with a ten-month fuel supply held in hull tanks. A light-sensitive cell switches the light on when required, while the operation can be monitored from a shore base over a UHF radio link.

◄ One of the four lightships that mark the Goodwin Sands, a dangerous stretch of shifting sands in the English Channel.

SEE ALSO: BUILDING TECHNIQUES • ELECTRICITY • EROSION • LIGHTBULB • REFLECTOR • WAVE MOTION

Lightning Conductor

Lightning is a visible electric discharge occurring in the atmosphere in areas highly charged with static electricity and is most usually associated with the thunder cloud cumulonimbus. Each thunder cloud is composed of a number of smaller clouds, or cells, each cell acting as an electric generator for up to an hour as a result of its powerful internal air currents. A cell can deliver several amperes (A) of electric current and can charge the cloud up to 50 million volts above ground potential. Lightning occurs when the charge has increased so much that the insulation of the air in the cloud breaks down.

If the lightning reaches Earth, a ground flash is the result. Electric measurements have shown that over 90 percent of ground flashes carry negative charge to Earth. High-speed photo-

▲ Lightning researchers at Cape Canaveral use a small rocket to trigger a bolt of lightning. The rocket was launched into a thunderstorm trailing a copper wire that acted as a lightning conductor—providing an easy path for the lightning to reach Earth. This technique allows researchers to measure the current and voltage of lightning strikes and to measure other parameters.

graphy has shown these negatively charged ground flashes to consist first of a leader discharge that travels downward from the cloud and displays much forking. This leader moves in a series of steps, each step having a length of about 160 ft. (50 m), with pauses between each step of about 50 millionths of a second, and it reaches the ground in a few thousandths of a second. When one of the branches of the leader is about 320 ft. (100 m) above Earth, upward leaders, or streamers, rise from the ground to meet it. Immediately after the first upward streamer has reached the leader, the negative charge collapses rapidly into the ground along the path of the streamer, and the main discharge is established. This main discharge, or return stroke, consists of a pulse of high current, typically around 20,000 A, that travels up the leader channel.

The first lightning conductor

When Benjamin Franklin, the philosopher, statesman, and scientist, first announced the invention of his lightning rod in 1753, he described its main function as being that of lightning prevention. He had observed that objects charged with static electricity in the laboratory could be discharged by holding a grounded metallic needle nearby, and he deduced that tall, pointed grounded rods on buildings would similarly discharge an overhead thunder cloud.

We now know that lightning conductors cannot release sufficient charge either to prevent lightning or to influence its production and that their sole function is the interception of ground flashes and the harmless dissipation to Earth of the current.

Cone of protection

Lightning conductors do not attract lightning. They do, however, provide a route of least resistance for the lightning to travel to Earth. This has the effect of protecting buildings from the potentially devastating effects of lightning strikes. Lightning can heat air to around 54,000°F (30,000°C), causing it to expand explosively. If lightning hits a building directly, this explosive effect can cause major structural damage. Lightning may also start fires and cause damage to electrical equipment such as televisions, computers, and telephone systems.

In the past, the range of protection lightning conductors gave to a building was thought to form a cone with an angle of 45 degrees to the vertical and with its apex at the top of the conduc-

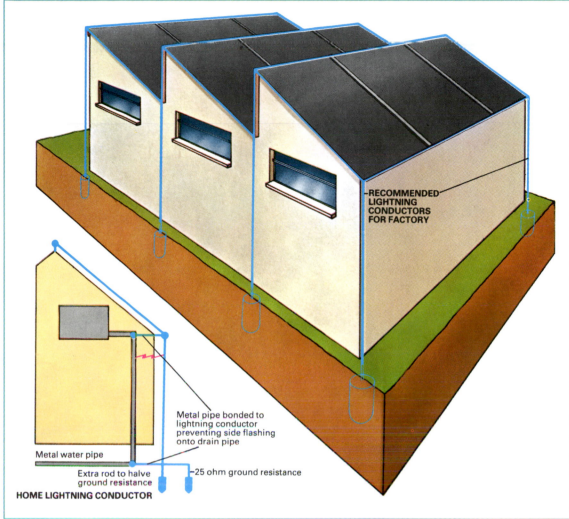

RECOMMENDED LIGHTNING CONDUCTORS FOR FACTORY

Metal pipe bonded to lightning conductor preventing side flashing onto drain pipe

Metal water pipe

Extra rod to halve ground resistance

25 ohm ground resistance

HOME LIGHTNING CONDUCTOR

LIGHTNING PROTECTION SYSTEM

Most modern building codes rarely recommend vertical rods, especially for buildings such as factories. Horizontal conductors along roof ridges and along vulnerable parts of the structure are best because they minimize the risk of side flash. On buildings with prominent vertical features, such as spires or pinnacles, a combination of vertical and horizontal conductors gives broader protection. The vertical conductors are placed on the spires and pinnacles and then connected to a grid of horizontal conductors that in turn lead to a series of down conductors.

tor. Any part of the building within this cone was thought to be safe from a lightning strike. Although this theory is still generally held to be true, lightning researchers have found that in some cases buildings have been struck on their sides in places within the cone of protection.

More sophisticated lightning protection systems, such as those used for historical buildings, may involve a series of vertical rods joined to horizontal conductors.

The down conductor

One or more down conductors may be led from a network of horizontal or vertical roof conductors, taking the shortest path to ground. The down conductor may be made of copper or aluminum wire 0.8 in. (2 cm) in diameter. The size of the down conductor is governed mainly by mechanical and corrosion considerations rather than by its current-carrying capacity. Although a lightning current can be very large, it is usually of such short duration that the heating effect is surprisingly insignificant, even in thin, high-resistance wires.

A good ground is essential for the satisfactory dissipation of the high impulse current from a lightning flash. The ground termination usually

consists of one or more metal rods driven into the soil, perhaps also with buried horizontal conductors in soils of low conductivity. Even with a good ground, however, other precautions are necessary. For example, with a single rod 1 in. (2.5 cm) in diameter and driven to a depth of 6 ft. (1.8 m) in soil of high conductivity, the ground resistance will be around 50 ohms. When passing a lightning current of 20,000 A, the voltage drop across the ground termination would be about one million volts. The whole down conductor would be at this voltage, and it could flash over into the protected building, which would still be at ground potential. This phenomenon is known as a side flash, and it is particularly hazardous when there are internal metallic services in the protected structure close to the down lead, especially if they are grounded separately. Side flashes are overcome by reducing the ground resistance as much as possible to minimize possible down-lead voltages and by connecting or bonding the down leads to any metallic services at risk inside the building.

SEE ALSO: CONDUCTION, ELECTRICAL • ELECTRICITY • THUNDERSTORM

Linear Motor

The usual shape of an electric motor is that of a cylinder, whether it be fed with alternating or direct current. Its job is to receive electric power input and to convert this, as efficiently as possible, into mechanical output by applying a twisting force to a central shaft so as to produce rotary motion. In perhaps 99 percent of all such machines, the outer part of the motor, a hollow iron cylinder having current-carrying coils, is the stationary part (the stator), usually secured to a bedplate on the floor. The inner cylinder, generally known as the rotor, is mounted on a bearing at each end of the machine.

Our understanding of the working principles of an electric motor (as with electromagnetism in general) is nothing more than the accumulated experience of the best ways of making such machines. There is no fundamental change in the action of a motor if it is built in such a way that its structure looks exactly like a rotary machine that has been sliced open along a radial plane and unrolled. Instead of producing a twisting force (or torque) on a rotary shaft, a linear motor produces force between primary and secondary members (the stator and rotor of ordinary motors) in a straight line.

Linear motors have found many uses in applications where accuracy and speed are required under heavy loads, such as in riveting or punching machines. Unlike conventional electric motors, they have only one moving part and do not need gears, ball bearings, or similar mechanical devices that are prone to wear or breakdown. Linear motors are also found powering conveyor belts, textile loom shuttles, and sliding doors. A more unusual type of linear motor can be found in an electromagnetic pump, which uses a liquid metal conductor instead of a solid one.

Types of motor

There are many different types of rotating electric motor, including induction, synchronous, reluctance, commutator (both AC and DC), and hysteresis motors. Each type has its linear counterpart. The most popular rotating motor, the induction motor, uses AC power directly and requires no brushes or rubbing contacts between stationary and moving parts. The robust nature of the rotor, which usually consists of copper or aluminum bars cast into slots in a steel cylinder and joined together at each end of the cylinder by a thick bar of the same metal as the bars, has resulted in over 95 percent of the world's electric drive power being of this type. For similar reasons, the linear induction motor has now also proved to be the most popular.

A glance at a linear motor shows at once that either its primary or secondary member must be extended or relative motion will separate the two very quickly. In the induction motor, it is less expensive to elongate the simpler cast secondary member, for it is cheaper to construct and does not require a supply of electric current. Even so, any substantial extension is expensive, and in 1903, the double-sided sandwich motor was developed, in which the secondary member was reduced to a single aluminum sheet.

This motor was rejected by industry on the grounds that because the magnetic field had to be

▲ Trains that run without rails are perhaps the most exciting example of linear motors in action. This Japanese experimental train achieved a world record speed of 342 mph (552 kph) in April 1999. Maglev trains, as they are called, work by the induction of magnetic force in electromagnetic coils lining the guideway that cause the train to levitate and glide at an

erator, consisting of a long tube surrounded by concentric coils. When the coils are fed with a polyphase supply, the result is a traveling electromagnetic wave. If a conductor is placed in the tube and the supply switched on, the conductor experiences a force and moves at the same velocity as the traveling wave. A powerful, fast-moving wave in a suitable tubular motor can be used as a missile launcher or some other kind of electromagnetic cannon.

Motor control

Linear induction motors are essentially constant-speed devices, and in most applications, a constant speed is no problem and can be an advantage. Despite this property, however, the speed of a linear induction motor can be controlled.

Four methods of speed control are frequency control, pole changing, adding a rotor or secondary resistance, and counter-rotor voltage control. Frequency control has become the most popular of the control methods, both because of its elegance (the speed of induction motors depends directly on the supply frequency) and because a ready-made device, the silicon-controlled rectifier, is available.

If the pole-changing method is used, individual stator coils are connected externally so that the polarity of adjacent coils may be made identical or opposite in polarity. If pairs of adjacent coils have the same polarity, the effective number of poles will be half the number when the coils have opposite polarity. In this situation, the synchronous speed will be doubled. The main drawback of pole changing is that control is not infinitely variable, and speed can be changed only in 2:1 steps.

Control by changing the rotor resistance is limited in its application to motors with a wound rotor. A simple external resistance applied to vary the motor speed can lead to considerable power losses, and extra equipment needs to be used to overcome this problem, adding considerably to the cost of the installation.

Linear motors in use

In practice, linear motors are extremely robust. Smaller motors can withstand immediate application of full voltage, but larger motors need to be protected from the large currents that occur during starting—often five times the running current is needed. If such large currents are allowed to flow through the windings, the motor may overheat, causing permanent damage.

A number of options are open to the designer of a large motor. If the starting load is to be applied only for a short period of time, an auto-

even distance above the track. The train also carries electromagnets in bogies fitted to its sides that repel the forces produced by the guideway magnets, and push the train forward. Because there is no physical contact, there are none of the mechanical stresses produced by conventional rail technology and maintenance costs are substantially lower.

driven through two air gaps plus the substantial thickness of nonmagnetic sheet that forms the secondary, its efficiency, power factor, power-to-weight ratio, and power-to-cost value were all bound to be much too low to be profitable. This belief continued until the late 1950s, when research at Manchester University, Britain, investigated some of the complex phenomena in linear motors, demonstrated how the motor's shortcomings could be made less severe than previously thought possible, and showed that in a number of applications the shortcomings were greatly outweighed by the advantages of direct linear drive.

A less common type of linear motor is the tubular motor. It resembles a linear particle accel-

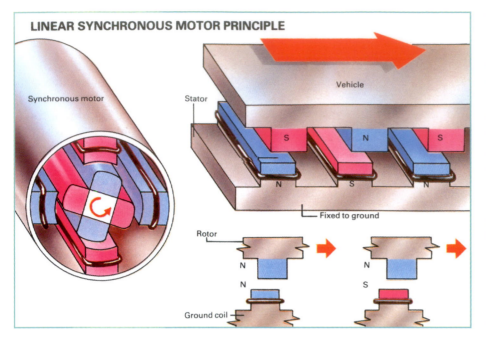

LINEAR SYNCHRONOUS MOTOR PRINCIPLE

Synchronous motor

Stator

Vehicle

S   N   S

N   S   N

Fixed to ground

Rotor

N

N

N

S

Ground coil

transformer—a transformer with primary and secondary windings as part of one coil—can be used to reduce the applied voltage by about 30 percent. The current is proportional to the square of the voltage, so the starting current will be reduced accordingly. A far simpler solution is to have resistors that can be switched in circuit during start-up to limit the current. Three-phase linear motors may be delta connected and thus will reduce both the voltage and the current drawn by the motor.

In addition to these preventive measures, sensors are usually employed to detect damaging temperature rises in use. Unfortunately if the sensors act to reduce power the linear motor will cease to function until it has cooled down—running a linear motor on drastically reduced power normally means that it fails to overcome gravity and/or friction.

Applications

Modern applications of linear motors may be divided into three classes. In the first class there are machines required to produce force with little or no movement. In the second, they are used to produce kinetic energy for such purposes as car-crash testing, rope testing, and metal forging. One particular machine that falls within this class was the electropult developed after World War II for catapulting aircraft. It never proceeded beyond the experimental stage, however, because of the invention of the steam catapult.

The third class contains the high-powered, high-speed motors currently being developed in Germany and Japan to propel high-speed vehicles. Here the efficiency of energy conversion is all-important. For this purpose there has been a

▲ The principle of the linear motor is essentially similar to that of a conventional motor, except that a linear motor provides motion in a straight line instead of in a circle. Linear motors are able to move the rotor relative to the stator without them coming into contact with each other, which reduces mechanical wear considerably.

▶ Linear motors have been used to produce high-speed train systems that work on the principle of magnetic levitation. The train is propelled forward by attractive or repulsive forces induced by electromagnets mounted in the train and the track.

return to the single-sided motor because the sandwich motor is unsafe at high speeds, owing to the secondary plate being flexible and the necessity of including temperature-expansion gaps at intervals along the track. Attention is also being focused on single-sided motors of the synchronous type, in which the magnetic field is created by DC currents in separately fed coils. The reason for this preference is that, although it is more complicated, the linear synchronous motor can run at a better power factor and higher efficiency and can be more easily integrated into a fully magnetic suspension system on the basis of the principle of the controlled electromagnet.

An interesting development consists of a twin-track motor in which the magnetic field paths are shortened by arranging them in planes transverse to the direction of motion. These motors are called transverse flux motors (TFM). One particular type of TFM has been designed in such a way that the moving member (which, unlike its rotary ancestor, can be either primary or secondary) can be freely suspended and guided by the same linear motor that drives it along. The resemblance to the action of bodies floating in flowing water has given rise to the name magnetic river for this type of motor, which may find a use in advanced materials-handling applications.

Linear motors have been used in conveyor belts, the linear movement imparted by this kind of motor being a far more elegant way of moving the belts than using the conventional rotating motor. Curtain rods and sliding doors have also seen the application of linear motors. In fact, sliding doors are possibly the largest application of linear motors in the world today. More surprising applications have included the electromagnetic pump. In this device, a conducting fluid, such as mercury or liquid sodium-potassium alloy (NaK),

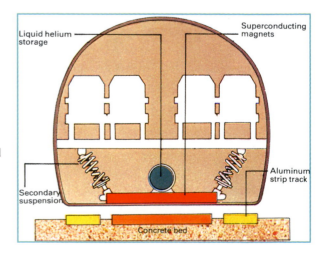

Liquid helium storage

Superconducting magnets

Secondary suspension

Aluminum strip track

Concrete bed

acts as the rotor. Experiments in Japan with a speedboat, using the electric properties of water and having coils arranged along the underside of the boat, were investigated but later abandoned. Development work on miniaturized linear motors for use in camera shutters has long been reported from Germany and Japan.

The world of robotics has been keen to apply linear motors both for gross movement—linear motors are being used to move industrial robots on production lines—and for moving limbs. Unfortunately, control problems appear to be limiting such applications. More promising is the use of linear motors in micromachines and fractal shape-changing robots. The latter are assemblies of cubes that can slide around and over each other to create differently shaped machines or structures. Normal electromagnets can be used to drive the robots, but tests are being carried out with much smaller superconducting magnets, magnetic chain drive linear motors, and rare earth linear motors to build robots that can operate at the mesoscopic scale (less than 1,000 nm).

Going off the rails

One of the more glamorous applications of the linear motor has been in the field of transport. Throughout the world, railway operators are hard pressed to compete with the high speed of passenger airplanes and the versatility that an ever-widening network of roads gives to motorists and bus operators, largely because of the cost of moving the enormous mass of steel that constitutes conventional trains and the modern trend of reducing the sizes of rail networks as economy measures. Many operators believe that the way to preserve the railways as a mode of transportation is to build lighter, faster, trains.

Already, speeds of about 155 mph (250 km/h) have been achieved by the light, rapid, comfortable train (LRC) in Canada and the Train à Grande Vitesse (TGV) in France. They, however, are conventional wheels-on-rail systems that required advanced technology to attain even such a modest speed. Steel wheels on a steel track have an upper speed limit owing to friction and instability. For high speeds, the tracks must be absolutely straight and, equally important, maintained that way. A train traveling at 310 mph (500 km/h), for example, would be derailed by the slightest imperfection in the track.

One way to achieve speeds higher than 155 mph is to reduce or eliminate friction between the train and the track and to find some means of steering the train. Magnetic levitation (maglev) offers a quiet system with no moving parts, apart from the train. Maglev is essentially the principle of the linear motor, in which electricity flowing

through a system of flat coils generates a magnetic field that drives the coils along a permanent, flat magnet. These magnetic forces can produce levitation either by attraction or by repulsion.

To use the repulsive force, north poles, for example, in the track would repel north poles in the train, causing it to glide without contact over the track. Both systems pose problems for the development engineers. The attractive system is inherently unstable, because the attractive force increases as the gap between rails and train is reduced. The current in the electromagnets must be monitored continuously so that the magnetic force can be varied automatically to maintain a constant gap between track and train. Magnet-to-rail spacings of 0.4 to 0.8 in. (10–20 mm) are usual. Larger gaps would be desirable but difficult to achieve, because extremely large power surges would be needed to restore the gap once it widened appreciably.

The repulsive system, by contrast, is much more stable. The power flowing through the magnets governs the height of the train above the track. Stronger currents increase the gap. A major problem, however, is that this system needs vastly stronger magnetic fields to provide enough force to counteract the weight of the train.

Problems such as these have delayed the development of magnetic levitation since the early 1900s, when a patent for the idea was first filed. Since then, three important technological developments have brought magnetic levitation within reach: new plastic composites have made ultralightweight vehicle bodies possible; superconducting magnets can provide extremely large magnetic fields; and electronic engineering can switch large currents rapidly.

▲ Testing types of magnets to guide, levitate, and propel trains at high speeds. Electromagnets, consisting of coils of conductor, are used extensively, but cryogenic superconducting magnets are best, as they are stronger and consume less power than conventional electromagnets.

If a conductor is cooled sufficiently, it becomes superconducting so that current continues to flow indefinitely without weakening. However, most superconducting magnets used in maglev trains are made from a niobium–titanium compound that generates a large amount of heat, which must be cooled to 4 K to maintain its superconducting properties. The magnets are kept superconducting by liquid helium refrigeration units mounted on the bogies.

The track is made from conducting coils into which superconducting magnets on the train induce a magnetic field. The two magnetic fields repel each other and levitate the train. Unfortunately, the system has two major problems. The first is that magnetism is induced in the track only when the train is moving. It becomes stronger as the speed of the train increases, but there is little lift at low speed. In practice, the train must be traveling at at least 46 mph (74 km/h) before the magnetic force is sufficient to raise the train, so an auxiliary wheel system has to be included.

The second problem is that in addition to providing lift, the induced magnetism also generates magnetic drag, which tends to hold back the train. At moderate speeds, this drag accounts for most of the total force against the train's movements, but becomes less important as speed increases, when aerodynamic drag increases rapidly. Both drag forces can be turned to advantage, however, as highly efficient braking forces.

A number of maglev train systems have been developed since the 1920s, but only two large-scale operations have come close to being implemented. The German Transrapid and the Japanese maglev systems have both built test tracks to carry out high-speed evaluations of their trains. Both have achieved speeds in excess of 310 mph (500 kph), with the Japanese train *MLX01* attaining a record 342 mph (552 km/h) in 1999. However, plans to start building Germany's first long-distance commercial passenger track in 2000 have been put on hold after objections to the cost.

Billions of dollars have been spent so far on maglev research, much of it in developing new superconducting magnets and cooling systems. The expense has led to doubts about its ever being implemented as an alternative to conventional railways. Its advantages are that, per trip, maglev consumes one-seventh the energy used by a 737 aircraft, it is more energy efficient than conventional railways, and because there is no contact with the track, it is cheap to maintain.

SEE ALSO: ELECTRIC MOTOR • ELECTROMAGNETISM • LOCOMOTIVE AND POWER CAR • MAGNETISM • VOLTAGE REGULATOR

Liquid Crystal

Liquid crystals are liquids that exhibit some of the structural order of solid crystals. Their discovery is attributed to the Austrian botanist Friedrich Reinitzer, who in 1888 reported that he had observed two apparent melting points for cholesteryl benzoate: one where solid crystals formed a turbid liquid—in fact, a liquid-crystal phase—and another where the liquid became transparent. Despite the age of their discovery, it is only in recent decades that liquid crystals have started to find useful applications in technology.

Principles and properties

In bulk, liquid crystals have cloudy appearances, rather like milk or honey. In thin films, such as those used in liquid crystal displays, they are almost completely transparent.

Materials that exhibit liquid-crystal properties have certain molecular properties in common. They are rod-shaped molecules that either have permanent electrical dipoles, with a positively charged end and a negatively charged end, or are easily polarized to form temporary dipoles. These are the properties that encourage the molecular alignments that underlie liquid-crystal behavior.

The molecules in a liquid crystal tend to line up along an axis called the director. The amount of orientational order in such a material is described by the order parameter, S, and the angle each molecule strikes with the director, θ. These two values are related as follows:

$$S = \tfrac{1}{2} <3cos^2\theta - 1>$$

where the angle brackets (< and >) indicate that the enclosed term is averaged for all molecules. The value of S for a typical liquid crystal is between 0.3 and 0.9. If all the molecules were aligned along the director axis, the value of S would be 1; in a perfectly random liquid, S is 0.

The molecular properties that encourage alignment are opposed by the randomizing influence of collisions between molecules, which tend to knock them out of alignment with the director. As temperature increases, these collisions become stronger and the amount of orientational order decreases. At a certain temperature, which depends on the type of liquid crystal, the orientational order suddenly falls to zero, indicating that the sample has become a conventional liquid.

Liquid crystals vary in the extent to which their molecules form layers perpendicular to the director and how the director changes between layers. These differences characterize three subclasses: smectic, nematic, and cholesteric.

◄ These goggles form part of a system for viewing three-dimensional images on a computer screen. The lenses are liquid-crystal light filters that alternate between transparent and opaque states so that the right lens is opaque when the left-eye image appears on the screen, and vice versa.

Subphases

Smectic liquid crystals are the most highly ordered of all the subclasses. In addition to their high degree of orientational order, the molecules of a smectic liquid crystal tend to line up side by side to form layers. In this respect, they show the greatest similarity to solid crystals.

In a nematic liquid crystal, molecules tend to arrange themselves with their long axes parallel to the director but take up any position along their axes with respect to adjacent molecules. As such, nematic liquid crystals exhibit a grain along the director but do not form layers.

Cholesteric liquid crystals form layers along the director rather than at right angles to it, which is the case for smectic liquid crystals. The director of each layer is sightly twisted relative to the directors of the adjacent plane so that, over a large distance, a continuous twist is observed to be superimposed upon the parallel arrangement. This property stems from a chirality, or "handedness," in the molecules of the liquid crystal.

Working range

All types of liquid crystals flow as a liquid but exhibit optical properties similar to those of solid crystals over a typical working temperature range of 23 to 149°F (–5 to 65°C). The lower temperature is determined by the point at which the material transforms from its solid state and becomes able to flow. In this state—the mesophase—liquid-crystalline materials exhibit anisotropy, which is a variation of properties depending on the orientation along which they are measured. In particular, liquid crystals show anisotropy in their ability to scatter and transmit light. At the upper temperature limit, the substance loses its anisotropy and behaves as an ordinary liquid. The exact lower and upper temperature limits depend on the chemical nature of the liquid crystal.

Dynamic-scattering displays

A dynamic-scattering display consists of a thin layer of nematic material sandwiched between glass sheets surface-treated so as to encourage the liquid-crystal molecules to align perpendicular to the glass. The display then becomes transparent, since the aligned molecules scatter no light.

Such a display is made opaque by applying an electrical field, causing the polar molecules of the liquid crystal to align parallel to the glass surfaces. If that were all that happened, however, the display would remain transparent as the molecules of liquid crystal continued to be aligned.

In practice, however, free ions in the liquid are drawn to the oppositely charged conducting surfaces. As they pass through the liquid, these ions cause localized disturbances in the electrical field within the liquid crystal. These disturbances result in small groups of molecules becoming randomly disoriented in a turbulent manner. Since the refractive index of a liquid crystal depends on its orientation, the boundaries between regions of the crystal that have different orientations present

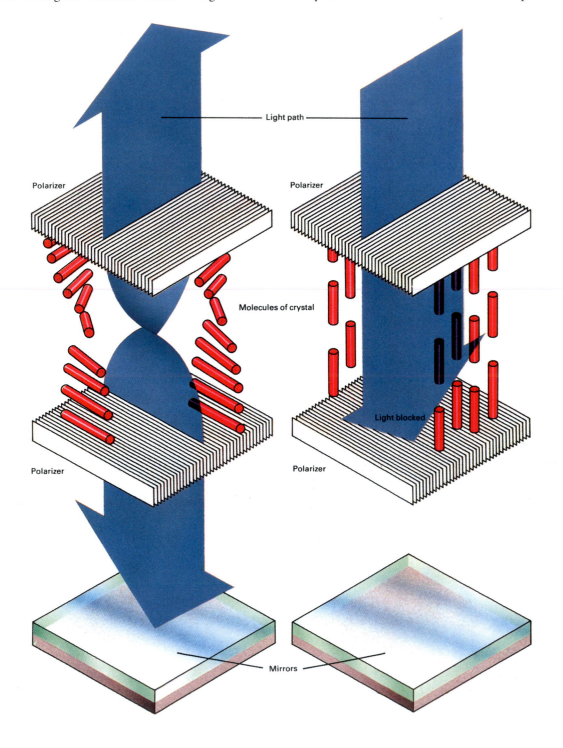

▶ One type of liquid-crystal display employs cholesteric liquids, which form into planes whose director axes trace a spiral along a line perpendicular to the planes. At rest (near right), this spiral twists the plane of polarized light between cross-polarized filters so that the display is transparent. Light then reflects off a mirror behind the display so that the display appears light. When subjected to an electrical field (far right), the molecules of the liquid line up along the field and are no longer able to rotate the plane of polarization of light between the filters. In this condition, the display absorbs light, resulting in a dark appearance.

Light path

Polarizer

Polarizer

Molecules of crystal

Polarizer

Light blocked

Polarizer

Mirrors

sharp changes in refractive indices—just as occurs in a finely ground powder. In this condition, the display takes on a milky or pearlescent appearance as it starts to scatter incident light.

Cholesteric displays

Displays that contain films of cholesteric liquids operate on a different principle from that described for nematic liquids. They make use of the fact that the regular twist in the molecule layers causes the plane of polarization of light passing through the liquid to be rotated. The angle of rotation depends on the exact type of material and the thickness of the liquid crystal film.

In one type of cholesteric display, the film of liquid crystal is held between two polarizing filters that are so arranged that light passes through the display when the liquid crystal is in its rest state. When a suitable potential is applied across the active parts of the display, the liquid-crystal molecules break out of their planar arrangement to line up along the field, after which the rotation of polarized light ceases to occur. The light entering through one polarizing filter ceases to be able to pass through the other polarizing filter, and that part of the display darkens.

In an alternative arrangement, the two polarizing filters are set to accept light at the same polarization angle. While the field is switched on, the display is transparent as the molecules line up along the field. In the absence of a field, the molecules assume their twisted planes and rotate incoming light such that it is absorbed by the second polarizing filter, thus darkening the display.

Display construction

The maximum size of a liquid crystal display, or LCD, is limited by the requirement for a uniform thickness of liquid-crystal film across the display area, and therefore depends largely on the quality of materials available. A four-digit clock display using nematic liquid might, for example, be constructed of seven-bar digits between two glass plates with surface dimensions of 3 x 1 in. (75 x 25 mm). The thickness of the liquid in the sandwich would be around 0.0001 in. (0.0025 mm), and the glass plates would be about 0.13 in. (3.3 mm) thick to ensure sufficient rigidity in the glass to maintain the correct gap in the sandwich.

The electrical fields used to activate a display are provided through transparent electrodes formed in the shapes of the characters or patterns to be displayed. The electrode material is typically a layer of tin oxide that has been sintered onto the glass, and the voltage is supplied through conducting areas that lead to contact areas along the edges of the glass plates.

Cholesteric displays differ from nematic (dynamic-scattering) displays only in the material that contains the liquid-crystal layer. Whereas nematic displays are sandwiched between plain glass, cholesteric displays use polarizing filters.

▲ In an LCD thermometer, different display elements become active as the temperature changes.

Applications

Liquid crystal displays have largely replaced other types of displays in battery-operated portable equipment, because they use around 0.1 percent of the power used by gas-discharge displays or light-emitting diodes and therefore conserve battery power.

LCDs are the only type of electronic display that can easily be read in high ambient light levels—even direct sunlight—making them particularly suited to use in aircraft and automobile instrument displays. However, LCDs must be illuminated to make them visible at night.

The simultaneously low operating voltage, low current demand, and low surface temperatures of LCDs make them useful in the potentially explosive atmospheres of mines and chemical plants, for example, because their operation is incapable of producing sufficient energy to initiate an explosion.

Liquid crystal displays are particularly suitable for use with microprocessors, since their operating voltages and very low power requirements are directly compatible with the output capabilities of such equipment. High resolution LCDs are increasingly used as the screens and monitors of televisions and computers—particularly for their portable versions—since an LCD screen is many times smaller from front to back than its cathode-ray-tube counterpart. The comparatively low power demand of an LCD is a particularly strong advantage for such applications.

▼ The digital LCD display of this exposure meter is more precise and easier to read than the analog needle displays of earlier devices of this type.

SEE ALSO: CLOCK • CRYSTALS AND CRYSTALLOGRAPHY • DIGITAL DISPLAY

Lithography

Lithography is a printing process that is based on the fact that grease and water do not readily mix. The image areas on a lithographic plate do not stand up in relief as in the letterpress process, and neither are they recessed into the plate as in gravure. The plate simply relies on the fact that the image areas attract a greasy ink while the non-image areas repel it. To prevent any ink from adhering to the nonimage, these areas are coated with gum and kept slightly damp, so another of the distinctive features of lithographic printing is that it involves the use of water as well as ink on the press. Before each impression is made, a litho plate must be dampened and then inked. First, rollers in the damping system distribute water from a water trough or fountain to the nonimage areas of the plate, then inking rollers transfer a film of ink from the ink reservoir or duct via a series of distribution rollers to the image areas of

the plate. The balance between the water and the ink applied in lithography is a crucial factor requiring great skill by the press operator.

Although lithographic printing was discovered in 1798 by a German printer, Alois Senefelder, it is only in recent years that the process has acquired such commercial importance. It has now overtaken letterpress as the major printing process, and its applications range from the small offset duplicating machines in offices to the large web-offset installations producing magazines and newspapers in color.

In the original lithographic process, the printing area was made by drawing directly onto a polished limestone surface with a greasy crayon, and these origins explain the derivation of the word lithography from the two Greek words, *lithos* meaning a stone, and *graphe*, a drawing. Litho stones were incorporated into flatbed presses, but

▲ Offset lithography is the most popular method of printing in use today. Because they use flexible rubber rollers, offset machines can be used to print onto many different materials including metals, cloth, leather, wood, rough and smooth paper, and plastics such as the candy wrappers being printed above.

today's fast litho presses all use the rotary principle, in which case litho printing surfaces must be made on thin, fairly strong, sheet materials that can be curved around the cylinder of a rotary press. A great variety of materials are used, including aluminum, zinc, plastics, paper, and combinations of metals such as chromium and copper. The most important of these plate materials is undoubtedly aluminum, which combines lightness, flexibility, and reasonable strength with excellent lithographic properties, relatively low cost, and recyclability.

Origination

A major factor in the growth of lithography has been its ability to use reproductions produced by phototypesetting techniques, which offer advantages over the older hot-metal typesetting systems. In phototypesetting, the text is input using a conventional keyboard along with control codes that specify factors such as size of typeface, emboldening or italicizing of the type, and column width. The input is stored on magnetic disks and then used to produce a photographic print of the set text. Early systems used a light beam to project a master image of the letters onto sensitized paper, but in modern systems, the letter shapes are stored in digital form. A cathode-ray tube or laser beam is used to write the letters onto sensitized paper, which is then developed to give the image.

The text is made up into pages with any pictures required, though page makeup can be carried out directly with some phototypesetting systems. Normally, pictures have their image broken down by a halftone screen. This breaks the different tones of light and dark into a series of small and large dots, but it is also possible to use the photographic grain structure directly. Alternatively, the image can be digitized and processed directly by the phototypesetting system. When the pages have been produced, checked, and corrected, they are then ready for use to produce the litho plates.

Where color work is involved, the original has to be separated to give individual negatives for each of the printing colors. For full-color (unlike monochrome or two-color) work the separation is to cyan (blue), magenta (red) and yellow elements along with a black component, and the individual negatives produced have register marks to ensure that the individual color elements can be lined up during printing. The separation process may be carried out photographically in a process camera using color filters or else done by electronic means with a scanner system.

▼ Layout of the Roland Parva two-color machine; some rollers are shown cut off halfway for clarity. Modern litho plates are usually presensitized and made of aluminum.

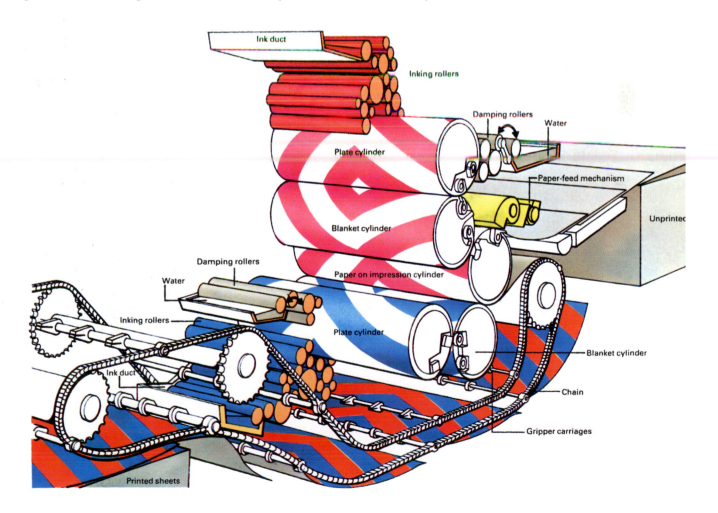

Ink duct

Inking rollers

Damping rollers

Water

Plate cylinder

Paper-feed mechanism

Blanket cylinder

Unprinted

Damping rollers

Water

Paper on impression cylinder

Inking rollers

Plate cylinder

Blanket cylinder

Ink duct

Chain

Gripper carriages

Printed sheets

The final stage of the page-makeup process is called imposition. All the pages to be printed are arranged so that when the sheet of paper is folded after printing, the pages fall in the correct sequence and are the right way up. This arrangement will vary depending on whether the pages are printed in sections of 4, 8, 16, or 32 pages and whether they are to be printed on a sheet-fed or continuous-web offset machine.

Litho plates

In their simplest form, litho plates can be made by drawing directly onto the metal surface with a greasy crayon, a method that is still used for limited editions of artists' lithographs. Another example of a direct-image plate is the short-run plate for an office duplicator made by typing onto a paper plate using a special ribbon on the typewriter. In both these cases, however, the litho image is very susceptible to wear, and the plate has a comparatively short press life. The real breakthrough for lithography came with its marriage to photography, and today, with few exceptions, litho plates used in the printing industry are produced by photomechanical means.

Most litho plates are made of aluminum. The surface of the metal is normally roughened or grained by mechanical or chemical means in order to increase its surface area and so improve its water-holding capacity in the nonimage area. This is taken a stage further in the use of anodized aluminum on which the aluminum oxide layer has been built up electrolytically to provide an extremely hard yet porous surface, which helps to ensure clean litho working and a long press life.

Platemaking

The original subject to be reproduced can be either negative or positive, with the image being transferred to the sensitized surface of the plate by a photographic process. Exposure of the plate causes the image area to become either more or less soluble (depending on the coating) in a particular solvent, with the more soluble areas being washed away in the developing process to leave the image. Plates are known as negative working or positive working, depending on whether exposure is made using a negative or a positive master.

A variety of coatings are used to sensitize the plates, with early coatings consisting of gum arabic or egg albumen sensitized with ammonium dichromate, which were poured onto the plate while it was being rotated—on a whirler—so they spread out to give a uniform thickness. Modern

▼ When the film pages have been output they are imposed into their printing order and checked for flaws on a light box. Any small marks, spots, or cut marks introduced by stripping in photographs or editorial corrections are removed by covering them with an opaque paint. The negatives then pass to a photolithography machine, exposing a light-sensitive printing plate to ultraviolet light. The plate is then treated with chemicals to fix the image before being attached to the printing press.

plates use other mainly synthetic coatings, such as polyvinyl alcohol, diazo compounds, and photopolymeric resins.

Surface plates

The exposed and developed coating of surface plates becomes the image that takes up the ink during printing. In making a negative surface plate, the coated plate is placed in a vacuum printing frame and the negative positioned accurately over it. The frame is closed and a vacuum applied to pull the negative into close contact with the plate for exposure to a powerful light source. The light passes through the clear areas of the negative to harden the plate coating, and the plate is removed from the frame and the image is developed.

The developing process depends on the plate coating. In the simple subtractive process, the unexposed areas are simply washed away to leave the light-hardened coating as the printing image. Alternatively, with additive plates, a developer is used to build up the image areas while also dissolving the unexposed coating and acting to make these unexposed areas more receptive to water. Positive plates are processed in much the same manner; the developing process removes the exposed area.

With surface plates, the image is slightly raised from the plate surface and is subject to wear during the printing process, so additive plates are normally limited to print runs of up to 50,000. Subtractive plates are more resistant to wear and can be used for runs of around 100,000, while some photopolymer plates can be treated to allow runs of a million or more copies.

Etched plates

In producing deep-etch litho plates, the coating is exposed to light through a positive. The unhardened areas are washed away, but in this case, the function of the hardened areas is not to act as the litho plate but to form a protective stencil while the image areas are lightly etched and then filled with a hard lacquer. Despite the name deep-etch, the image areas are only about 0.0003 in. (0.008 mm) below the general level of the plate. The fact that the image is slightly recessed, however, makes it more resistant to wear and hence better able to stand up to press runs, which can often exceed 100,000 copies.

Bimetal plates take advantage of the fact that oil and water do not wet all metals with the same ease. An oleophilic (oil-loving) metal, such as copper, is used for the image and a hydrophilic (water-loving) metal, for example, chromium, for the nonimage areas. The method of platemaking

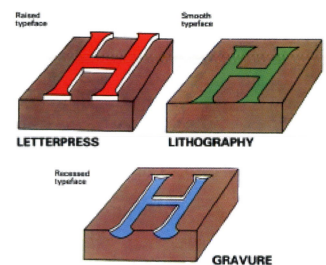

◀ Letterpress, offset litho, and gravure typefaces. In letterpress printing, the printing surface is raised; in offset litho, it is flush with the rest of the plate; in gravure printing it is engraved into the plate, as its name implies, forming a well into which the printing ink collects.

is similar to that used in the deep-etch process, but the purpose of etching is to remove a thin layer of chromium to leave bare copper exposed to form the image. Although bimetallic plates are more expensive than those described earlier, they are far more resistant to abrasion, and they are capable of press runs exceeding a million impressions.

Other types of plates

Although most litho plates are produced by photographic processes as described above, increasing use is being made of other platemaking processes, particularly in connection with the processing of text and images that are held in a digital form using a computer. For example, with electrostatic plates, the image is first formed as an electrostatic charge pattern on a photoconductive surface (normally a drum). The charge image is allowed to attract toner particles that are then transferred to a plate and heat fused or fixed to give the printing image. Alternatively, a photoconductive coating can be applied directly to the plate, the nonexposed areas being removed after the toner has been applied and fused to the plate surface.

Laser systems, also known as computer-to-plate systems, can be used to scan originals for platemaking or to produce plates directly from data stored in a computer without the need for an intermediate film stage. The laser can be used to write the image to a photoconductive plate as in the electrostatic process, or the image can be formed as a transfer from a pigment-coated mask softened by the heating effect of the laser.

Offset printing

All modern lithographic printing is offset printing, that is, the plate does not transfer ink directly to the paper but first offsets the image onto a rubber blanket from which it is printed onto the

◀ A litho typeface that has been inked with a water-repellent ink and is surrounded by a film of water on the print plate.

▶ Making a negative working surface litho plate. The negatives are mounted on a plastic film in the correct layout, and the film is cut and peeled away in the image areas. The layout is placed in a vacuum frame together with the plate, and the plate is exposed.

paper or some other substrate. The offset principle was first used for the printing of tin plate in order to overcome the problems met in printing directly from metal to metal, but it is now used for all substrates. Indeed, the word offset has become synonymous with lithography, and this association is unfortunate, because the offset principle is also used in letterpress and even in gravure printing. The use of an offset blanket reduces the wear on a litho plate, and its resilience makes it possible to print fine halftone images on a wide variety of papers, including those with fairly rough surfaces. Another advantage of printing offset is that the image on the plate can be the right way round and not wrong-reading, as in any direct printing process. Offset blankets consist of several layers of woven fabric laminated with thin layers of synthetic rubber and are made in various thicknesses and combinations of hardness.

Although flatbed offset presses are generally used for proofing purposes, all production machines use the rotary principle. The basic printing unit of a sheet-fed offset litho press consists of a plate cylinder, a blanket cylinder, and an impression cylinder. The plate is clamped around the plate cylinder, and with each revolution of the machine, it first comes in contact with a damping roll and then with the inkers. The paper passes between the blanket and the impression cylinder, but it does not touch the plate. Sheet-fed offset presses are commonly available with two, four, or six printing units for color work. In some machines, several sets of plate and blanket cylinders are arranged around a single common impression drum. Another arrangement is the perfecting, or blanket-to-blanket, press, where both sides of the paper are printed in a single operation. Here a pair of blanket cylinders are arranged to run against one another, the paper passing between the cylinders so that each blanket acts as the impression cylinder for the other blanket. Several such perfecting units can be connected in series for multicolor perfecting.

Web-offset printing

Web offset presses print on a continuous web, or length of paper, which is fed into the machine from a reel. Each printing unit is basically the same as those on sheet-fed presses, but they can be combined in a variety of different ways to give alternative print combinations. For example, a single web can be printed in full color on one side and black on the other side, or two webs can be run in a single machine, one in full color and the other in black, the two webs being folded together into pages after printing so that the color is spread through the black and white section. Applications for large web offset presses include newspapers and magazines, while smaller models are increasingly replacing sheet-fed machines for general offset litho work.

FACT FILE

- Honore Daumiér, considered by many to be the greatest 19th-century lithographer, was sent to jail for a lithograph he produced in 1824 caricaturing the king as a monster devouring France's wealth.

- In 1832, the Thomas de la Rue company patented the first British chromolithographic process, which was used to produce colored playing cards.

- Electron-beam lithography is used to draw circuit patterns onto microchip materials. The computer-controlled electron beam can move at a rate of up to 10 million steps per second.

SEE ALSO: ALUMINUM • DESKTOP PUBLISHING • ENGRAVING AND ETCHING • INK • PHOTOGRAPHIC FILM AND PROCESSING • PRINTING

Lock, Canal

Navigable waterways must be level to enable canals or ships to sail them, but the land around them can rise or fall substantially. Thus, a boat sailing on a canal or river or entering a dock may have to move from one level to another. The simplest device for this purpose is a pound (or chamber) lock. The general form of the modern lock is that of an open-topped chamber, with watertight gates at each end. Once the boat is inside, the gates are shut, and the water level in the lock rises or falls (depending on whether the boat is ascending or descending). When the water in the chamber has reached the level of the adjoining waterway (either up or down), the appropriate gate is opened to allow the boat to leave the lock.

Locks have a history going back at least 2,000 years, although the earliest types were not pound locks. One factor limiting the navigability of rivers is shallow water, so dams were often built to increase the depth. Part of each dam would be removable, enabling boats to be winched upstream through the gap or swirled downstream by the current. The removable part is called a flash lock; the entire structure is a navigation weir. Its use was twofold: the impounded water not only increased upstream depths, it could also be released in a surge to assist vessels in shallow water downstream. Locks of this type existed in China in 70 C.E., and their use later spread—they were built into watermill weirs as well. Although this solution reduced disputes between millers and boatmen, the problem could not be settled until the adoption of the pound lock, whose closed chamber minimizes the water loss from the higher level. In 984 C.E., the first known example of a pound lock was built in China, operated by raising or lowering gates at each end (now called guillotine gates). Europe's earliest pound lock, which can be

▲ A ship enters a lock on the Panama Canal. The chambers can hold vessels up to 1,000 ft. (305 m) long and 112 ft. (34 m) wide.

dated precisely, was built in 1373 at Vreeswijk, Holland, and it also had guillotine gates.

Most modern locks have an improved type of gate invented by the Italian inventor Leonardo da Vinci in the 15th century for a canal in Milan, Italy. They turn on hinges, like doors, and each end of the lock has two such gates that meet to form a V pointing upstream, giving them the name miter gates. One advantage of miter gates is that since the V shape points upstream, they are self-sealing. When there is a difference in water level between one side and the other, the pressure holding the gates together is at its greatest.

Ancient locks were often built entirely of wood, but stone or brick chambers became standard. Gates were usually wooden and lasted up to 50 years. To fill and empty the lock, hand-operated sluices were fitted to the gates, but it was later found that mounting them in conduits bypassing the gates gave a smoother water flow.

Where steep rises have to be negotiated, locks are built continuously with the upper gates of one acting as the lower gates of the next. The resulting structure is called a flight of locks and many examples exist from two steps (three sets of gates) to the mighty Neptune Staircase on the Caledonian Canal, Scotland, which consists of eight locks in one structure with nine sets of gates.

Construction

Modern lock construction can be seen to be a refinement of older locks, with concrete usually used for the chamber and welded steel for the gates. Hydraulic power or electricity is used to operate the gates and sluices. As locks have grown in size to admit larger vessels, so—on canals— water loss from higher to lower levels has increased. To overcome this problem, pumping may be employed, or economizer locks are built that have small reservoirs alongside the chamber to store some of the water emptied from it. This water is later used to refill the lock. Outstanding examples of this type are on the Rhine-Main-Danube canal linking Germany's waterways to those of southeastern Europe. Here, multiple side reservoirs allow savings of up to 60 percent of the lock water. The locks are 623 ft. (190 m) long, 39 ft. (12 m) wide and have rises up to 82 ft. (25 m).

In the 19th century, locks rarely had rises above 30 ft. (9 m), but today's largest industrial lock has a rise of 138 ft. (42 m). It is at Ust-Kamenogorsk, in Kazakhstan, and lifts 1,600-ton (1,450 tonne) vessels past a hydroelectric dam. The chamber, 328 ft. (100 m) long and 56 ft. (17 m) wide, takes half an hour to fill or empty. The lower gate does not extend to full height; it moves vertically to seal a tunnel through which ascending vessels enter the lock.

◄ A flight of locks on the Rideau Canal near Ottawa. The miter gates are operated by winches (seen at one side) rather than by hand.

The Panama Canal, opened in 1914, also has large locks. These locks have miter gates up to 82 ft. high and can accommodate vessels 1,000 ft. (305 m) long and 100 ft. (30 m) wide, taking only eight minutes to fill or empty.

Gates

Early dock entrance locks closely resembled 18th century canal locks, with brick or masonry chambers, timber miter gates, and manual operation. A dock entrance lock rarely needs a rise over 20 ft. (6 m), but the draft of ocean-going vessels requires that the gates be very deep. Many modern gates are miter gates, but others are hinged along their lower edge (flap gates), moved sideways on rails (traversing caissons), or floated into place (floating caissons). All are made of hollow welded steel permanently ballasted with concrete. Operating ballast may be required and is provided by pumping water in or out of the gate's interior.

Although deep-water terminals are replacing enclosed docks for the largest ships, many massive dock entrances exist. Enclosed docks are unnecessary if the tidal range is less than about 13 ft. (4 m), so many major ports do not have entrance locks. Among the ports where locks are necessary are Bremerhaven, Germany, which has a lock 1,220 ft. (372 m) long and 148 ft. (45 m) wide, and Antwerp, Belgium, which has one 1,180 ft. (360 m) by 148 ft. (45 m). The time taken to operate them is more dependent on maneuvering the large ships than on actually filling the lock—it can take up to 90 minutes. Unless a suitable natural water supply exists at a higher level, water must be pumped back up into the dock to compensate for water lost during the locking process.

SEE ALSO: Boat building • Canal • Compressor and pump • Dock • Ship • Water

Lock, Security

◀ A bronze lock-plate and hasp from the Roman period in France.

The earliest known mechanical fastening for a door is the wooden Egyptian lock, in use 4,000 years ago. Specimens have been found in the pyramids, and this type of lock is depicted in ancient bas-relief sculptures. It is a pin-tumbler lock in which the bolt is hollowed out; the key is a curved, flattened wooden stick with pins projecting from the end. When the key is inserted into the lock and levered upward, the pins push upward on pins projecting down into the bolt from a fixed staple, allowing the bolt to be withdrawn. These locks were made up to 2 ft. (0.6 m) long.

Another prevalent type of ancient lock, found in China and other parts of the world, is a padlock that works on a spring-barb principle. The bolt has an indentation (sometimes a reverse projection) into which a leaf spring snaps and is held fast. The key, a plain strip of metal, is slid in, depressing the spring, drawing the barbs together, and releasing them from the indentation so that the bolt can be withdrawn.

Yet another primitive lock is a screw-action padlock. Here the key is an ordinary male screw, and as it is turned, the barrel is withdrawn and the shackle released. This type of lock was used throughout Europe.

Warded locks

From these descriptions, it is easy to see that early locks were no more than an inconvenience to any burglar. The first locks made of metal that attempted to provide security by requiring a key of peculiar configuration were the warded locks, first made by the Romans and common in Europe by the 13th century. The wards are obstructions inside the lock; the bit of the key must be made to bypass the wards of the particular lock. The sliding or pushing motion of the key now gave way to the familiar modern turning motion. Sometimes the keys were made pipe-shaped to fit over a fixed pin, in which case the lock could be operated from one side only, or else they were made solid with a projecting bit that could enter the lock from either side. The Romans made keys small enough to be worn as finger rings.

Lock making soon became a skilled trade, and an extraordinary range of ward designs were produced. Sometimes they were combined with springs to hold the bolt shut, against which the key was turned. A back-spring lock was produced in which a key, passing the wards, pushed the spring off the bolt with a clicking sound; this lock was actually less secure than the ancient Egyptian lock, because the bolt could be forced back by any pressure applied to its end. Skeleton keys could be made that would open a variety of warded locks.

Modern locks

The security provided by modern locks began in the 18th century, when the tumbler lock was invented. Basically, the tumbler is a lever, or pawl, that fits into a slot on the bolt; the key lifts the latch. In its simplest form, the tumbler can be

▶ A modern mortise lock. This lock can be operated by a key from the outside or by a spring-operated lever from inside, and double-locked by a pin on the inside.

raised by a pick or a skeleton key, but in 1778, an Englishman, Robert Barron, invented the double-action tumbler, in which two (later, more than two) tumblers must be raised, each to exactly the right height to clear its slot. (If any tumbler is raised too high, it catches in another slot above, so that the bolt still cannot be drawn.) This was the great modern advance in lock security, and the multiple lever is still the basis of most locks made today. An interesting variant on the Barron tumbler lock was the detector device, patented by the British inventor Jeremiah Chubb in 1818, also still in use today. If this type of lock is tampered with, a lever stays in the raised position so that the bolt cannot be withdrawn until the correct key is turned backward. This gives notice to the keyholder that someone has been trying to open the lock with the wrong key.

In 1784, the British inventor Joseph Bramah patented a lock that operated with a pipe-shaped key with notches of varying lengths. The Bramah lock includes a notched diaphragm plate and a number of spring-loaded radial slides. The key pushes the slides down until they match with the notches on the diaphragm, allowing the barrel of the lock to be turned. These types of lock were operated using small keys and had intricate mechanisms, making them expensive to manufacture. In order to lower costs, Bramah designed cutting machines that produced the parts mechanically.

Today, the most common lock used to fasten the front doors of houses is the Yale lock, a cylindrical pin-tumbler design that combines the best features of many locks, including the ancient Egyptian wooden one. It was invented in 1848 by Linus Yale from Connecticut and improved by his son. The rotation of the plug in the cylinder is prevented by five pins that extend into the hollowed-out bolt of the Egyptian lock. The pins are divided into upper and lower halves; the lower half of each is called the tumbler, and the upper half is called the driver. Each tumbler is a different length from the others, and the same is true of the driver halves. Only a key with the correct serrations can lift all five tumblers to the correct height to allow the plug to turn, thus operating the bolt. The pin tumblers are spring loaded so that they are always in the locking position except when the proper key is inserted. The Yale lock is fairly difficult to pick and offers reasonable security under ordinary circumstances.

Combination locks

The bolt or shackle in a combination lock has slots in it. A number of rings (tumblers) are provided with numbers or letters around the outside and projections on the inside, which fit the slots. The rings must be lined up correctly in order for the shackle to be withdrawn. If the lock has three rings with one hundred numbers on each, there are a million possible combinations, only one of which will open the lock. The combination lock has been known in Europe since at least the 16th century, but its origins are lost. The modern vari-

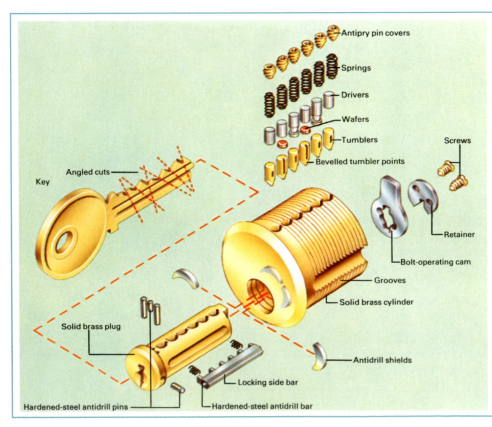

CYLINDER LOCK

The cylinder lock was invented by Linus Yale in 1848 and is based on the pin-tumbler mechanism used by the ancient Egyptians 4,000 years ago. The Yale cylinder lock is the most common form of domestic lock, often used to secure the front doors of houses. Locksmiths attempt to stay one step ahead of criminals by designing locks that are ever more sophisticated. This effort has led to a number of technical improvements to the cylinder lock. As this cross section shows, cylinder locks have lugs that prevent the tumblers from rising if the wrong key is inserted in the lock or if anybody attempts to pick the lock. Angled cuts in the upper portion of the key also help to deter picking. Antidrill devices reduce the risk of criminals gaining entry by destroying the lock mechanism.

Labels in illustration: Antipry pin covers; Springs; Drivers; Wafers; Tumblers; Screws; Bevelled tumbler points; Angled cuts; Key; Retainer; Bolt-operating cam; Grooves; Solid brass cylinder; Solid brass plug; Antidrill shields; Hardened-steel antidrill pins; Locking side bar; Hardened-steel antidrill bar

ety has a dial on the front that is turned back and forth until the rings inside are lined up. Most combination locks are designed so that the combination can be changed occasionally for security.

Safes

Safes usually have combination locks because they have no keyhole into which explosives can be inserted to blow the safe. Sometimes they also have time-lock devices so that they cannot be opened during certain hours, even by someone who has the combination. The most secure safes depend on alloy steel cladding that can be burned through only by electric arc-cutting torches—a process that takes many hours.

Electronic lock

Since the 1970s, it has been possible to make buildings secure during closing hours with electronic locks that works on the same principle as the push-button telephone. The locks have several numbered buttons on the outside, and a predetermined sequence of numbers operates the lock. The advantages of this type of lock for properties that must allow access to repair and maintenance personnel at odd hours are that no keys are required, the lock is as tamper-proof as a combination lock, and the combination sequence can be easily and frequently changed.

Recognition technology

Every person has voice patterns that are different from any other person, and computer software has been developed that recognizes these differences. This advance has led to the use of voice recognition to operate locks that may be used to secure doors but may also be used to prevent unauthorized use of computers. Similarly, various parts of the human body have characteristics that are unique to each person, and these characteristics can be used to create computer-operated systems that allow entry to a building or use of certain equipment only to authorized individuals or groups of people. Among currently available recognition systems are those that use differences in the iris and retina of the eye, the lines on a palm or finger, and the appearance of a face. All of these systems scan a specific area to create digitized information that may then be compared to a database of similar information on authorized staff.

The future of much of this technology is in the area of information security to protect industry against theft and fraud. Devices already available include a computer mouse that recognizes the fingerprints of its authorized user.

▲ This lock uses retinal recognition technology to restrict access to authorized people. The lock recognizes the differences between one human retina and another and uses this information to restrict access to buildings or information systems to people included on its database.

SEE ALSO: SECURITY SYSTEM • VOICE RECOGNITION AND SYNTHESIS

Locomotive and Power Car

The first railways were constructed in the 16th century, but motive power was provided by animals or stationary engines until the early 19th century when the first locomotives came into use. They were all steam powered, and steam dominated railway traction for some 150 years. However, the thermal efficiency of steam engines is comparatively low, and increasing fuel costs resulted in the gradual adoption of other forms of motive power, notably diesel locomotives and electric traction. Such locomotives also tend to have a higher availability than steam engines, which need a considerable amount of routine maintenance to keep them in service.

Provided that the traffic is heavy enough to repay the heavy costs of electrification, electric trains are the most economical to operate. But where trains run less frequently over long distances, the cost of electrification is prohibitive, and diesel traction is employed. Steam locomotives are still used in some countries where suitable fuel is available at low cost, while the increasing cost of petroleum products has resulted in renewed interest in more refined designs of steam locomotive.

A number of other drive systems, including steam and gas turbine and gasoline engines, have been used in railway engines, but they are not generally competitive with diesel traction. An increasing trend with passenger services is the introduction of integrated trains with multiple drive units incorporated in the carriages rather than separate locomotives, as in Britain's Intercity 125 or the French Train à Grande Vitesse (TGV).

Classification

Steam locomotives are classified according to the number of wheels. Except for small engines used in switchyards, all modern steam locomotives had leading wheels on a pivoted bogie or truck to help guide them around curves. The trailing wheels helped carry the weight of the firebox. For many years the American standard locomotive was a 4-4-0, having four leading wheels, four driving wheels and no trailing wheels. The famous Civil War locomotive, the General, was a 4-4-0 as was the New York Central Engine No. 999, which set a speed record of 112.5 mph (181 km/h) in 1893. Later, a common freight locomotive configuration was the 2-8-2. An alternative classification commonly used in Europe counts the axles instead of wheels, and this is further developed by using letters to distinguish different drive wheel combinations. Thus, A represents one driven axle, B two axles, C three axles, and D four axles

◀ It was wood-fired steam engines such as this that hauled trains across the American Wild West in the years after the first transcontinental railroad was completed in 1869.

so that, for example, a 2-8-2 becomes a 1-D-1. The same system is used for the classification of diesel and electric-powered locomotives with the additional suffix "o" being applied to axles that are individually driven.

Steam locomotives

Early development of locomotives was concentrated in Britain, and the first locomotive to run on rails was built by Richard Trevithick for the Penydarren Tramroad in Wales in 1804. It proved too heavy for the cast iron rails of the time and was subsequently used as a stationary engine. A number of other locomotives were built for various applications with mixed success, and in 1815, George Stephenson patented the idea of direct drive from the cylinders by means of cranks on the drive wheels instead of through gear wheels, which imparted a jerky motion, especially when wear occurred on the coarse gears. Direct drive allowed a simplified layout and gave greater freedom to designers.

In 1825, only 18 steam locomotives were doing useful work. One of the first commercial railways, the Liverpool & Manchester, was being built, and the directors had still not decided between locomotives and cable haulage, with railside steam engines pulling the cables. They organized a competition that was won by George Stephenson in 1829 with his famous engine, the *Rocket*.

Locomotive boilers had already evolved from a simple flue to a return flue model, and then to a tubular design, in which a nest of fire tubes, giving more heating surface, ran from the firebox tube plate to a similar tube plate at the smoke-box end. In the smoke box, the exhaust steam from the cylinders created a blast on its way to the chimney that kept the fire up when the engine was moving. When the locomotive was stationary, a blower was used, creating a blast from a ring of perforated pipe into which steam was directed. A further development, the multitubular boiler, was patented in 1872 by Henry Booth, treasurer of Liverpool & Manchester, and incorporated in the *Rocket*. After 1830, the steam locomotive assumed its familiar form, with the cylinders level or slightly inclined at the smoke-box end and the fireman's stand at the firebox end.

As soon as the cylinders and axles were no longer fixed in or under the boiler itself, it became necessary to provide a frame to hold the various components together. The bar frame was used on the early British locomotives and exported to the United States, where it evolved from wrought iron to cast steel construction, with the cylinders mounted outside the frame. The bar frame was superseded in Britain by the plate frame, with cylinders inside the frame, spring suspension (coil or laminated) for the frames, and axle boxes (lubricated bearings) to hold the axles.

As most railroads produced their own locomotive designs, a great many characteristic types developed. Some designs with cylinders inside the frame transmitted the motion to crank-shaped axles rather than to eccentric pivots on the outsides of the drive wheels; there were also compound locomotives, with the steam passing from a first cylinder or cylinders to another set of larger ones.

Steel boilers

When steel came into use for building boilers after 1860, higher operating pressures became possible. By the end of the 19th century, 175 psi (12 bar) was common, with 200 psi (13.8 bar) for compound locomotives. It rose to 250 psi (17.2 bar) later in the steam era. (By contrast, Stephenson's *Rocket* developed only 50 psi, 3.4 bar.) In the 1890s, express engines had cylinders up to 20 in. (51 cm) in diameter with a 26 in. (66 cm) stroke. Later diameters increased to 32 in. (81 cm) in places like the United States, where locomotives in general were built larger.

Supplies of fuel and water were carried on a separate tender pulled behind the locomotive. The first tank engine, carrying its own supplies, appeared in the 1830s. Separate tenders continued to be common because they made possible much longer runs. While the fireman stoked the firebox, the boiler had to be replenished with water by some means under his control; early engines had pumps running off the axle, but there was always the difficulty that the engine had to be running. The injector was invented in 1859. Steam from the boiler went through a cone-shaped jet and lifted the water into the boiler against the greater pressure there through energy imparted in condensation.

Early locomotives burned wood in the United States, but coal in Britain. As British railway laws began to include penalties for emission of dirty black smoke, many engines were built after 1829 to

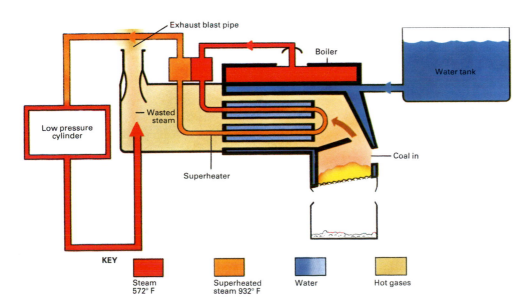

TRADITIONAL STEAM ENGINE

Exhaust blast pipe

Boiler

Water tank

Wasted steam

Low pressure cylinder

Superheater

Coal in

KEY

Steam 572° F

Superheated steam 932° F

Water

Hot gases

◀ In a traditional steam locomotive, steam passes into the cylinders to produce power. Exhaust steam emitted from the chimney creates a draft to draw out the combustion products. For every ton (0.9 tonnes) of coal burned, 10 tons (9 tonnes) of water are evaporated. Most steam engines haul their own supply of fuel and water, which is carried in a separate tender towed behind the locomotive.

burn coke. Under Matthew Kirtley on the Midland Railway, the brick arch in the firebox and deflector plates were developed to direct the hot gases from the coal to pass over the flames so that a relatively clean blast came out of the chimney and the cheaper fuel could be burned.

Valve gear

Valve operation on most early British locomotives was by Stephenson link motion, dependent on two eccentrics on the driving axle connected by rods to the top and bottom of an expansion link. A block in the link, connected to the reversing lever under the control of the driver, imparted the reciprocating motion to the valve spindle. With the block at the top of the link, the engine would be in full forward gear, and steam would be admitted to the cylinder for perhaps 75 percent of the stroke. As the engine was notched up by moving the lever back over its serrations (much like the handbrake lever of a car), the cutoff was shortened; in midgear, there was absolutely no steam admission to the cylinder, and with the block at the bottom of the link, the engine was fully in reverse.

In 1844, the Belgian inventor Egide Walschaert created a valve gear that allowed more precise adjustment and easier operation for the driver. An eccentric rod worked from a return crank by the driving axle operated the expansion link; the block imparted the movement to the valve spindle, but the movement was modified by a combination lever from a crosshead on the piston rod.

Superheating

Steam was collected as dry as possible along the top of the boiler in a perforated pipe or from a point above the boiler in a dome and passed to a regulator that controlled its distribution. The most spectacular development in steam locomotives used for heavy haulage and high-speed runs was the introduction of superheating. Steam at 175 psi (12.3 bar), for example, was heated to 371°F (188°C) and superheated a further 200°F (93°C), resulting in the steam expanding much more readily in the cylinders, so 20th-century locomotives could work at higher speeds and increased power. Steel tires, glass-fiber boiler lagging, long-lap piston valves, direct steam passage, and superheating all contributed to the last phase of steam locomotive performance.

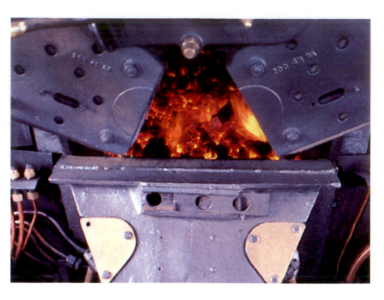

▲ The boiler of a modern steam locomotive, viewed from the footplate. Coal feed is automated; other modifications to the basic design that greatly improve efficiency include computer-timed valves and improved exhaust systems.

The largest steam locomotives were articulated, with two sets of drive wheels and cylinders using a common boiler. The sets of drive wheels were separated by a pivot; otherwise, such a large engine could not have negotiated curves. The largest ever built was the Union Pacific Big Boy, a 4-8-8-4, used to haul freight in the western United States.

Diesel locomotives

Diesel locomotives have several advantages over steam engines. They are instantly ready for service and can be shut down for short periods, whereas it takes some time to heat the water in the steam engine, especially in cold weather, and the fire must be kept up while the steam engine is on standby. The diesel can go farther without servicing as it consumes no water; its thermal efficiency is four times as high, allowing further savings of fuel. Acceleration and high-speed running are smoother with a diesel, and thus, there is less wear on rails and roadbed. The economic reasons for turning to diesels were overwhelming, especially in the United States, where the railways were in direct competition with road haulage over very long distances.

The most common type of diesel locomotive is the diesel electric, in which the diesel engine drives a generator to produce electricity that is supplied to traction motors on the locomotive axles. In most modern designs, the generator is a three-phase alternator, with a solid-state rectifier system being used to convert the AC into DC for the traction motors. Engines are generally V-type with both two- and four-stroke cycles being used, often with turbocharging for higher efficiency and power output.

The traction motors are carried on the undercarriage parallel to the axles, and the drive is transmitted through a reduction gear. Speed control is achieved by a switch-gear system that alters the winding characteristics of the drive motors to give maximum torque for starting, gradually changing the connections as the speed increases. Further control is achieved by adjustment of the excitation current of the generator to vary the power output.

Hydraulic drive systems are also used on diesel locomotives, with a fluid flywheel connected between the engine and the driving gears. In some designs, alternative gear ratios are provided to give a choice of speeds.

Electric traction

The first use of electric power for railway traction was in 1834, but this and other early attempts relied on batteries, which were heavy and had a limited output before recharging was needed. Modern electric locomotives draw their power from an external source through a third rail mounted alongside the track or an overhead wire system, or catenary. With third-rail systems, the current is collected by a shoe, while overhead wire systems use pantographs; in both cases, the circuit is completed through the locomotive wheels and the running track.

Both DC and AC power supplies are used, with DC systems being favored in many early systems because they allowed the use of proven DC traction motors. The development of efficient and reliable rectifier systems made the use of AC systems more feasible, with 2,500 V single-phase AC at 50 Hz being used in most modern systems. However, there are still a number of other systems in use, ranging from 600 V AC third-rail arrangements through 3,000 V DC overhead wire to 1,500 V AC at 16.66 Hz.

Drive arrangements for electric locomotives are generally similar to those of diesel electric units, but with the diesel engine replaced by a transformer and rectifier system and thyristor switching used for speed control. In Europe, some electric locomotives are run over networks that include a number of different electrification systems, the change between systems being made without the train having to stop.

Gas-turbine powered trains

During the 1960s, trains powered by gas turbines were developed in the United States and were used on services between New York City and Boston, as well as between Toronto and Montreal. These trains were made with light aluminum bodies, reducing the amount of power needed, and the small size of the turbines allowed them to be incorporated into the design of the carriage rather than occupy a separate locomotive. Rising fuel costs in the 1970s, however, made gas-turbine trains increasingly expensive to run, and they have since been replaced by more conventional locomotives.

Tilting trains

The design of trains that tilt as they go around curves has enabled trains to travel at faster speeds on existing tracks, avoiding the need to build costly new straight tracks. The first tilting train prototype was designed by Fiat in Italy as long ago as 1970, and practical models were first used

▼ Eurostar high-speed trains at Waterloo International Station, London. These trains operate on the Channel Tunnel route that connects London with Paris and Brussels.

by the Italian State Railway in 1976 to run between Rome and Ancona. The first high-speed tilting trains were introduced in 1987 and can travel at speeds up to 155 mph (250 km/h). These trains automatically tilt by means of hydraulic or electromechanical tilt actuators—hence the name "Pendolino," or "little pendulum." This pendulum action always positions the carriages at the optimum angle for speed and comfort when negotiating curves. The only alteration needed to existing tracks is to bank them slightly to help the train's instruments detect the curve. The Spanish tilting train designed by Patentes Talgo is currently in use in the United States running on routes such as Seattle to Portland.

High-speed trains

The electric powered Japanese Shinkansen, or bullet, train, was one of the earliest high-speed trains; current models are capable of speeds up to 160 mph (260 km/h). The fastest passenger train in service is the French TGV, also electric powered, which has established a world rail-speed record of 320.3 mph (515 km/h). The German Inter City Express (ICE) trains, which may be either diesel or electric powered, are capable of running at speeds of up to 174 mph (280 km/h). All of these trains run on dedicated lines, adding considerably to the initial construction costs. Germany, however, has recently introduced a tilting version of the ICE train and thus has broadened the range of routes it can operate on.

FACT FILE

■ The first locomotive to move passengers along a rail in the United States was named Tom Thumb. Weighing just over one ton (0.9 tonnes), it exerted slightly more pulling power than a single horse.

■ The Royal George, built in 1827 by Timothy Hackworth, was the most powerful steam railway engine of its time. It could haul 130 tons (117 tonnes) at the speed limit of 5 mph (8 km/h).

■ The most powerful steam locomotives ever built were the Union Pacific Big Boys of 1941, with an output of 6,300 horsepower and a load capacity for gradient work of 4,000 tons (3,600 tonnes).

■ The first U.S. passenger service was hauled by Best Friend of Charleston. The boiler exploded in 1931 when the fireman shut the safety valve to stop the noise of the steam.

▲ The Japanese Shinkansen, or "bullet," trains are some of the fastest trains currently in service. Developed in the 1960s, the latest models operate at speeds up to 160 mph (260 km/h).

SEE ALSO:

Cog railway • Electric motor • Gas turbine • Internal combustion engine • Mass transit and subway • Railroad system • Steam engine • Thyristor

Logarithm

A logarithm is a different way of representing a number but is integrally linked with the nature of numbers in general. An enormous range of numbers, from the minutest fractions to the largest figures, can be encompassed by a range of logarithms that can be handled easily. They are used extensively in science, engineering, and mathematics.

Numbers

We are accustomed to counting numbers to the base of ten. We have ten fingers and numerical symbols—zero (0), one (1), and so on up to nine (9). With them we can represent a number of any size. For any integer number (a whole number) greater than nine but less than 100, two characters placed side by side are required. Three characters specify any integer between 100 and 999.

This system of numbers is easy to understand and simple to use. It is one of the first things taught in school and essential to all transactions, especially those involving money—maybe a child's first practical experience with numbers.

Such a system, however, becomes extremely cumbersome with large numbers—they become incomprehensible and unwieldy. It is easy to envisage ten people but the idea of 1,000 people is more difficult. The population of the world is over six billion and is baffling even when written as 6,000,000,000.

The same difficulty is encountered with extremely small numbers. One-tenth can be written as 0.1, one-hundredth as 0.01, but one-millionth, which is 0.000001, is already unwieldy.

Powers and logarithms

There is a simple way to represent very large and very small numbers—using powers. One hundred is equal to 10 multiplied by 10 and can be more easily written as 10^2. This number is read "ten squared" and means ten to the power two.

Similarly, one million is ten multiplied by ten five times. Therefore one million is ten to the power six, written as 10^6.

This system greatly shortens the space required to describe large numbers and can be extended down to the smallest fraction. As one hundred is 10^2, ten is 10^1 (ten to the power one) and one is 10^0 (that is, ten to the power zero—in fact, any number to the power zero is one). Proceeding to still smaller numbers (less than one) the power becomes negative. For example, one-tenth (0.1) is 10^{-1} (ten to the power minus one), one-hundredth (0.01) is 10^{-2}, and one-millionth is 10^{-6}.

It is not necessary, however, to keep on writing the base number if it is understood. The power alone is then sufficient to describe the original number and this power is called the logarithm of that number (to the base 10). Thus six is the logarithm to the base ten of one million and minus two is the logarithm of one-hundredth (0.01). The logarithm of ten is one and the logarithm of one is zero. The brevity of this system can be demonstrated by the fact that logarithms between +6 and –6 represent numbers between one million and one-millionth.

Logarithmic tables

We do not always handle numbers as convenient as 10 or 100 or 0.001, but every number, integer or not, has a logarithm. For example, the logarithm of 554.6 to the base ten will lie between 2 (which is 100) and 3 (which is 1,000) and must therefore include decimal places. Such a logarithm is not easily determined using pen and paper, and so logarithmic tables (or log tables for short) have been devised to make the task easier. The logarithm of 554.6 from log tables is 2.744 to three decimal places. To convert a logarithm back into a number, log tables can be used in reverse.

▲ On some electronic equipment, volume can be increased logarithmically. Amplification is measured in decibels on a logarithmic scale.

Antilog tables have been devised to make these conversions easier. Today, logarithms can be easily calculated using a pocket calculator.

Applications of logarithms

Logarithms enable complicated multiplications and divisions to be performed by simple addition and subtraction. For example, 100 x 10,000 equals 1,000,000. Put another way, $10^2 \times 10^4 = 10^6$. The two powers to the left of the equals sign add up to the power on the right. In other words, two numbers can be multiplied by adding their logarithms and finding the antilog of this sum. Division is the subtraction of one log from the other.

A slide rule operates on this principle. It consists of two logarithmic scales, one of which can be moved. Multiplications and divisions are determined by adding and subtracting along the scales.

One practical application of logarithms is in the Richter scale used to measure the magnitude of earthquakes. Earthquakes vary greatly in their magnitude, and a logarithmic scale helps to compress the range of values.

Logarithms to other bases

Once the logarithm of a number has been established in principle, it is possible to use any base. For example, 64 is two multiplied by two five times—that is, 2^6 (two to the power six). Thus, the logarithm of 64 to the base two is 6. Similarly, the logarithm of ½ to the base two is –1, and ¼ is –2. Because 2^0 equals one, the logarithm of 1 to the base two is 0.

Natural or Naperian logarithms

In the application of logarithms there is one number so important that it is even given its own symbol—e. This is the exponential number, and e = 2.71828 to five decimal places. It is important in calculations concerning natural growths; that is, growth that is continuous rather than in stages. For example, the compound interest on $1 is calculated in yearly stages knowing the annual interest rate. In one year the sum has grown to $ (1 + r/100), where r is the yearly interest rate as a percentage. This sum is then the new sum for the next year's calculation; therefore, after two years the initial sum has grown to $ (1 + r/100)^2.

After n years, it has grown to $ (1 + r/100)^n— this is growth in stages. If the interest rate is 100 percent per year, then at the end of the first year, the $1 has increased to $2, after 2 years $4, 3 years $8, 4 years $16, and so on.

Now, consider reviewing the interest on the sum twice yearly—thus reducing the gaps between updating the accumulated sum. The interest rate per half year is 50 percent (still 100

percent per year) and the sum accumulated at the end of one year is $ (1 + 50/100)^2, which is $ (1.5)^2, or \$2.25. Consequently, with interest reviews more frequent than once yearly, the sum accumulated is larger. Increasing the reviews per year will not, however, lead to ever-increasing accumulations over the yearly period. As the number of reviews per year become infinitely frequent, the accumulated sum over the year rises more slowly and tends toward \$2.71828, that is, e.

To demonstrate this fact, with four reviews per year with an interest rate of 25 percent per quarter year, the accumulated sum at the end of one year is $ (1 + 25/100)^4, which is $ (1.25)^4, or \$2.44. With eight reviews per year it is $ (1.125)^8, which is \$2.565, 16 reviews is \$2.64, and 32 reviews \$2.675. This figure is approaching e.

Natural, or Naperian, logarithms are logarithms to the base e and are used wherever natural growth functions are encountered. For example, the voltage across the plates of a capacitor being charged through a resistor increases in a certain exponential way that when represented mathematically will include powers of e.

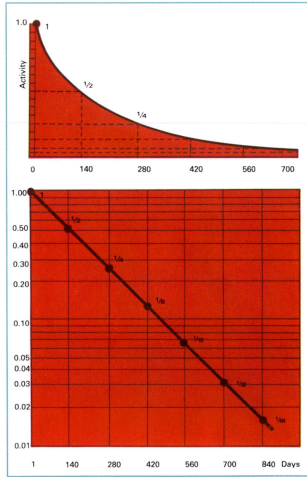

LOGARITHMIC GRAPHS

Polonium is a radioactive element with a half-life of 140 days (the time in which its activity is halved). An ordinary graph of activity against time is curved, but plotting the graph on logarithmic graph paper produces a straight line. Logarithms are also used in a process called carbon dating, which archaeologists use to calculate the age of specimens containing the radioactive isotope carbon-14.

SEE ALSO: ELECTRICITY • MATHEMATICS • RADIOISOTOPIC DATING • RESISTOR • SEISMOLOGY

Logic

The study of logic is a branch of philosophy; its purpose is to improve the validity of reasoning. The history of formal logic in the Western world is generally thought to have begun with the Greek philosopher Aristotle, although logical thinking and clear reasoning certainly existed long before. The development of logic gathered pace in the 17th century through the contributions of great thinkers such as Francis Bacon, Gottfried Leibniz, and René Descartes.

In 1847, two mathematicians—George Boole and Augustus de Morgan—independently proposed forms of algebra to represent logical expressions. Seven years later, Boole published *The Laws of Thought*, which set forth the first practical means of expressing logic in algebraic form. Boolean algebra, as it is now called, considers only two values—zero and one—and thus is ideal for the binary processes of computers, communications systems, and a multiplicity of microprocessor-controlled devices. More flexible operation of such devices is achieved by the use of "fuzzy" logic, which caters for probability values between the absolutes of zero ("definitely not") and one ("definitely"). Feedback circuits complement logic circuits by providing information about the system under the control of the logic circuits of a processor—by measuring the temperature of water in a washing machine, for example.

Logic applies to a broad spectrum of situations, and human use of logic in everyday scenarios is frequently subconscious. The conscious application of the principles of logic to problem analysis is a powerful problem-solving tool.

Hardware

Any binary logic component must have two stable states that correspond to the one and zero of Boolean algebra. The earliest calculating machines were entirely mechanical, with different values being represented by distinct mechanical settings. The first computers used relay logic, in which the two states of relay coils—energized or not—corresponded to one and zero.

In electronic computers, microcircuits on silicon chips replace relay circuits. Some of these circuits are called latch circuits, since they can be switched between two stable states by an electrical signal and remain locked in a given state until switched by a new signal. The microprocessors of modern computers have many millions of such circuits, while microprocessors that control simpler devices have numbers of logic circuits that match the complexity of their intended functions.

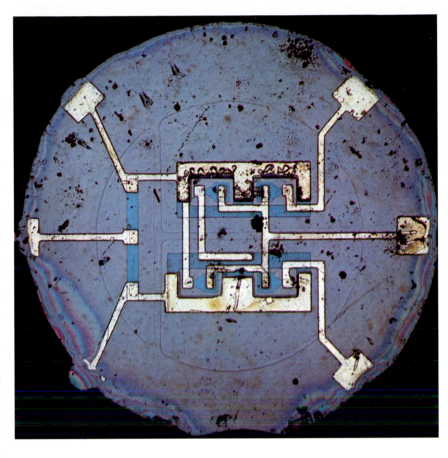

Signals pass between the interconnected circuits of a microprocessor, often performing billions of logic operations each second.

The signals that activate and deactivate logic circuits are largely at the discretion of the circuit designer. While one type of circuit might be activated by an "on" signal that consists of a 12 V pulse and deactivated by an "off" signal of 0 V, another device might be activated by a signal of –5 V and deactivated by a signal of 5 V.

In a fluid-logic device, the flow of a gas or liquid changes to represent the two states required to perform logic operations. A typical fluid-logic device has an input channel and two output channels in the form of a narrow Y. The form of the channels is such that, between switching operations, fluid flows smoothly from the input port to one or other of the output ports. Two narrow ports, located at right angles to the input port at the center of the Y, admit rapid bursts of fluid that switch the main flow between output ports.

Logic functions

The three basic logic functions are AND, OR, and NOT—upper-case letters help distinguish when these words refer to logic functions. These functions, and their various combinations, are sufficient to perform any logic calculation.

▲ This photomicrograph shows the first monolithic logic circuit, introduced in 1961. The circuit is an example of a latch circuit, which can be switched between two stable states by electrical signals.

BLOCK DIAGRAMS AND TRUTH TABLES

Circuit designers use block diagrams to show the connections between the basic components of complex logic circuits. In such diagrams, each operation is represented by a block, or labeled box (below left). By convention, the inputs connect to the left side of the block, and the outputs connect to the right.

While block diagrams are useful for tracing the sequence of operations in a complex logic circuit, the relationship between the possible input permutations and their associated outputs is best represented in a truth table (below right). In the first example below, possible input values, labeled A, B, and C, are listed in the first three columns from the left. The corresponding outputs for an AND circuit appear in the right-hand column of the table.

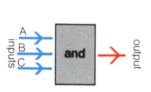

inputs			output
A	B	C	
0	0	0	0
0	0	1	0
0	1	0	0
0	1	1	0
1	0	0	0
1	0	1	0
1	1	0	0
1	1	1	1

Alternative output values for two or more different operations may be listed in adjacent columns at the right of such a table. The example below shows the results for two alternative operations—OR and EXCLUSIVE OR—in separate columns. Such representations help clarify the differences between functions. In the case of OR and EXCLUSIVE OR, the truth table reveals that the OR function gives an active (1) result if more than one of the inputs is active, whereas the EXCLUSIVE OR function returns an inactive (0) result in such cases.

Truth tables can also help engineers identify unlabeled logic circuits. In such cases, all the possible combinations of input signals are fed into the test circuit, and the corresponding outputs are measured. The nature of the logic circuit under investigation can then be identified by comparing its experimental truth table with standard truth tables for known logic functions.

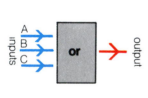

inputs			output	
A	B	C	or	ex or
0	0	0	0	0
0	0	1	1	1
0	1	0	1	1
0	1	1	1	0
1	0	0	1	1
1	0	1	1	0
1	1	0	1	0
1	1	1	1	0

Of all the logic functions, NOT has the simplest block diagram and truth table. It has a single input, and the output value is always the inverse of the input value, so the truth table has only two rows and two columns.

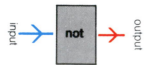

input	output
0	1
1	0

AND function

The AND function requires two or more input values and produces a single output value. The output is active if all inputs are at an active level; the AND function is then said to be satisfied. If one or more of the inputs is inactive, then the output of the AND function will also be inactive. The active and inactive states are represented by the values 1 and 0, respectively.

The AND function is analogous to a simple electrical circuit that has an electric lamp connected to a suitable power source through two or more switches in series. The lamp will glow — assume its active state—only if all of the switches are closed—in their active states. If any of the switches are open, the lamp fails to light.

OR functions

In common with the AND function, OR functions require two or more inputs and have one output. In contrast to an AND function, the output of the simple OR function becomes active if any one of the inputs is active.

Extending the analogy of the electric lamp in a circuit, the OR function corresponds to a circuit in which all the switches are wired in parallel. The lamp glows (is active) if any of the switches are closed (active). Only if all the switches are open will the lamp remain dark (inactive).

There is, however, a second type of OR function: the EXCLUSIVE OR function. This function becomes active if one—but only one—of its inputs becomes active. If a second input becomes active, the function is no longer satisfied, and the output then becomes inactive.

NOT function

In contrast to the AND and both OR functions, the NOT function has only one input. It also has one output. The NOT function inverts the state of a signal, so an active input results in an inactive output, whereas an inactive input results in an active output. The NOT function is sometimes described as an inverter or negator function.

NAND and NOR functions

Of all the possible combinations of logic functions, two occur so frequently that they have acquired their own function names. These are the NAND and NOR functions.

The NAND function (*NOT + AND*) consists of an AND function followed by a NOT function. The result is a function whose output is active when any or all of its inputs are inactive.

The NOR function (*NOT + OR*) consists of an OR function followed by a NOT. Its output is active only when all its inputs are inactive.

Latch circuits

A latch circuit is a complex of logic components, called gates, that has two states between which it can be switched by the appropriate sequences of input signals. One such circuit is the RS–NAND latch, which has two inputs—the set line (S) and the reset line (R)—and two NAND gates. The set and reset lines each provide one input to one of the NAND gates, and each NAND gate's output provides the second input for the other NAND gate through a feedback line.

In the two normal states of an RS–NAND latch, both R and S lines provide active inputs, and one or the other of the NAND outputs is active. The states are switched—the active output deactivated and the inactive output activated—by switching off the input to the NAND gate whose output is inactive. That input is then switched on again to avoid the possibility of both inputs being switched off, which would make the behavior of the latch circuit unpredictable.

The output of the NAND gate fed by the set line is denoted Q, and the output of the NAND gate fed by the reset line is denoted Q'. If, for example, Q is active, the latch can be switched by switching off the R signal. This satisfies the NAND gate attached to the R line, making Q' active. While Q' is active, Q remains inactive since the combined active inputs from Q' and S fail to satisfy the NAND condition. The latch stays in this condition until, with R active, the S signal is switched off, reversing the latch.

Latches are also known as triggers, bistable multivibrators, flip-flops, and toggles. Their many applications include use in memory devices, where their ability to retain a given state is used.

Boolean algebra

Boolean algebra is a convenient way of expressing and manipulating statements of logic. In Boolean algebra, any variable that can be expressed as one of two alternatives is known as a logical variable or Boolean element. Each variable of a given system is assigned two characters—X and $\overline{X}$, for example—where $\overline{X}$ presents the alternative state to X, and is called the complement of X. ($\overline{X}$ is read "not X" or "X bar.")

In Boolean algebra, AND is often replaced by a multiplication sign (x or .). This corresponds to the mathematical treatment of probabilities, where the probability of two independent events both occurring is equal to the multiplication product of the individual probabilities. In a similar way, OR is replaced by the addition sign (+), which also corresponds to the treatment of probabilities. Together with the complement, these symbols represent the basic logic functions.

◄ An engineer wires a prototype circuit board. Such a board typically contains several logic circuits, whose working parts are miniaturized electronic components.

One application of Boolean algebra is in the analysis of switching circuits. Consider the simple example of a stairwell light controlled by two switches: one upstairs, one downstairs. The two switches are joined by a pair of wires: one connected to the upper terminal of each switch, the other to the lower terminal. The circuit that provides power for the lamp is complete if both switches are in the same position: up or down.

If Boolean elements A and $\overline{A}$ represent "upstairs switch in up position" and "upstairs switch in down position," respectively, and B and $\overline{B}$ represent equivalent statements for the downstairs switch, then the conditions for the lamp to be lit are stated as follows:

$$X = A.B + \overline{A}.\overline{B},$$

where X means "the lamp is lit" and the equals sign represents "if." A similar analysis of more complex switching circuits sometimes reveals redundant switches that can be removed to make a less complicated arrangement.

Boolean search queries

Many Internet search engines use Boolean type of notation to refine searches of the World Wide Web. In effect, a search query of the type "red riding hood" is the command "find Web pages that contain the words *red* OR *riding* OR *hood*." Such a search can be made more specific by including an addition sign before each word, so "+red +riding +hood" searches for the words *red* AND *riding* AND *hood*. The search can be further refined by including the term "-automobile"—meaning "NOT automobile" to eliminate car-related pages attracted by the term *hood*.

SEE ALSO: Computer • Fluidics • Internet • Switch • Telephone system • Washing machine

Loom

The loom is among the most ancient of devices. It was in use in 4500 B.C.E., according to evidence found in tombs, and probably long before that. Hand looms are still used for weaving in developing countries throughout the world, the way they were in the English cottage industry until 200 years ago. They are also used in hobby and handicraft activities. Modern high-speed industrial looms work on the same basic principles.

In a piece of woven cloth, the lengthwise threads are called the warp. The threads that go across are called the weft, woof, or shoot. The edge of the cloth is called the selvedge. In modern industrial weaving, the selvedge is about ¼ in. (6 mm) wide and may contain a woven trademark.

In the loom, the warp threads are held in tension by the machine. In the simplest, most common pattern, called plain or tabby weave, every other thread is pulled upward and the rest are pulled downward. This separation of the threads into two sheets is called shedding, and the space between is called the shed. The weft thread is passed through the shed; this step is called picking, and each weft thread is called a pick. Then the pick is beaten in (pushed up tightly into the weave) and the upper and lower sheets change places so that they hold the pick in the weave. The beating in is accomplished by the reed, a screen or gate made of wire, so called because it was originally made of reeds. The batten is the part of the machinery that operates the reed. The batten is sometimes called the sley, and sleying is threading the warp threads through the reed. Thus, the operation of the loom is a continuous cycle of shedding, picking, beating in, shedding, picking, and so forth.

History

Primitive weaving was a slow process analogous to darning. The earliest loom probably comprised sticks in the ground to hold the thread with the operations carried out by hand. Thousands of years ago, shed sticks were invented to form the shed and keep the sheets separate. Before that it would have been necessary to accomplish shedding by hand, one thread at a time.

The next improvement was the invention of the heddle, or heald shaft. Again, we do not know when this took place. At first, the heddle may have been a stick with a hole in it; later it became a piece of wire with an eye in it, and still later a strip of metal with a hole. The heddle is mounted vertically at the front of the machine; there is usually a heddle for each warp thread. The thread passes through the hole in the heddle and the

◀ Hand-operated looms are still common in some parts of the world, as is this carpet-making loom in Iran.

shed is formed by raising and lowering the harness (frame that holds the heddles). In more complicated weaving patterns, the heddles are raised and lowered in various combinations according to the pattern. The pattern is supplied to the weaver on graph paper.

On primitive looms there were several ways of providing tension on the warp. On the weighted loom, the warp threads were hung over a crossbar with weights on the ends. In the backstrap loom, the operator had a strap tied around his or her back and added tension by leaning back. The pick was passed back and forth through the shed by hand with the thread wrapped around a stick; in modern looms, the weaver uses a shuttle, which in its simplest form is a hollowed-out piece of wood containing the weft package (a cone or spool of thread).

The heddles and the shuttle were operated by hand until recent times, except that a single harness could be operated by foot, an innovation that first occurred in the East. Throughout the medieval period in Europe, looms were simple machines, but in the 13th century the shaft loom appeared, also copied from an oriental idea. This design has a number of heddles suspended above the loom from a shaft and operated by a treadle. This makes more weaving patterns possible, because each shed variation can have its own heddle rod.

In modern times, improvements to the loom have consisted of ways to conveniently or automatically operate the heddles and the shuttles and finally to use steam or electricity to drive the machine. Automating the shuttle is one of the many ideas to which Leonardo da Vinci gave some thought. Real progress, however, was not made until the 17th century, and the process of development has continued until the present day. The improvement in textile machinery together with the invention of the steam engine sparked off what we call today the industrial revolution.

Draw loom

The draw loom was invented to create the intricate patterns that the shaft loom was not capable of weaving. The draw loom can make a greater variety of sheds, because in addition to heddles, it has slip cords tied to the warp threads. They were operated at first by a draw boy, who sat on top of the machine and pulled the cords in various combinations according to the pattern. His reliability entirely dictated the regularity of the pattern. The draw loom was improved gradually until the Jacquard loom was perfected.

Jacquard loom

The Jacquard is a device mounted on a loom for weaving intricate patterns and figured designs in cloth. It was invented in 1805 by the Frenchman Joseph Marie Jacquard and immediately revolutionized the weaving industry. By 1812, there were 11,000 of these looms in France alone, and Jacquard's original principle is still in use today with only minor improvement.

Jacquard, who was born in the silk-weaving town of Lyon, was a draw boy himself on a draw loom when he was young. Attempts had already been made to eliminate the need for a draw boy. The first, introduced in the 17th century, was by controlling the cords with levers worked by an assistant beside the loom.

In 1725, the French inventor Basile Bouchon devised a method of selecting the cords automatically. Each cord was threaded through a needle. Every time the shuttle was about to be passed through, a cylinder punched with rows of holes, one for each needle, was slid along to touch the row of needles. There was a roll of paper wound around this cylinder; the sequence of the pattern was recorded on it in the form of holes fitting over those on the cylinder. If a needle met a hole, it passed into the cylinder, through it, and was not moved. If it met an unpunched space, it was forced outward by the movement of the cylinder. The assistant now pressed a pedal, operating a device that caught the needles that had been moved and pulled the cords attached to them. The shuttle was then passed through, the roll of paper was wound on one space, and the cycle began again. This device eliminated mistakes but still needed an assistant. Furthermore, the paper kept tearing. Three years later, the inventor

A 19th century Platt power loom. Power-operated looms did not become common until the 19th century, but now some industrial machines run at well over 200 picks a minute.

Falcon improved upon this design, replacing the paper roll with an endless chain of stiff punched cards strung together.

The next step was taken in 1745 by Jacques de Vaucanson. He built an experimental loom where the movement of the cylinder pulled the cords directly, without the need for an assistant. But the machinery for this arrangement was so complicated and unreliable that it never caught on.

Not long after this attempt, Jacquard was born. His first invention was an automatic net-making machine, which earned him a reputation that caused him to be summoned to Paris to over-

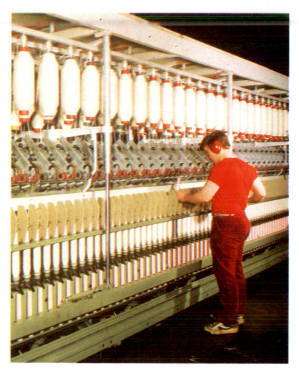

The 20th century saw many developments in loom technology. Many processes once done by hand are now carried out automatically.

haul Vaucanson's original loom, which had been preserved by the Conservatoire des Arts et Métiers, (Institute of Arts and Crafts). He immediately set out to produce a workable version.

Jacquard's device

Compared with earlier attempts, Jacquard's device was fairly simple. Each pull cord attached to a warp thread was topped by a hook. These hooks were caught and pulled by a bar (called the griff or griffe), which was moved by a foot pedal operated by the weaver himself. But any of these hooks could be moved out of the way so that the griff missed it by a needle and punched card

device similar to that of Falcon's machine. The perforated cylinder around which the chain of cards was wrapped was replaced by a long revolving box of square cross section; it pulled the cards around more positively and they could lie flat against it, which made the whole machine stronger and more reliable. The foot pedal that raised the griff also turned the box around.

Jacquard's machine was an instant success. The Lyon weavers, who thought it would put them out of work, tried to drown the inventor in the River Rhône. But the next year, the French government bought the patents and paid Jacquard a pension, plus royalties on each machine made.

▼ The operation of a loom. Left: Shedding, in which the top and bottom warp threads are opened for the insertion of the weft. Top right: Beating up—the closing of the weft pick with the main part of the woven cloth. Center right: Weft insertion—the weft is propelled across the loom by means of a slinging action from an overpick or underpick device.

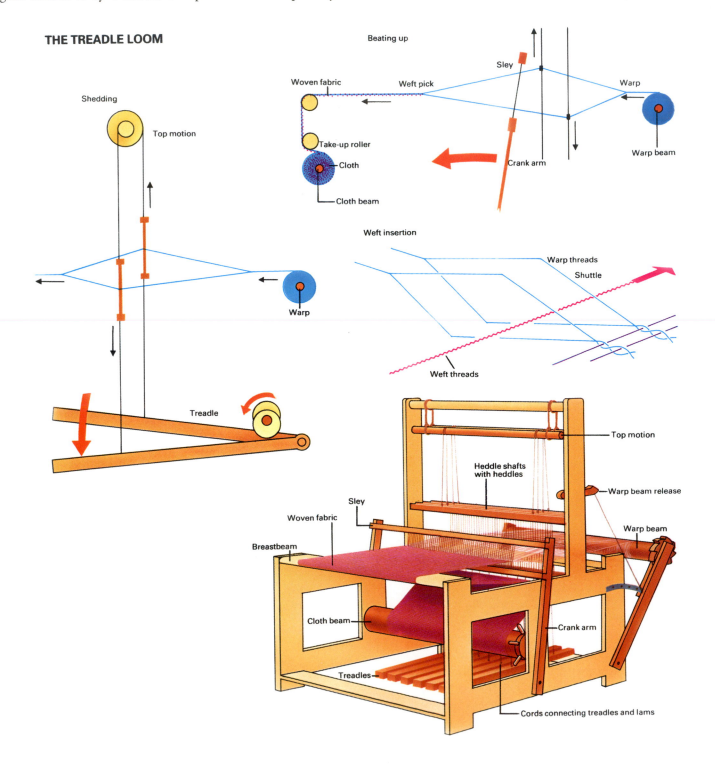

THE TREADLE LOOM

Shedding
Top motion
Treadle

Beating up
Woven fabric
Weft pick
Sley
Warp
Take-up roller
Cloth
Cloth beam
Crank arm
Warp beam

Weft insertion
Warp threads
Shuttle
Weft threads

Warp

Top motion
Heddle shafts with heddles
Warp beam release
Warp beam
Sley
Woven fabric
Breastbeam
Crank arm
Cloth beam
Treadles
Cords connecting treadles and lams

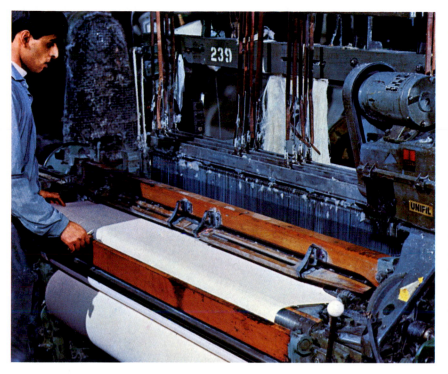

gle picks or odd numbers of picks of a certain color, since no fully automatic machines have been built that can do this. The shuttle contains a supply weft package and is propelled across the loom by means of a slinging action from an overpick or an underpick device, which pivots in a short, powerful arc from above or below the shuttle.

Automatic looms

Most modern looms are of the automatically replenishing type. Looms that automatically replaced the shuttle when the weft package was used up have been superseded by an improved type that replaces the bobbin of weft in the shuttle when it is at rest in the shuttle box at the side of the machine, with no break in production. Sensors determine when the weft is about to run out and the fresh bobbin is inserted, ejecting the old one.

Shuttleless looms

The noise level in textile mills is extremely high, and the advantage of shuttleless looms is that they are quieter as well as potentially faster. There are three types: dummy shuttle, rapier, and fluid jet. All of these types have the weft package stored at the side of the machine.

The dummy shuttle is a small steel projectile that travels back and forth on a track. It has a gripping spring in the back end and takes the weft with it. It returns more slowly than it travels across, so some machines have several dummies going at once. Several picks a second are possible.

The rapier is essentially a piece of wire with an eyelet in the end. Some rapiers are flexible steel tapes that are reeled up at the side of the machine. The latest design has a double rapier; one rapier carries the weft from one side of the machine and another rapier meets it half way. Transfer takes place inside the shed. The rapier is not as fast as the dummy shuttle.

In the fluid-jet machine, nothing enters the shed but the weft itself; it is propelled from a nozzle by a jet of air or water. Since the propelling pressure is not great enough to pull the weft off the bobbin, the machine has an additional device that draws the yarn off ahead of time, storing it loosely so that it can be propelled at zero tension. The water jet is more efficient than mechanical systems, but can be used only with waterproof (synthetic) fibers and machines built of non-corrosive materials.

Automated looms

The flying shuttle was invented in 1733 by an English maker of broadcloth, John Kay. Because of the width of the cloth, the broadcloth weaving process required two operators to pass the shuttle back and forth through the shed. Kay realized that automatic operation would make better cloth, because there would be no need to stop the shuttle and reach through the shed, which resulted in imperfections. He devised a driver attached to the batten so that the weaver could send the shuttle in the right direction by sharply pulling a cord.

Other inventors devised mechanical arms for the shuttle, spring-loaded beating-in devices, overhead cranks to operate the heddles, and so on. These devices all had to be combined with means of feeding the machine with thread and winding up the finished cloth. One mechanically limiting factor was that the shuttle speed had to be much faster than the other operations. Power-operated looms did not become commonplace until the 19th century, but today, some industrial looms are able to run at speeds of considerably over 200 picks a minute. The majority of modern industrial looms consist of three distinct types: hand replenished, automatic, and shuttleless.

Hand-replenished looms

For weaving special patterns or fabrics, the power-operated looms of the 19th century have been refined to a high degree. They run more smoothly and more safely, but not much faster, than their predecessors. Hand-replenished machines are particularly useful for inserting sin-

▲ A cotton-weaving loom in Lancashire, Britain. This automatically replenishing loom has several full bobbins ready at the side. It senses when a shuttle bobbin is almost empty, then ties the new weft onto the old, with no break in production. The sensors may be mechanical, electric, or optical. An air-suction device extracts any loose ends before they become woven into the fabric.

SEE ALSO: CLOTHING MANUFACTURE • FLOOR COVERING • SPINNING • TEXTILE

Loudspeaker

◀ This unusual loudspeaker clearly shows the different elements that are required for high quality reproduction of the full range of recorded frequencies, from a tweeter at the top for the reproduction of high-range frequencies, a large midrange speaker in the middle, and a woofer at the bottom for the reproduction of low-range frequencies.

A moving-coil loudspeaker (speaker) consists of a light circular (or elliptical) diaphragm, or cone, freely suspended from a metal frame by springy suspensions both around its edge and near the center. Firmly attached to the center of the cone is a cylindrical former and wound on this is a coil of wire called the voice coil. The former and coil are positioned between the poles of a magnet. The early speakers used electromagnets and were energized by a direct voltage derived from the amplifier, but permanent magnets of iron or ceramic materials are now used. When a signal is applied to the coil, a force is exerted according to the theory of electromagnetism: the coil is a current-carrying conductor in a magnetic field, and being rigidly attached to the diaphragm causes it to move. The movement of the diaphragm closely follows variations in the electric signal and sets up sound waves.

Enclosures

The audible frequency range extends from about 30 to 16,000 cycles per second (Hz) or more, and it was known long before the first cone loudspeakers were developed that certain problems arose when radiating such a wide range of fre-

In the 1920s, discoveries were made that allowed sound waves to be recorded and reproduced by electric means. Before that time, the record player worked on simple mechanical principles. As the pickup (or sound box) traced the record, the mechanical vibrations of the needle were coupled to a flared horn mounted on top of the instrument, and this horn produced the sounds directly. Later, however, the theories of electricity became more closely allied to those of acoustics (the science of sound), and pickups were made that became known as transducers, because they converted energy from one form into another; that is, the tiny mechanical movements of the needle on the record were translated into an electric signal. Such an electric signal could be amplified by the newly developed vacuum tube amplifier, but it could not be fed to an acoustic horn. Hence, some means had to be found of converting an electric signal back into sound waves.

Probably the most important single contribution to the development of the loudspeaker came from the American engineers C. W. Rice and E. W. Kellogg, who in 1925 described the first hornless loudspeakers and whose work led to the establishment of this new device. The system they described has remained essentially unchanged.

ELECTROSTATIC LOUDSPEAKER

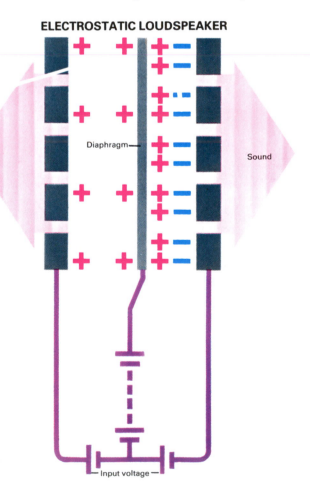

Diaphragm

Sound

Input voltage

▶ Electrostatic speakers move the diaphragm by electrostatic forces. This system can reproduce subtle tonal qualities of music with great accuracy. However, at low frequencies, when diaphragm movements are large, there is the danger of the two polarized plates touching. Hence, the low-frequency performance of the system is somewhat restricted.

quencies. First the sound from the rear surface of the cone had to be isolated from that of the front, otherwise sounds leaving the two surfaces would cancel each other at low frequencies. Second, sounds are not radiated in all directions but become concentrated in a narrow beam at high frequencies. This effect would be more noticeable with large-diameter diaphragms. To improve reproduction and efficiency at low, or bass, frequencies, a loudspeaker is mounted in an enclosure or cabinet.

Today, the speaker is often mounted in a sealed cabinet, which is packed with sound-deadening material to isolate sound radiation from the rear surface of the cone. This acoustic suspension speaker is less efficient, that is, it requires more power from the amplifier, but gives good bass response from a conveniently smaller enclosure. In other designs, the rear radiations are arranged to aid those from the front. An example of this type is the tuned, or reflex, enclosure, where a vent or port at the front magnifies the sound pressure at a specially tuned bass frequency range. The labyrinth, or transmission line, enclosures guide the back radiations to the front of the cabinet, where they augment the speaker's front radiation.

Single loudspeaker units are used in radios, television sets, and portable record players, but for sound reproduction of the highest quality, more than one speaker is required to cover the full audible frequency range. Quite small units, with cone diameters of around one inch, are often used to cover the treble frequency range. Such small diaphragms overcome the problem of narrow directional radiation, and their design can be optimized to give a more accurate response than a single large cone. High-frequency speakers do not need enclosures, because their cone movements are very small. This allows the rear of the frame to be sealed, so that their operation is not affected when mounted in low-frequency enclosures.

In a modern loudspeaker system of high quality, there might be a bass unit (or woofer) about 10 in. (25 cm) in diameter, covering the range from 30 Hz to about 500 Hz; a mid-range unit about 6 in. (15 cm) in diameter working from 500 Hz to around 4 kHz; and a small high-frequency (or tweeter) unit for the treble range. The speakers are fed from an electric filter or crossover circuit that divides the audio spectrum appropriately between units. Considerable attention is paid to designing systems that produce a single integrated sound, rather than a collection of separate sound sources. Many modern speaker systems use tweeters with a domed diaphragm, which is more rigid than a cone and so gives a more accurate response.

Other types

Other types of loudspeaker were developed in the 1950s and have since become established alternatives for certain applications.

The ribbon loudspeaker, used for high-frequency reproduction, uses a magnetic field in which is placed a light metal ribbon, two or three inches long and about ⅜ in. (9 mm) in diameter. The ribbon acts as both voice coil and radiator, but because it is so small, an acoustic horn is often used with it to improve efficiency. Its very tiny mass allows very accurate reproduction of subtle transient sounds, because there is so little energy stored in the light ribbon diaphragm.

The electrostatic speaker has proved successful as a full-range system. In this speaker, the diaphragm is a light, taut metal, or metal-sprayed plastic, sheet mounted close to a similar but fixed plate. A very high direct voltage (several thousand volts) is connected between the plates. This voltage polarizes the system and creates an electrostatic force between the two plates, which are perforated to allow sound radiation to take place. The signal from the amplifier is connected between the plates via an isolating transformer. When a signal appears, the electrostatic force between the plates is modified or modulated, causing movement of the diaphragm and hence radiation of sound. Because the diaphragm is light and tightly stretched, it moves accurately and can reproduce the subtle tonal qualities of music with near perfect fidelity.

One recent development is the flat-panel speaker, which uses a central magnet and coil to radiate tiny vibrations across the surface of a thin panel. This speaker produces a 360 degree distribution of sound rather than the more focused sound of a conventional loudspeaker.

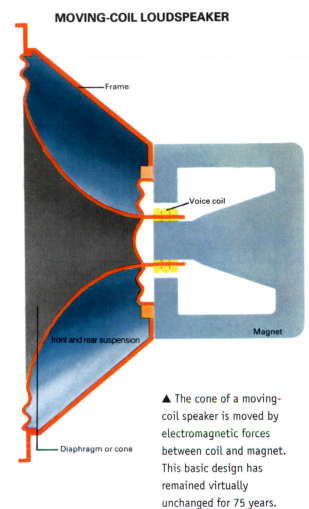

MOVING-COIL LOUDSPEAKER

Frame

Voice coil

Magnet

front and rear suspension

Diaphragm or cone

▲ The cone of a moving-coil speaker is moved by electromagnetic forces between coil and magnet. This basic design has remained virtually unchanged for 75 years.

SEE ALSO: ACOUSTICS • ELECTROMAGNETISM • HI-FI SYSTEMS • SOUND REPRODUCTION • TRANSDUCER AND SENSOR

Low-Emission Road Vehicle

Concern over the effects of pollution caused by the burning of fossil fuels has led to increased interest in alternative forms of energy, and one of the main areas of research is in developing automobile engines that produce low levels of pollution. Lowering levels of pollution can be done in a variety of ways; two of the most promising sources of clean energy are electric and hydrogen power.

Electric vehicles

Vehicles powered by electricity are often thought of as a new development, but as long ago as 1837, Robert Davidson of Aberdeen, Scotland, built an electric carriage powered by a crude iron–zinc battery and driven by a very simple electric motor, which contained all the basic elements of the modern electric vehicle.

The advent of the lead–acid battery allowed the first commercial battery-operated vehicle to be introduced in 1881 by the Paris Omnibus Company. London had its first electric bus in 1888, and the world's first mechanically propelled taxicabs, were built in 1897 by W. C. Bersey for the London Electric Cab Co. Ltd., and operated for two years.

The most commonly used fuel for vehicles is oil, in the form of gasoline, diesel fuel, or aviation fuel. Oil is a nonreplenishable resource, and oil-burning engines are complex, noisy, and pollu-tion-creating. Electricity, however, is available from many sources and can provide quiet, vibration-free transport without creating pollution. Electric vehicles may be divided into two classes: those that are continuously fed electric power from an external source (such as electric trains, trams, trolley buses, and fairground dodgem cars) and those that carry their energy source internally. Externally powered electric vehicles normally pick up their power from either an electrified rail or an overhead conductor. Some London commuter trains use both—they pick up current from an electrified third rail as they run through the city subway network, but once they break the surface on the edge of town, a pantograph is raised to make contact with an overhead wire that provides the necessary power during the rural portion of their journey.

Internally powered electric vehicles present severe design problems in many applications. They stem from the amount of energy needed to accelerate the vehicle, allow it to climb hills, and overcome wind and frictional resistance. Using traditional lead–acid batteries, an automobile with performance comparable to its gasoline-driven equivalent would have a very limited range. The range cannot easily be extended by adding more batteries, since the extra weight will demand more power for acceleration and climbing and therefore

▼ The city of Coventry in England has introduced an electric-car project to reduce the urban pollution resulting from conventional gasoline-powered cars.

result in only a small increase in range. Some automobile manufacturers have attempted to produce electrically powered versions of standard production vehicles, but these typically need to fill most of the trunk and/or rear passenger space with batteries. The weight of these batteries often results in poor ride and handling characteristics. Since electric traction motors tend to be more efficient than gasoline engines, they produce less waste heat and so cannot be used to supply interior heating requirements. If interior heating or air-conditioning is needed, a lot more battery power will be required.

There are some applications where poor acceleration, low top speed, and lack of range are unimportant. A number of specialized vehicles have been designed to exploit these areas, including local delivery vans, golf buggies, wheelchairs, and mobile industrial robots. A lot of research is being directed toward producing a small, electric-powered personal commuting vehicle. Gasoline-driven vehicles are at their most inefficient when used for short journeys through heavy traffic, and they bring problems of congestion both on roads and in parking lots. If a suitable electric vehicle could be produced, it would bring substantial environmental benefits but consumers cannot be expected to move to a vehicle that has a performance and convenience significantly worse than they get now.

Improved performance

The performance of electric vehicles can be improved by either reducing the amount of power that they require or by increasing the amount of energy that can be stored in a given size and weight of battery. Energy usage can be minimized by careful electrical and mechanical design. Motors, speed-control equipment, gearing, wheel bearings, tires, and lubricants can all influence overall efficiency. Extra energy savings can be gained by using regenerative braking, a system that allows the motor to be used as a generator in order to recharge the battery during braking, converting most of the vehicle's kinetic energy into usable chemical energy in the battery rather than waste heat in the brakes. The use of materials with a high strength-to-weight ratio and the application of aerodynamic principles to the exterior shape can also reduce energy requirements. Research into batteries with high energy-to-weight and energy-to-volume ratios has yielded

▲ This small electric car is one of a fleet of experimental electric taxis at a recharging station in Amsterdam.

some interesting designs but nothing immediately suitable for general use. Fuel cells powered by liquefied hydrogen and oxygen need cryogenic (very low temperature) fuel tanks while sodium–sulfur batteries require elevated temperatures and hence expend a lot of energy.

Recharging

With the exception of hybrid vehicles mentioned below, all internally powered electric vehicles need to be periodically recharged from a stationary source. Electric delivery vehicles, for example, are normally plugged into powered chargers at their depots each night. Some experimental vehicles use battery packs built around easily removable pallets, allowing quick replenishment. For the full benefits of this system to be realized, all pallets will need to be standardized.

Hydrogen-powered vehicles

Hydrogen as a source of power has many advantages over other fuels: it burns at a high temperature, contains much more energy than a similar weight of gasoline, and creates far less atmospheric pollution. Unlike gasoline, there is no free (uncombined) hydrogen on Earth and only a little in the atmosphere. However, there is no shortage of the raw materials required to produce it. All that is needed is water plus energy in some other form—and there are many promising processes being developed.

Storage

For hydrogen to be used successfully as a fuel for vehicles, it is necessary to be able to store it ready for use. Currently, the most common way of storing hydrogen is to liquefy it—the boiling point of hydrogen is $-423°F$ ($-253°C$)—with a cooling system to maintain the storage conditions. This technique, however, is not suitable for automobile application, because the cooling system has to be kept running continually for as long as the tanks contain hydrogen. One solution to this problem being researched by the National Renewable Energy Laboratory (NREL) in the United States is a solid-state storage system in which the hydrogen is chemically or physically bonded to a solid material such as carbon. This system has the potential to store more hydrogen per unit volume than liquid hydrogen and can do this at higher temperatures than conventional liquefied hydrogen. The hydrogen is released from the carbon by

◄ Mercedes Benz hydrogen powered buses have been in use for several years in Germany.

changing the pressure and temperature levels of the cell. Another system is the hydrogen fuel cell, in which electrons are stripped from hydrogen and used to produce electricity directly. This system is considered by some researchers to be the most promising means of using hydrogen to power cars.

Engines

Hydrogen can be used to power internal combustion engines, but these engines run only at about 20 percent efficiency. An alternative is the hybrid engine. In this instance, the hydrogen powers an internal combustion engine that is used to generate electricity that in turn powers an electric engine. Although this may seem complicated and inefficient, this systems allows the internal combustion always to be operating at its optimum speed; the electricity it produces is stored in a battery and drawn upon as the electric engine requires it. Already there are gasoline-powered cars that operate on this system, such as the Toyota Prius, that provide energy savings of between 10 rond 20 percent. A similar system could also be powered by hydrogen.

Safety

One factor that has restricted the use of hydrogen as a fuel is the risk of the mixture, of hydrogen and air exploding. One example often cited is the destruction of the *Hindenburg* airship, which caught fire when landing at Lakehurst, New Jersey, in 1937. In this case, though, the hydrogen (used for lift rather than as a fuel) was contained in easily damaged fabric gas bags. Storing hydrogen in tanks or in solid-state fuel cells should create no greater a risk of fire than gasoline—which is itself a highly flammable substance. In addition, hydrogen is lighter than air and so tends to disperse readily, and if it does catch fire, the fireball tends to move rapidly upward and so away from the vehicle.

Applications

Hydrogen-fuelled buses are already in use in Germany and in North American cities such as Vancouver and Chicago. Iceland plans to introduce hydrogen buses by 2002 as part of a wider project to increase its use of hydrogen. Hydrogen can be made cheaply and cleanly on Iceland owing to its abundant supply of hydroelectric power. Other initiatives include joint projects between General Motors and Toyota to explore the possibilities for low-emission vehicles including the design of fuel cells using hydrogen.

SEE ALSO: AUTOMOBILE • BATTERY • BUS • ELECTRIC MOTOR • ENERGY RESOURCES • FUEL CELL • HYDROGEN

Lubrication

Lubrication is the process of controlling friction to reduce the wear of surfaces in rubbing contact with each other, such as those in bearings and gears, by introducing a lubricant between the surfaces. Many different materials, including liquids, solids, and gases, can be used as lubricants; the most common are mineral oils, which are products of oil refining. Whichever lubricant is used, there are three basic modes of lubrication: boundary lubrication, fluid-film lubrication, and mixed lubrication.

Boundary lubrication

Boundary lubrication usually occurs either under conditions of high load and low sliding speed between two surfaces or if there is insufficient

▲ A liquid lubricant being squirted onto a drilling bit. Lubricants act to reduce friction and so reduce wear and tear on moving parts, as well as reducing the amount of energy needed to power machines. Lubricants may also help to prevent materials from overheating.

lubricant because of unfavorable surface geometry. The entire load is carried by a thin, multimolecular layer of lubricant between the surfaces.

Many animal and vegetable fats and oils can provide effective boundary lubrication and significantly reduce friction and wear. The lubricating agent in all these natural organic substances is a fatty acid (an organic acid derived from a hydrocarbon) of high molecular weight, such as stearic or oleic acid. The molecules of these fatty acids are long-chain compounds that can attach themselves to suitably reactive metal surfaces with sufficient strength to maintain adherence during rubbing contact. This reaction produces a soap film of low shear strength, protecting the metal and reducing friction. Unrefined mineral oils do not contain a large percentage of fatty acids and are therefore not very good boundary lubricants. Refined mineral oils, however, with an addition of from 0.5 to 5 percent fatty acids are effective boundary lubricants.

Solid lubrication

Various solid lubricants can also be used to provide boundary lubrication, particularly in hostile environments or where contamination must be minimized. Typical solid lubricants are molybdenum disulfide (MoS_2), graphite, and polytetrafluoroethylene (PTFE). These materials are used to provide a surface film of low shear strength between two sliding surfaces. In graphite, the bonds between atoms in a layer are strong, but the bonds between one layer and the next are weak. This allows the layers to slide over one another and in this way function as a lubricant. In addition, graphite has a high melting point of over 5400°F (3000°C) and so can be used in situations that require great resistance to heat. Molybdenum has a layered structure similar to graphite, while PTFE is a carbon-fluorine polymer, more familiarly known as Teflon, that is used to create nonstick surfaces on cooking utensils. Soft metals, such as tin, lead, and indium, may also be used as solid lubricants.

Fluid-film lubrication

The best way to minimize surface damage of rolling or sliding contacts in machines is to separate the solids completely by a film of lubricant. The lubricant can be a liquid or a gas, and the load-supporting film can be created by the motion of the surfaces or by supplying the fluid under pressure, as in hydrostatic bearings. The main feature of fluid-film lubrication is that the surfaces are separated by a fluid film that is considerably thicker than the surface films formed by boundary lubricants.

Friction is caused only by viscous shearing of the lubricant and is reduced to about one-tenth of the value that would be achieved by boundary lubrication. The main factors that have an effect on the formation of fluid films are the load, the relative speed of the surfaces, the lubricant viscosity, and the density, if the lubricant is a gas.

The theory of fluid-film, or hydrodynamic, lubrication is based on the experimental work of Beauchamp Tower, who developed suitable methods for lubricating railway axle bearings in 1883. The conclusions of this work led the British engineer Osborne Reynolds to formulate his classical theory of fluid-film lubrication in 1886. The rotation of a shaft in its bearing will demonstrate the principle of hydrodynamic lubrication. There must be some clearance in the bearing so that the shaft can rotate, and thus when the loaded shaft is stationary, it is positioned eccentrically. As the shaft rotates within its bearing, lubricant is drawn into the convergent channel between the shaft and bearing and causes an increase in pressure. This in turn pushes the shaft back to its central position and maintains a film of lubricant between the shaft and the inner surface of the bearing. Under some conditions, such as start up and shut down, a film will not exist, and boundary lubrication will occur.

Because of the extremely high pressures that occur in some bearings, local elastic deformation of the surfaces leads to a condition known as elastohydrodynamic lubrication. This is the principle mode of lubrication in many gears, rolling bearings, cams, and some soft rubber seals. The effects of operating temperature and pressure on the lubricant have to be considered when designing a hydrodynamic bearing. In some systems, boundary and fluid-film lubrication can exist simultaneously, and this combination is called mixed lubrication.

A further method of lubrication is the use of gases such as air, steam, and liquid-metal vapors, which in many ways are similar in their properties to liquid lubricants. The main differences are that gases are much more compressible and much less viscous than liquids and so are not used in situations where the lubricant must be able to bear heavy loads. One application is in air bearings, which find uses in such areas as diamond turning, graphite milling, and prescription-optics machining. Often gas lubricants are used in equipment where gases are already being used, such as in dental drills and air turbines.

Lubricants

Plain mineral oils are used in many lubrication systems, but because of the demands of modern high-speed machinery, they are often enhanced with additives. A mineral oil is a mixture of

◀ Greasing a slipway prior to the launch of a ship. The grease has a very high compression strength and a high tenacity so that it adheres to the slipway. Grease is a viscous form of lubricant; greases are generally mineral oils thickened with a metallic soap (a metal salt of an organic acid) or clay. Additives are sometimes used, as with oils.

◄ An oil rig uses a mixture of mud, water, and chemicals for lubrication, pumped through the steel pipe to the drill beneath the ocean floor.

hydrocarbons having an average molecular weight ranging from about 150 for a light machine oil to about 1,000 for a heavy gear. Oils are usually rated according to their viscosity, and the Society of Automotive Engineers (SAE) has devised a series of numerical values each of which represents a range of viscosities. Thus, an oil whose SAE value is 30 will have a viscosity in the range 0.2 to 0.3 ft.^{2} per sec. (0.0180–0.0280 m^2/s) at 77°F (25°C). By using appropriate additives, oils can be formulated that will have different SAE values under different conditions; they are called multigrade oils.

Common additives include viscosity-index improvers, which counteract the tendency of oils to become thinner as temperature increases; pour-point depressants, which improve fluidity at low temperatures; antioxidants, which prevent the formation of sludge by reaction of the oil with atmospheric oxygen; antiwear additives, which neutralize the corrosive acid gases present in the exhaust of internal combustion engines; extreme pressure additives, which improve the ability of an oil, for example, a hypoid gear oil, to maintain lubrication in high-pressure conditions; and dispersants, which prevent the build up of particles, such as carbon particles, on the lubricated surfaces.

Assessing lubricants

The appropriateness of a lubricant to a particular job can be assessed in a number of different ways. The flash point, for example, tests the temperature at which a lubricant ignites in the presence of a flame. It is important in machinery that uses highly flammable materials. The pour point is the temperature at which a lubricant ceases to flow. It may influence the choice of a lubricant that has to operate at low temperatures. Other tests include the penetration number, which indicates the film characteristics of grease lubricants, and neutralization number, which is a measure of pH in new oils and oxidation degradation in used oils.

Sealed bearings

Under certain conditions it is advantageous to use a more viscous form of lubricant, for example, in bearings that are lubricated and sealed for life, and in dirty environments where maintenance is difficult; for this purpose, greases have been developed. Greases are generally mineral oils thickened with a metallic soap (a metal salt of an organic acid) or clay. Additives can be used as with oils. Calcium or lime greases are satisfactory for lubricating plain and rolling bearings at low speeds, but for higher speeds, sodium- or lithium-based greases are preferred.

In extreme conditions, such as in aero engines where very high temperatures are encountered, it is impossible to provide the right characteristics with a lubricant based on mineral oil. More expensive synthetic lubricants are then used, typically esters, diesters (compounds obtained by reacting acids with alcohols), or silicones.

Auto lubrication

Lubrication of automotive engines serves not only to reduce friction and wear of the moving parts but also to disperse heat, reduce corrosion, and help the sealing action of the piston rings.

Modern lubrication systems used in diesel engines and four-stroke gasoline engines have developed by stages from the crude total-loss systems used in the early internal combustion engines. In these early systems, the driver operated a manual pump, which delivered oil to the crankcase, from where it was splashed around the engine by the moving parts. The oil in the engine was eventually lost, by being burned in the cylinders or by leakage through joints and bearings, and then it was replenished by further operation of the pump. This method was replaced by a pump system in which oil was pumped to a trough beneath the crankshaft, where it was picked up by scoops on the big-end bearing caps and carried to the bearings.

In most modern engines, oil is carried in an oil pan, or sump, and fed to the moving parts by a pump via a filtration system. The oil pan usually forms the lower part of the crankcase and fulfils the combined duties of reservoir and cooler.

▲ In this cutting machine, water is being used as a lubricant as well as a coolant.

filter through the perforations in the cylinder, passes through the filter element, and leaves through a central outlet tube.

Typical full-flow filters retain all particles over 15 microns in diameter, 95 percent of all particles over 10 microns, and 90 percent of all particles over 5 microns. During use, the elements eventually become blocked and therefore less efficient, and so have to be replaced periodically.

Distribution

From the filter, the oil, at a pressure of about 40 to 60 psi (2.76–4.14 bar) in modern engines, is fed to a main passage or gallery, which is connected by drillings in the cylinder block to the moving components, such as the main bearings, camshaft bearings, valve rockers, and timing gears. After passing through the main bearings, some of the oil drains back into the oil pan, and the rest passes through drillings in the crankshaft to the big-end bearings. Cylinder walls and gudgeon pins are generally lubricated by oil thrown out of the big-end bearings or else via an oil channel in the connecting rod.

In engines where high oil temperatures are expected, an oil cooler may be installed in the pressurized circuit. On some high-performance engines a dry sump system is employed. In this system, oil is retained in a storage tank, which may also function as a cooling radiator. The oil is pumped to the engine through a filter and then scavenged by a second pump in the oil pan and returned to the tank.

In most two-stroke gasoline engines, the crankcase is used to provide initial compression of the fuel–air mixture and cannot be used as an oil pan. In these engines, lubrication is usually provided by adding a small percentage of oil to the fuel.

Cooling is achieved because the sump protrudes into the airstream below the vehicle and can be improved by adding cooling fins to increase the surface area. The pump is normally fitted to the crankcase and its drive is taken from the camshaft or the crankshaft. The commonest forms of oil pump are the gear type, using intermeshing gears to pump the oil up, or the rotor type. The rotor-type pump has a rotor mounted off-center within the casing, and sliding vanes around the edge of the rotor carry the oil from inlet to outlet.

Filters

Oil usually enters the pump through a strainer submerged in the oil that is designed to trap any large particles of dirt. The oil then passes through a fine filter, either the bypass or full-flow filter. In the bypass system, some of the flow is fed to the filter and then returned to the oil pan, while the rest is fed directly to the engine. Full flow filters handle all the pump's output before delivery to the engine, and incorporate a relief valve that allows oil to bypass the filter if the element becomes blocked.

Filter elements can be made from various materials but must be capable of restricting the flow of fine particles without restricting oil flow. A common filter element comprises resin-impregnated paper folded into a multipointed star enclosed in a perforated cylinder. Oil enters the

Gauges

To monitor the performance of a pressurized system, many vehicles have oil-pressure gauges. They are connected to the main oil gallery by a thin pipe, and any drop in oil pressure or persistent low pressure will warn the driver that there is either a fault in the lubrication system or else a lack of oil in the system. On many modern cars, the oil gauge has been replaced by a warning light that comes on when the oil pressure is low. The light is connected to a pressure-operated switch in the oil gallery, whose contacts close when there is insufficient pressure in the system.

SEE ALSO: FRICTION • HYDRODYNAMICS • INTERNAL COMBUSTION ENGINE • OIL REFINING • TRANSMISSION, AUTOMOBILE • VISCOSITY

Lumber

Because of the widespread use of and the resulting demand for wood, the lumber industry is very important worldwide. Wood remains the most popular building material in the world, while the paper industry uses huge amounts of wood pulp as its raw material. In the United States, lumberjacks cut some 10 billion cu. ft. (0.3 billion m³) of timber each year, and in Canada the figure is 4 billion cu. ft. (0.1 billion m³).

Historically, peak lumber production in the United States was reached in the early 1900s. Although output has now declined slightly, annual production has remained fairly constant except for a shortfall during the depression years.

Geographical variations

The west coast now produces half of the U.S. lumber output. Output from the southern states generally has declined but still accounts for some 30 percent of U.S. output. However, there is one exception in the South. Output from the South Atlantic states has grown in response to the increase in demand for softwoods—especially since the introduction of processes for pulping southern pine for paper. In contrast, New England and the mid-Atlantic states have witnessed a decline from their peak output of about 20 percent of U.S. production at the beginning of the century to less than 5 percent.

Lumbering techniques

Lumbering techniques have to be carefully considered because of the possible environmental damage and long-term damage to the forest. In Canada, in particular, there have been worries about clear felling, the traditional practice where whole forests were felled completely. Although this method is quick, easy, and cheap compared with other felling methods, it leaves no cover for seedlings, which are vital if the forest is to grow again.

Other problems stem from the waste matter (slash) from felling. A forest floor covered with slash is a serious fire hazard. Methods of log transportation have also been reconsidered, as dragging, or skidding, in which logs are raised at one end and then dragged through the forest, tears up the ground and will destroy any seedling trees in the way.

Modern felling involves more expensive singling out of trees but does have the great long-term advantage that the overall health of the forest is preserved. Careful transportation to roads, railways, or waterways ensures that seedlings are not destroyed.

◀ Cutting timber in western Australia. The tree is first undercut on the side of the fall, then either a two-person saw or a power saw is used on the opposite side to fell the tree.

Waterways

The lumber industry has strong links with waterways. Logs are often floated downstream to sawmills and other timber-processing plants. Transporting lumber in this way has the great advantage that the cost is minimal. The total weight of harvested timber can be colossal, so more conventional forms of transportation are often excluded on cost grounds.

Often the complete range of timber-processing plants is built at one location to economize further on transportation. For example, it is common to find sawmills, paper mills, and plywood plants close together. With this concentration of plants, partially manufactured materials rather than just wooden planks can leave the industrial areas.

Hardwoods and softwoods

Wood is usually categorized as hardwood and softwood, although sometimes the differences are blurred. Most softwood trees are characterized by spiky leaves and are usually coniferous—the larch, a deciduous tree, being an exception. Common softwoods include cedar, Western red, hemlock, pitch pine, Parana pine, western white pine, Sitka spruce, lodgepole pine, and yellow cedar.

Hardwood trees, on the other hand, are mostly deciduous species with broad, flat leaves—but there are exceptions, such as yew and holly. Where softwoods have branches that form at the

◀ These logs will be left on a frozen river until they can be floated downstream in spring.

same level, hardwoods have branches that form at different levels, with never more than two branches at the same level. Common hardwoods include beech, ash, elm, mahogany, gabon, utile, sapele, ramin, and Japanese oak.

Softwoods are usually produced from intensive forestry schemes; hardwoods often occur at random and grow naturally. Random distribution increases the prices of hardwoods, because felling and collection of such trees are difficult. Hardwoods grown intensively take longer to grow than softwoods and also increases their price. Their greater cost to the consumer means that many hardwoods are used mainly as veneers over cheaper timbers. In recent years, the hardwood eucalyptus has become increasingly popular owing to its relatively rapid rate of growth.

Forestry techniques now allow specific kinds of trees to be grown in response to general trends in demand, although the timescales involved in growing trees rule out much opportunism in the marketplace. Woods with special purposes can also be grown in preference to more general purpose timbers, although climate remains the most important factor in determining which trees can be grown and the profits that can be made from the timber.

The trunk

Mature wood from the center of the tree trunk is called the duramen, usually referred to as true wood or heartwood. This is the best quality wood, with better dimensional stability and less

vulnerability to insect attack than wood from the other parts of the tree. The cells in the duramen contain little sugar and starch, which are found in the growing outer layers of the tree.

The outer layers are called the alburnum, or sapwood, and are lighter in color than the duramen. They are also softer and spongier. The starch and sugar contained in the alburnum make it far more susceptible to insect attack. Altogether, the alburnum is a less desirable product than the duramen.

Until recent years, alburnum was used for packaging materials—such as boxes and crates—but was rarely used for anything more permanent. However, with the rising cost of lumber, the situation has changed. Alburnum is now used in furniture and construction, but modern improvements in seasoning and treating timber have made such use possible without putting the resulting furniture or buildings at risk.

Producing planks

The process of turning an uncut tree trunk into planks is known as conversion. Conversion involves two stages—sawing and seasoning.

As little time as possible should be wasted after the wood has arrived at the sawmill, because if left too long, the outer layers of the trunk will dry out and crack. A sawmill will aim to cut the trunk—uneven growth means that branches are rarely used commercially—with as little wastage as possible and also will allow the cut wood to season properly, either in the open air or in a kiln.

There are two popular ways of cutting timber into planks. The first is called plain sawing. It is the most common and simplest way to produce planks, but the resulting grain pattern—called the figure—is often thought uninteresting, and it has the disadvantage that the planks may distort.

Plain sawing may be done by the flat cut, that is, the trunk is cut into slices that still have the wavy outside edge of the trunk. A slightly more complex variation on the flat cut is billet sawing. Here, the outside of the log is trimmed and the remainder cut into thick planks or billets, which are then sawed into thinner ones.

If the planks being produced need to show an attractive grain structure, the more wasteful and labor-intensive process of quarter sawing is used. Aside from the fine grain structure produced in the resulting planks, they are also stronger and less prone to warping than those produced by plain-sawing methods.

The finest and most expensive timbers are usually cut into veneer thicknesses so that attractive facings can be applied to cheaper timbers. Plywood and blockboard are also manufactured from veneer-thickness timber.

Modern techniques of milling may use lasers to scan the wood. This information is processed by a computer that calculates the best way of cutting the wood to get the maximum amount of lumber with the minimum amount of wastage. In addition, the use of stronger metals, such as high-grade steel, to make circular cutting saws enables the saws to have a thinner edge. This means that less sawdust is produced and so less wastage.

◀ Increased automation has helped the timber industry to meet the world demand for lumber.

▶ Floating logs down inland waterways is a quick and cheap way of getting them to the mill. Sometimes the logs are assembled into rafts like these, which can then be towed by tugs. In the background are barges full of tree trimmings.

Seasoning

Once sawed, the planks have to be seasoned. This is the process of making the wood dry out so that its moisture content is the same as that of the atmosphere. If the wood is allowed to season naturally by being left stacked outdoors, its moisture content reduces to about 15 to 17 percent. The resulting wood is suitable for outdoor use and general construction work. If this timber is brought indoors, however, it will continue to season and dry out, resulting in shrinkage and warps.

Kilns may be used to force seasoning by heating. Moisture content is further reduced by this means, but ideally, timber for indoor use needs to be left in the room in which it is to be used for as long as possible before working with it.

Pressure-treated lumber

One problem with wood as a building material is its susceptibility to attack by insects, bacteria, and fungi, which can seriously reduce its durability. This is especially true when the wood is in contact with the ground. Pressure treating of lumber attempts to overcome this drawback by a process in which chemical preservatives are forced under pressure into the fiber of the wood. This process ensures that all of the wood is impregnated. Lumber may be simply soaked in preserving chemicals, but this method is less effective, as the chemicals do not reach the core of the wood. The most common chemical used for pressure treating is chromated copper arsenate (CCA), which effectively kills many of the insects and fungi that attack wood and thus extends the wood's lifespan by up to several decades.

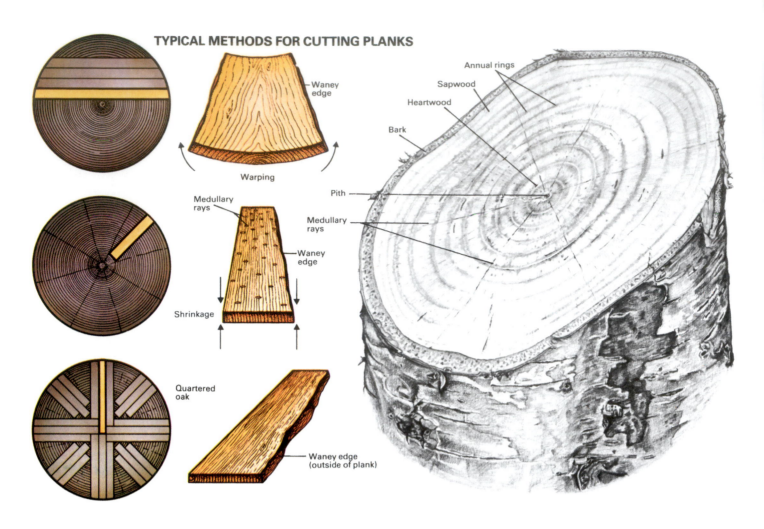

TYPICAL METHODS FOR CUTTING PLANKS

Waney edge

Warping

Medullary rays

Waney edge

Shrinkage

Quartered oak

Waney edge (outside of plank)

Annual rings

Sapwood

Heartwood

Bark

Pith

Medullary rays

▲ Above left: methods of cutting planks. Above right: a cross section of a log showing the heartwood, sapwood, and medullary rays—cells conducting food and moisture to and from the sapwood.

FACT FILE

■ *When treated with anhydrous ammonia in either gaseous or liquid form, hardwood strips can be cold bent. The treated timber is bent to the required shape and held firmly in position. In a short time the ammonia dissipates into the air, leaving the bends set in the wood.*

■ *The Canadian logging industry uses huge gas-filled balloons to lift heavy weights of timber clear of the cutting site and to transport them to road vehicle loading positions without having to negotiate forestry tracks through standing trees.*

■ *Laminated wood components are stronger than lumber and can be made in sections substantially larger than the largest pieces of lumber. The Jai-Alai Fronton amphitheater in Florida has a clear-span roof 245 ft. (75 m) wide, supported by 12 laminated wooden arches, each weighing more than 15 tons (13.5 tonnes).*

Pulp

Wood pulp for making paper is divided into two classes, with the cheaper wood pulp being produced by breaking down logs against a grindstone. The process needs a great quantity of water and forms a fibrous mass. This kind of pulp is primarily used in the manufacture of newsprint and other low-quality papers. Paper made in this way still contains all the wood's impurities, which is why newspapers discolor after a short period.

Better-quality papers are manufactured by a chemically based process. The bark is first removed from the logs, then the logs are fed into a machine that breaks them into small chips. The chips are fed into a digester and boiled under pressure with an acid or an alkali, a process that removes everything from the wood except the pure cellulose. This is removed from the digester, washed, and bleached using chlorine dioxide (ClO_2) to give the desired degree of whiteness.

Wood pulp is also used in cigarette filters, while cellulose extracted from pulp is used to make artificial fibers, such as rayon.

SEE ALSO: BIOFUEL • ENERGY RESOURCES • FIBER, SYNTHETIC • FORESTRY • KILN • PAPER MANUFACTURE • WOOD COMPOSITE

Index